GOD AND RELIGION
IN THE
POSTMODERN WORLD

Essays in Postmodern Theology

DAVID RAY GRIFFIN

STATE UNIVERSITY OF NEW YORK PRESS

Published by
State University of New York Press, Albany

©*1989 State University of New York*

*For information, address State University of New York
90 State Street, Suite 700, Albany, NY 12207*

Library of Congress Cataloging-in-Publication Data

*Griffin, David Ray, 1939-
God and religion in the postmodern world : essays in postmodern
theology / David Ray Griffin
p. cm.—(SUNY series in constructive postmodern thought)
Includes index.
ISBN 0-88706-929-0. ISBN 0-88706-930-4 (pbk.)
1. Theology—20th century. I. Title. II. Series.*

BT26.G75 1989   88-12357
230'.09'04—dc 19   CIP

God and Religion
in the Postmodern World

SUNY SERIES IN
CONSTRUCTIVE POSTMODERN THOUGHT
DAVID RAY GRIFFIN, EDITOR

David Ray Griffin, editor, *The Reenchantment of Science:
Postmodern Proposals*

David Ray Griffin, editor, *Spirituality and Society: Postmodern Visions*

David Ray Griffin, *God and Religion in the Postmodern World:
Essays in Postmodern Theology*

for my parents,
Troy and Ella Griffin,
in Hermiston, Oregon

CONTENTS

Introduction to SUNY Series in Constructive Postmodern Thought

The rapid spread of the term *postmodern* in recent years witnesses to a growing dissatisfaction with modernity and to an increasing sense that the modern age not only had a beginning but can have an end as well. Whereas the word *modern* was almost always used until quite recently as a word of praise and as a synonym for *contemporary*, a growing sense is now evidenced that we can and should leave modernity behind—in fact, that we *must* if we are to avoid destroying ourselves and most of the life on our planet.

Modernity, rather than being regarded as the norm for human society toward which all history has been aiming and into which all societies should be ushered—forcibly if necessary—is instead increasingly seen as an aberration. A new respect for the wisdom of traditional societies is growing as we realize that they have endured for thousands of years and that, by contrast, the existence of modern society for even another century seems doubtful. Likewise, *modernism* as a worldview is less and less seen as The Final Truth, in comparison with which all divergent worldviews are automatically regarded as "superstitious." The modern worldview is increasingly relativized to the status of one among many, useful for some purposes, inadequate for others.

Although there have been antimodern movements before, beginning perhaps near the outset of the nineteenth century with the Romanticists and the Luddites, the rapidity with which the term *postmodern* has become widespread in our time suggests that the antimodern sentiment is more extensive and intense than before, and also that it includes the sense that modernity can be successfully overcome only by going beyond it, not by attempting to return to a premodern form of existence. Insofar as a common element is found in the various ways in which the term is used, *postmodernism* refers to a diffuse sentiment rather than to any common set of doctrines—the sentiment that humanity can and must go beyond the modern.

Beyond connoting this sentiment, the term *postmodern* is used in a confusing variety of ways, some of them contradictory to others. In artistic and literary circles, for example, postmodernism shares in this general sentiment but also involves a specific reaction against "modernism" in the narrow sense of a movement in artistic-literary circles in the late nineteenth and early twentieth centuries. Postmodern architecture is very different from postmodern literary criticism. In some circles, the term *postmodern* is used in reference to that potpourri of ideas and systems sometimes called *new age metaphysics,* although many of these ideas and systems are more premodern than postmodern. Even in philosophical and theological circles, the term *postmodern* refers to two quite different positions, one of which is reflected in this series. Each position seeks to transcend both *modernism* in the sense of the worldview that has developed out of the seventeenth century Galilean-Cartesian-Baconian-Newtonian science, and *modernity* in the sense of the world order that both conditioned and was conditioned by this worldview. But the two positions seek to transcend the modern in different ways.

Closely related to literary-artistic postmodernism is a philosophical postmodernism inspired variously by pragmatism, physicalism, Ludwig Wittgenstein, Martin Heidegger, and Jacques Derrida and other recent French thinkers. By the use of terms that arise out of particular segments of this movement, it can be called *deconstructive* or *eliminative postmodernism.* It overcomes the modern worldview through an anti-worldview: it deconstructs or eliminates the ingredients necessary for a worldview, such as God, self, purpose, meaning, a real world, and truth as correspondence. While motivated in some cases by the ethical concern to forestall totalitarian systems, this type of postmodern thought issues in relativism, even nihilism. It could also be called *ultramodernism,* in that its eliminations result from carrying modern premises to their logical conclusions.

The postmodernism of this series can, by contrast, be called *constructive* or *revisionary.* It seeks to overcome the modern worldview not by eliminating the possibility of worldviews as such, but by constructing a postmodern worldview through a revision of modern premises and traditional concepts. This constructive or revisionary postmodernism involves a new unity of scientific, ethical, aesthetic, and religious intuitions. It rejects not science as such but only that scientism in which the data of the modern natural sciences are alone allowed to contribute to the construction of our worldview.

The constructive activity of this type of postmodern thought is not limited to a revised worldview; it is equally concerned with a postmodern world that will support and be supported by the new worldview. A post-modern world will involve postmodern persons, with a postmodern spirituality, on the one hand, and a postmodern society, ultimately a postmodern global order, on the other. Going beyond the modern world will involve transcending its individualism, anthropocentrism, patriarchy, mechanization, economism, consumerism, nationalism, and militarism. Constructive postmodern thought provides support for the ecology, peace, feminist, and other emancipatory movements of our time, while stressing that the inclusive emancipation must be from modernity itself. The term *postmodern*, however, by contrast with *premodern*, emphasizes that the modern world has produced unparalleled advances that must not be lost in a general revulsion against its negative features.

From the point of view of deconstructive postmodernists, this constructive postmodernism is still hopelessly wedded to outdated concepts, because it wishes to salvage a positive meaning not only for the notions of the human self, historical meaning, and truth as correspondence, which were central to modernity, but also for premodern notions of a divine reality, cosmic meaning, and an enchanted nature. From the point of view of its advocates, however, this revisionary postmodernism is not only more adequate to our experience but also more genuinely postmodern. It does not simply carry the premises of modernity through to their logical conclusions, but criticizes and revises those premises. Through its return to organicism and its acceptance of nonsensory perception, it opens itself to the recovery of truths and values from various forms of premodern thought and practice that had been dogmatically rejected by modernity. This constructive, revisionary postmodernism involves a creative synthesis of modern and premodern truths and values.

This series does not seek to create a movement so much as to help shape and support an already existing movement convinced that modernity can and must be transcended. But those antimodern movements which arose in the past failed to deflect or even retard the onslaught of modernity. What reasons can we have to expect the current movement to be more successful? First, the previous antimodern movements were primarily calls to return to a premodern form of life and thought rather than calls to advance, and the human spirit does not rally to calls to turn back. Second, the previous antimodern movements either rejected modern science, reduced it to a description of mere appearances, or assumed its adequacy in principle; therefore, they could base their calls only on the negative social and spiritual effects of modernity. The current movement draws on natural science itself as a witness against the adequacy of the modern worldview. In the third place, the present movement has even more evidence than did previous movements of the ways in which modernity and its worldview *are* socially and spiritually destructive. The fourth and probably most decisive difference is that the present movement is based on the awareness that *the continuation of modernity threatens the very survival of life on our planet.*

This awareness, combined with the growing knowledge of the interdependence of the modern worldview and the militarism, nuclearism, and ecological devastation of the modern world, is providing an unprecedented impetus for people to see the evidence for a postmodern worldview and to envisage postmodern ways of relating to each other, the rest of nature, and the cosmos as a whole. For these reasons, the failure of the previous antimodern movements says little about the possible success of the current movement.

Advocates of this movement do not hold the naively utopian belief that the success of this movement would bring about a global society of universal and lasting peace, harmony, and happiness, in which all spiritual problems, social conflicts, ecological destruction, and hard choices would vanish. There is, after all, surely a deep truth in the testimony of the world's religions to the presence of a transcultural proclivity to evil deep within the human heart, which no new paradigm, combined with a new economic order, new child-rearing practices, or any other social arrangements, will suddenly eliminate. Furthermore, it has correctly been said that "life is robbery": a strong element of competition is inherent within finite existence, which no social-political-economic-ecological order can overcome. These two truths, especially when contemplated together, should caution us against unrealistic hopes.

However, no such appeal to "universal constants" should reconcile us to the present order, as if this order were thereby uniquely legitimated. The human proclivity to evil in general, and to conflictual competition and ecological destruction in particular, can be greatly exacerbated or greatly mitigated by a world order and its worldview. Modernity exacerbates it about as much as imaginable. We can therefore envision, without being naively utopian, a far better world order, with a far less dangerous trajectory, than the one we now have.

This series, making no pretense of neutrality, is dedicated to the success of this movement toward a postmodern world.

David Ray Griffin
Series Editor

PREFACE

Like many other current books, this one seeks to return theological reflection to the public domain. While I hope that the essays herein will be found interesting to my fellow theologians and philosophers of religion, they were originally written for two types of readers: those nonmodern people who are intensely interested in religious or spiritual issues but who have found traditional theology incredible and modern theology irrelevant, and those fully modern people who, because of the assumptions they have imbibed from modern culture, have dismissed religious spirituality as well as theology. To the former, I propose a form of theology that is very different from traditional theologies and that takes seriously many beliefs and practices generally dismissed or ignored by modern theologians. To the latter, I propose a worldview that is more coherent than the modern worldview and more helpful ethically; at least this is the claim.

By *theology* I mean rational reflection about what we take to be holy, that is, of ultimate importance for its own sake. For various reasons, this type of reflection has dropped out of the public domain in the modern world, especially in the United States, this most modern of all nations. The results have been unfortunate at best, disastrous at worst. All decisions finally imply convictions about the holy, or matters of ultimate importance. Because we do not reflect together as a people about what we believe to be holy in this sense, we have no means for our policies to be shaped by our deepest intuitions and our highest thoughts about this most fundamental question. Our public policies are more likely to be shaped by the narrow self-interest of the most powerful segments of our society and thereby to reflect values that we would, upon reflection, consider to be only quasi-holy, even demonic.

One of the main dimensions of the postmodern age into which we are moving is a rejection of the modern approach to religious belief, which either denied its truth *a priori* and wholesale or restricted its relevance to the private domain. The postmodern consciousness believes that religious intuitions should have at least equal weight with sensory, mathematical, and logical intuitions in constructing a worldview, and that it is irrational to declare the specifically religious dimension of our worldview irrelevant to public life. One reason for this latter claim is that public and private life really cannot be separated.

Questioning the modern privatization of religion does not necessarily betoken a desire for a theocracy or some other form of religious state. That impulse is more premodern than postmodern. The postmodern discontent with modernity raises, instead, a most difficult question: Is it possible to move toward a form of theology that would through its intrinsic merits evoke a sufficiently broad response that the values implicit in it would replace the values of the modern worldview that have dominated public policy?

The phrase "through its intrinsic merits" is crucial. Unlike premodern theology, whose ultimate appeal is to authority and which, on the basis of this appeal, excuses various types of incoherence and experiential inadequacy, postmodern theology makes its claims in terms of its internal coherence, its adequacy to experience, and its illuminating power. This principle is hereby suggested for the evaluation of all potential public theologies: A public theology must be able to pass public scrutiny. And to pass public scrutiny is to pass those tests that are more or less explicitly applied to any account presented for public acceptance, whether it be an elaborate scientific theory or a story to a trial jury: Is the account self-consistent? Is it adequate to all known facts? Does it tie several known facts together in a new, illuminating way? And (ideally) does it illuminate previously unknown facts? My efforts surely fall far short of these austere ideals. But I and others will be helped if critics will point out how my proposals are deficient when judged in terms of these ideals, rather than, say, when judged in terms of the modern dogmas that they challenge.

Each of the chapters, except the introduction, was originally written as an independent essay for a particular occasion. I have, therefore, referred to the chapters as *essays*. Although I have removed some of the repetition that was present in their original form, much remains. I seek to justify it in the customary ways, saying that the remaining repetitions were necessary to keep the integrity of each essay, and that I hope most of the ideas expressed two or more times are sufficiently novel or difficult to make the repetitions more helpful than annoying.

Because I am editor of the series in which this book appears, a word may be in order about the relation between the series in general and the theological position enunciated in this book in particular. The "constructive postmodern thought" of the series title is intended broadly enough to encompass a variety of positions, as evidenced by the contributions to the first two volumes. The introductions I wrote for those volumes and especially the introduction to the series are intended to be acceptable, at least for the most part, to the various members of this movement. The theological stance articulated in the present volume, by contrast, is my own particular position, written as one member among others of this movement. It is not *the* statement of the specifically theological dimension of the series. None of the other contributors to the series should be assumed without further ado to share my position on any particular issue. Everything I have said here is consistent with the general stance of the series; but that general stance does not imply everything said here.

Chapter 3 is a greatly revised version of "Creativity in Post-Modern Religion," which was published in *Creativity in Art, Religion, and Culture*, Michael H. Mitias, ed. (Amsterdam: Editions Rodopi B.V., 1985). Two alternate versions of chapter 6 have been scheduled for publication elsewhere, although the final section of it is entirely new. Chapter 7 is a moderately revised version of "Faith and Spiritual Discipline: A Comparison of Augustinian and Process Theologies," published in *Faith and Philosophy* 3/1 (January 1986).

I wish to thank John Cobb and my wife, Ann Jaqua, for reading this book in manuscript form and making many helpful suggestions. I am also grateful to Geneva Villegas for typing several versions of each chapter, to Erline Goodell of the Center for a Postmodern World and Gary London and Nancy Howell of the Center for Process Studies for bibliographical assistance, to Elizabeth Moore of SUNY Press for guiding this book through production, and to William Eastman of SUNY Press for the fact that this series exists. Thanks are in order, finally, to those members of the Center for a Postmodern World who talked me out of my original title, "Beyond Nihilism and Supernaturalism," and especially to Frank Kelly for suggesting the present title.

I dedicate this book to my parents, who have, from the beginning, been as supportive of my efforts as any parents could be. I'm glad I chose them.

1

INTRODUCTION: POSTMODERN THEOLOGY

Theology fell from grace in the modern world. Having been the "queen of the sciences" in the middle ages, it is now not generally counted among the intellectually respectable disciplines.[1] A leading biologist jokes that only theology may exceed exobiology (the study of extraterrestrial life) in being a "great subject without a subject matter."[2] The reference on an editorial page to an argument as "theological" usually means that the proponent defends a faith-commitment in the face of overwhelming disconfirming evidence, employs meaningless distinctions, or both. The way to refer disparingly to those who formulate rationales and strategies for nuclear weapons is to call them "nuclear theologians."

In intellectual circles, theology is generally thought to consist of two types. One type is conservative-to-fundamentalist theology, which is based on appeals to supernatural revelation that will not withstand historical scrutiny and which makes assertions about the world that are disproved by science. The other type is modern liberal theology, which avoids contradicting modern historical and scientific knowledge by not asserting anything significant; it uses the word *God*—if indeed it uses it at all—in a Pickwickian way to put a religious gloss over secularism's nihilistic picture of reality. Because conservative-to-fundamentalist theology is unscientific,

1

and modern liberal theology is vacuous, both can be ignored. Because these two types of theology have constituted the whole of the public image of theology, the conclusion has been that theology as such could be ignored. The fate of theology in the modern period should be no surprise, for two reasons. The first is that God, transcendent values, and the human soul (with freedom), which are at the heart of any significant religious vision based upon the biblical tradition, are not allowed to play a role in the universe by the "modern scientific worldview," at least in its second form, which emerged in the eighteenth century and became dominant in the latter part of the nineteenth. (The distinction between the first and second forms of the modern worldview will be explained in chapter 2.) Within this context, theologians have seemed forced either to reject or ignore science and its worldview, thereby being antiscientific, or to accept them, thereby having a theology without God, transcendent values, and a self-determining soul. There *has* been a third form of theology, which challenged the modern worldview in the name not of an antiscientific authoritarianism but of a more fully rational understanding of reality. Its proponents, however, have not been very many or very visible, and its divergencies from modern liberal theology have been minor and/or timidly stated. That this third form of theology has been left out of the public image, which is necessarily drawn in broad strokes, is therefore understandable.

The second reason theology has been peripheral in the modern world is that it has been considered irrelevant. Modernity has had its theology-substitutes. A theology is an articulation and defense of a community of faith's path to salvation. In modern liberal society, salvation is to be achieved through material progress, which comes about through the marketplace and scientific technology. Economics and natural science, buttressed by the philosophy of science, comprise the two main branches of the modern substitute for theology. The science of economics explains how the market works, almost magically—as if it were guided by an invisible hand—to turn private greed into public good. Economics thereby embodies a distinctively modern form of the doctrine that divine providence works in mysterious ways. Far from being pure theory, economics provides a counterpart to practical theology, telling us how best to cooperate with grace (the marketplace). Liberal political theory, according to which the state allows the market considerable autonomy, and even subordinates itself to it, is a central feature of this practical doctrine.

Natural science, the other main branch of modernity's theology-substitute, provides the basic truth about the nature of the universe, replacing all previous theologies and their false doctrines of revelation. Modern philosophy of science provides the counterpart to what Roman Catholics have called "fundamental theology" and Protestants "apologetics." That is, it shows the scientific method to be the most reliable channel through which truth is revealed. In its most fundamentalist and representative forms, such as logical empiricism, the modern philosophy of science has insisted that science is the one true way for discovering truth and the one true body of doctrine. The god of science is a jealous god, allowing no other gods before it: metaphysics and common sense, as well as theology, are denounced as "unscientific."

Theology, in short, has been peripheral both because the modern worldview prevents a theological vision from being simultaneously significant and rational, and because the distinctive form of the religious quest for salvation embodied in modern society created substitutes for theology. Having been rendered impossible and irrelevant, theology was bound to fall on hard times.

As suggested in the introduction to this series, however, a postmodern world appears to be dawning. Negatively, confidence is waning in the materialistic worldview and in salvation through material progress. Positively, a postmodern worldview is emerging, supported by many scientists and scientific developments, and great interest in postmodern forms of community and spiritual life is becoming manifest.

In this new context, the place and nature of theology can be expected to change. Because of the renewed interest in religious spirituality as the foundation for both individual and social life, theology can be expected to return to the center of public discussion in the postmodern world. Neither of the two forms of theology that were dominant during the modern period can play this public role. But, of course, they will not be dominant in the postmodern world. The emergence of a postmodern worldview, supporting and supported by a postmodern science, provides the context in which a postmodern theology can be accepted. This postmodern theology articulates a genuinely religious vision of the world, unlike modern liberal theology, without taking an antiscientific, antirational stance, unlike modern conservative-to-fundamentalist theology. This postmodern theology can build upon the third form of theology, mentioned above, which challenged the modern worldview in the name of a more rational, more empirical, description of reality. In the new context, however, it can be bolder without seeming to go beyond the pale (to the theologians themselves as well as their readers).

The essays in this book constitute an example of a postmodern theology and thereby a proposal for the direction theology should take in the postmodern period. Whereas all the volumes in this series are theological in a broad sense of the term, the essays in this volume are theological in the stricter sense, dealing with ideas of God, religion, creation, science and theology, the human soul, immortality, spiritual discipline, and ethics. In the remainder of this introduction, I indicate the distinctive features of this postmodern theology.

With regard to the question of God, postmodern theology involves a naturalistic theism, which is equally distinct from the supernaturalistic theism of premodern and early modern theology and the nontheistic naturalism of the late modern worldview. A naturalistic worldview has been widely equated with a nontheistic view; even if the term *God* is used by naturalists, it would not refer to a personal being distinct from the world who exerts causal influence in it. The affirmation of such a divine reality has been assumed to involve supernaturalism. For example, it is almost universally said that science, because it deals only with natural causes, cannot deal with divine causation. Divine causation is assumed, by definition, to be supernatural causation. Against both of these modern assumptions, postmodern theology proposes a naturalism that is theistic, and a theism that is naturalistic. This naturalistic theism, or theistic naturalism, is developed in several of the chapters, especially 4, 5, and 8.

Epistemologically, postmodern theology is based on the affirmation of nonsensory perception. This nonsensory form of perception is said not only to occur—which is shocking enough to the modern mind—but also to be our *fundamental* mode of relating to our environment, from which sensory perception is derivative. This affirmation challenges one of the main pillars of modern thought, its sensationism, according to which sense-perception is our basic and only way of perceiving realities beyond ourselves. The primacy of nonsensory perception, or what Alfred North Whitehead called *prehension*, lies at the root of his contribution to postmodern theology. This postmodern primacy of prehension undergirds and develops the "radical empiricism" that is William James's main contribution.

This radical, nonsensationist empiricism lies behind the naturalistic theism already mentioned, and the closely related affirmation of the direct (if vague) perception of norms or values, which restores ethics and aesthetics to the realm of cognitive discourse (in which assertions capable of being true or false are made). This radical empiricism equally lies behind other distinctive features of postmodern theology, mentioned below, through which it differs both from traditional supernaturalism and modern nihilism.

The importance of this epistemic point cannot be overstated. The dogma that our experience is *wholly* mediated through culturally conditioned filters, especially linguistic filters, so that there can be no prelinguistic experience of anything, let alone God or norms, pervades the social sciences and the humanities. Postmodern theology's recognition (as it sees it) of nonsensory perception allows for *a dimension or element of perceptual experience that is not a product of culturally conditioned frameworks and is therefore common to us all.* Because this postmodern primacy of prehension is so fundamental, it is recurred to time and again throughout the volume. (The type of "postmodern theology" that is based on the *denial* of prelinguistic experience is discussed below.)

Equally distinctive is the postmodern treatment of nature. At the root of the modern worldview, along with the sensationist doctrine of perception, was the mechanistic idea of nature. This mechanistic idea of natural entities forced most modern minds to choose between dualism and materialism, both of which are extremely problematic. Dualism left the modern mind unable to explain its relation to its body; materialism led the modern mind to deny itself.

Modern thought, when it took its sensationist epistemology even more seriously than its mechanistic view of nature, *did* come up with alternatives to dualism and materialism, namely the phenomenalisms of Hume and Kant and the idealisms of Berkeley and Hegel. But these views are equally problematic, in that they refuse to affirm the real existence of the natural world studied by natural science and presupposed in everyday life. They have accordingly had little effect outside philosophical and theological circles.

Postmodern theology is based on another alternative, *panexperientialism*, in which feeling and intrinsic value are attributed to all individuals comprising nature. Our ineradicable realism is thereby honored, in that dogs, cells, and molecules are said to be real in the same sense in which we are real, while both dualism and materialism are avoided. This panexperientalism is the ontological basis for naturalistic theism, which seems so strange to the modern mind, given this mind's assumption that experience is not natural. If modernity has had trouble thinking of the human soul as natural, all the more could it not think of a cosmic soul as a natural reality and its interaction with the world as part of the natural process. Postmodern theology, by contrast, with its assumption that experience is fully natural, finds it natural to speak of a divine, all-inclusive experience.

Along with experience, the other key term in the postmodern doctrine of nature is *creativity*. The two terms should be used together: all experience is creative experience. Creativity is, in fact, considered the ultimate reality, which is embodied by all individuals, from God to electrons. That it is embodied in a plurality of finite individuals is as essential as that it is embodied by the divine individual. This idea is the essential presupposition behind postmodern naturalistic theism, according to which God could not possibly be the sole possessor of creative power, and cannot interrupt or unilaterally control events in the world. On this basis, postmodern theology, while agreeing with modernity that the problem of evil undermines supernaturalistic theism, argues that theism itself, if naturalistically conceived, is fully compatible with the reality of genuine evil. Chapter 3 develops the idea of creativity and applies it to a wide range of religious issues, some of which are treated more fully in other chapters.

Postmodern theology's naturalistic theism, along with its distinctive doctrine of nature, provides the basis for a new understanding of the relation between science and theology. This issue is illustrated in chapter 5. Postmodern theology rejects the modern assumption that evolution and a theistic doctrine of creation are necessarily antagonistic to each other. Theology need not choose between rejecting evolution, perhaps in the name of a supernaturalistic "creation science," and capitulating to an atheistic, nihilistic (for example, neo-Darwinian) account of evolution, with talk of divine creative activity either dropped or relegated innocuously to another "perspective" or "language game." Postmodern theology proposes a way of speaking straightforwardly about theistic evolution.

Postmodern theology is also quite distinctive in combining a high doctrine of human nature with an ecological approach to nature, in which intrinsic value is attributed to all entities. Chapter 2 explains the way the postmodern worldview allows us to recover the sense of "The Importance of Being Human," which has been lost in the modern period. It shows that an ecological viewpoint need not lead to equalitarianism, according to which all things, from humans to microbes, perhaps even electrons and rocks, are assumed to have equal intrinsic value. The key ideas here are degrees of intrinsic value, the directionality of evolution toward organisms with greater intrinsic value, and a divine perspective in which intrinsic as well as ecological value is cherished.

At the center of the postmodern reappraisal of the human being is a new way of speaking of the human mind or soul. Key ideas here are nature as a hierarchy of creative experience and the primacy of nonsensory perception. These ideas form the basis for chapter 6, which will surely be the most startling to modern readers, in that the possibility of life after death is affirmed within a naturalistic worldview. "Naturalism" for the modern mind has *meant* the rejection of any survival of bodily death. To believe in life after death, from the modern perspective, is to believe in the supernatural: the human mind is not the sort of thing that could live apart from its body naturally, that is, apart from a supernatural act.

Given postmodern assumptions, however, the possibility of life after death can be affirmed without abandoning a naturalistic standpoint. This standpoint is naturalistic not only ontologically, requiring no supernatural intervention, but also epistemically, requiring no leap (or supernatural gift) of faith. Postmodern theology here appeals to evidence, albeit a kind of evidence— parapsychological—much scorned by modern minds. Even most of those calling for an "empirical theology" do not have *this* type of empirical evidence in mind! The closedness of the modern mind to this kind of evidence points back to the very origin of the modern worldview. The mechanistic view of nature and the sensationist doctrine of perception were adopted by early modern minds in large part to declare that action at a distance and extrasensory perception could not happen naturally, thereby ruling out a naturalistic interpretation of the Christian miracles. Postmodern openness to evidence for extrasensory perception and psychokinesis reflects the very heart of its differences from both early modern supernaturalism and late modern naturalism.

One of the most important features of postmodern theology is its potential for overcoming that division between religious liberals and conservatives (including fundamentalists) which was inevitable in the modern period. Modernity presented religious thinkers with a forced choice: *either* let experience and reason be decisive for the content of one's faith, in which case it will become increasingly vacuous, *or* maintain a robust faith by basing it upon the authority of scripture and tradition, allowing experience and reason a merely subservient role. This forced choice was due to the peculiarly modern conceptions of experience and reason. Because *experience* in modern thought was basically sense-experience, modern empiricism was a superficial empiricism, which ruled out contact with any spiritual realities behind sensory appearances. *Reason* largely meant thinking that conformed to the modern worldview. A liberal approach, meaning one in which received beliefs are tested by experience and reason, thereby inevitably led to a thin theology, one that provided an inadequate basis for personal morality, public policy, and for answering the question of the meaning of life in the face of personal and global tragedy.

In this context, a reassertion of the authority of the scriptures (and perhaps tradition) appeared to be the only way to maintain "a faith worth having." A significant theology seemed to require a conservative method. Postmodern theology shows that this is no longer true. Within the context of the postmodern worldview, with its radical empiricism, a liberal method supports a significant theology with robust doctrines of God, providence, and even life after death. The main reason for adopting an authoritarian method is overcome. People no longer have to choose between having a meaningful faith and being fully empirical and reasonable.

Another important, if less unique, feature of postmodern theology is its movement toward overcoming the separation between theory and practice, a separation that exemplifies the modern penchant for dividing our thoughtful relations to reality into disciplines. Postmodern theology seeks to make explicit the ways in which theological truth is *liberating* truth. While practical issues are touched on in earlier chapters, especially 2 and 3, they become the focus of chapters 7 and 8. I suggest in chapter 7 that postmodern doctrines of God and the soul provide a new basis for spiritual discipline, which had been undermined by the atheistic materialism of modernity and even to some extent by the supernaturalism of medievalism and early modernity. Within postmodern naturalism, spiritual discipline is neither impossible, because the soul has significant power to shape itself, nor irrelevant, because the effectiveness of divine grace in the world is not unilaterally determined by God.

In chapter 8, the subject is liberation from demonic forces in the public realm, especially imperialism, nuclearism, and, more generally, militarism. The central idea here is that, given our religious desire to imitate the supreme power of the universe, naturalistic theism will tend to produce a different type of human beings than have supernaturalism and materialism, both of which portrayed the supreme power as coercive omnipotence. Whereas those modern doctrines tended to produce either crusaders or power-politic realists, naturalistic theism, with its doctrine of divine persuasion, will tend to produce pacific souls. The choice of *pacific*, as distinct from *pacifistic*, is deliberate. The latter term generally connotes the renunciation of violence as a matter of ethical principle. While there is nothing in postmodern theology that opposes pacifism in this sense, and even much that can support it, the concern here is not with an ethical principle but with a type of soul. Pacific souls are those that *want* to live in peace with their fellow creatures, who will therefore naturally seek forms of social order that promote peaceable relations, and will naturally seek peaceful resolutions of the inevitable conflicts that remain. Some of them may also want to live by and advocate an absolutist pacifist ethic, but that is another matter, not broached here.

Although I have not directly addressed the issue in any of the essays in this volume, postmodern theology is supportive of feminist or postpatriarchal theology. The nondualism, the primacy of nonsensory perception, the presence of divinity and creativity throughout nature, the divine as soul of the world, the divine persuasion, the divine receptivity, and the reunion of theory and practice have all been endorsed by feminist theologians as central elements for a postpatriarchal theology.

What is called *postmodern theology* here is obviously very different from much that goes under this name. In the other major type of philosophy and theology to which the term postmodern is often applied—which is called eliminative or deconstructive postmodernism in the introduction to the series—all the points highlighted here are denied, namely God, nonsensory and prelinguistic perception, the perception of objective values, the self-determining human soul, and the universality of creativity and experience. By eliminating God, the self, and all objective value and meaning, this form of thought simply carries modern thought to its logical conclusion, and is therefore really ultramodern rather than postmodern. It could better be called *mostmodern theology*. In following out Nietzsche's insight that the death of God leads to nihilism, this ultramodernism brings out the nihilistic implications that were present in the modern worldview from the outset. The postmodern theology of this book stands in contrast to this nihilistic postmodernism as well as to the modernism whose nihilistic implications are drawn out by it. (The contrasts between these two forms of postmodern theology are treated at length in a companion volume, *Varieties of Postmodern Theology*.)

The fact that I am a Christian theologian raises another question: Is postmodern theology (as portrayed here) a specifically Christian theology, or is it a philosophical (or "natural") theology, which could provide a foundation equally well for Jewish, Christian, or Islamic theologians—and perhaps even Buddhist, Hindu, and Primal theologians? There is, I hope, some truth in both answers.

On the one hand, postmodern theology is a philosophical theology, which states its claim to be accepted as true—or at least as less untrue than other available positions—solely in terms of the criteria used in scientific and philosophical reasoning at its best, that is, self-consistency, adequacy to the relevant facts, and illuminating power. (In philosophy, in distinction from the special sciences, the *relevant* facts include, of course, *all* the facts of experience.) Anyone who, on reading this book, concludes that postmodern theology is really *philosophy* is correct in this sense. It argues for its positions in terms of strictly philosophical criteria, making no appeal to special revelation to support its truth-claims. It indeed aspires to be recognized as a more adequate philosophy than any position that seeks to make sense of our experience without speaking of God.

Postmodern theology does, to be sure, appeal to religious experience. It makes this appeal because the reality of this type or dimension of experience is among the facts to which any position aiming for comprehensiveness must be adequate, and also because, by explicitly calling itself theology, it focuses on just those issues that are at the center of specifically religious concerns. But this appeal to religious experience involves no appeal to an extrinsic authority, whose truth-claims are to be accepted apart from their capacity for illuminating our common experience. Nor is this appeal, in principle at least, to one tradition of religious experience to the exclusion of others. Postmodern theology in principle provides a framework in terms of which each religious tradition could interpret its own more particular emphases, because this framework has drawn upon, say, Primal, Buddhist, and Christian experiences from the outset. (I stress *in principle* because, although this feature is already somewhat true of postmodern theology, it is much more an ideal for the future than a present achievement.)

Whereas there is a sense, then, in which postmodern theology (as developed here) is not specifically Christian, there are other senses in which it is. None of us has that all-inclusive, impartial perspective which is to be ascribed to the divine center of reality alone. We necessarily see reality from a particular perspective, which both selects and distorts while it reveals. This particular perspective will, to a great extent, be a function of the particular tradition in which we stand (which may be the product of several traditions, such as Hebrew, Greek, Christian, Egyptian, Roman, Anglo-Saxon, Christian-Protestant-Disciple, and modern-American, in my own case). This postmodern theology necessarily reflects a Western Christian perspective on the nature of reality. Not only were its two primary philosophers, Alfred North Whitehead and Charles Hartshorne, the products of Western Christian civilization, they were also sons of Anglican priests. They did study other philosophical-religious traditions, especially Buddhism, and sought to make their positions adequate to Buddhist as well as Christian insights, and several Buddhists have testified to their partial success in this regard. But there is no doubt that their philosophical visions, conceptualities, and valuations are more Christian than they are Buddhist.[3]

Accordingly, although postmodern theology is a philosophical (or natural) theology, it can more accurately be called a *Christian* philosophical (or natural) theology: even though it appeals only to the criteria that are appropriate to natural theology, which is a branch of philosophy, the questions it asks and the features of experience it consciously notices in answering them are influenced from the outset by its birth in a Christian cradle.[4]

The postmodern theology in this volume is Christian in an even more specific sense. Central to my own perspective is the conviction that the divine character, purpose, and mode of agency have been decisively manifested through Jesus of Nazareth. Within a framework of naturalistic theism, this conviction does not involve any metaphysical claims about God's unique presence or action through Jesus that a Jew, a Moslem, or even a Hindu or Buddhist could not in principle accept (if it be a Buddhist who finds the nonsubstantial deity of postmodern theology not incompatible with Buddhist emptiness). For example, a naturalistic christology could not describe Jesus as the second person of the trinity in a human body or, less crudely, as in any manner involving a divine mode of presence or agency that differed metaphysically from that in all other people. Such an interruption of the normal God-world relation is precisely what naturalistic theism rules out. Nevertheless, because of my belief in the decisive manner in which the character, purpose, and mode of agency of the soul of the universe was expressed through that portion of the history of the universe we call Jesus, I refer to Jesus in a normative way that would not be natural to a theologian of another tradition. Likewise, because I assume the majority of those who will read these essays are Christian, at least more Christian than anything else, I sometimes use "more authentically Christian" as a criterion for commending the naturalistic form of theism over the supernaturalistic. (A Buddhist postmodern theologian could use "more authentically Buddhist" in a similar manner. He or she would, of course, to some extent emphasize different aspects of postmodern theology than have I.)

The mention of Whitehead and Hartshorne raises yet another question, given the fact that the form of theology based on their theology has long been called *process theology*. Is *postmodern theology*, as developed here, just a new name for process theology?[5] That is to some extent true; most of what is here portrayed as characteristic of postmodern theology could equally well be used to illustrate process theology. Nevertheless, more is involved than simply a new name. While postmodern theology (as exemplified here) could equally well be called process theology, not all process thought could equally well be called postmodern. In the first place, one can be a process philosopher or theologian without giving explicit and thematic attention to the contrast between premodern, modern, and postmodern, and showing how process thought provides a solution to distinctively modern problems and recovers some premodern truths and values.

In the second place, a tendency has existed among many process thinkers to modernize Whitehead, that is, to reject, ignore, or at least not bring out the implications of just those features of his position that are distinctively postmodern. For example, a position called "Whitehead without God" has been proposed.[6] Whitehead's allowance for action at a distance is usually not mentioned, let alone emphasized. One proposal would, in fact, modify his position so as to disallow any direct influence of the noncontiguous past upon the present.[7] This interpretation would mean that, when the "many become one," only the immediately past many are directly involved, which is a considerable dilution of Whitehead's basic principle, which holds that, when the many become one, they are "increased by one." This modernized Whitehead provides no basis for the cumulative power on the present of past repetitions of a form, which Carl Jung's archetypes and Rupert Sheldrake's formative causation require.[8] Although few if any Whiteheadians have rejected the notion of nonsensory prehension, few have applied the doctrine to the question of "extrasensory perception" in the usual sense of that term. Nor have many Whiteheadians, including theologians as well as philosophers, built on Whitehead's recognition that his philosophy allows in principle for the continuation of the soul after bodily death, so that the question is to be decided by empirical evidence. (Some Whiteheadians have, in conversation, even denied the possibility of such continuation on the grounds that a "mental pole" always requires a "physical pole." Their equation here of the soul exclusively with "mentality" and the body exclusively with the "physical" is a wholly non-Whiteheadian use of those terms, which they in other contexts recognize.) Few process thinkers have applied the correlation between higher experience and greater creative power to the issues of spiritual discipline, psychokinesis, or survival. Finally, few process theologians have developed the doctrine of God with an eye to the question of pacifism, or what I call the development of pacific souls. My use of the term *postmodern* calls attention to the fact that the contrast between modern and postmodern theology is thematized, that the distinctively postmodern elements in Whitehead's metaphysics are accepted and emphasized, and that other postmodern possibilities are developed.

2

THE IMPORTANCE OF BEING HUMAN: A POSTMODERN VISION

A widespread conviction exists in our time that many of our most important qualities are in imminent danger of being lost. Historians can show that this feeling is not unique to our time. In our century, however, the concern seems to be more widespread, more intense, and more enduring. It makes sense, therefore, to ask about the root cause of this crisis, and what we can do, if anything, to preserve and strengthen what we consider our most valuable human qualities.[1]

The root cause of our crisis, I believe, is the modern worldview. The early sections of this essay explain this belief. The last section points to a postmodern worldview that should help.

I. PERSONS, IMPORTANCE, AND WORLDVIEWS

The kind of persons a society produces depends on the society's sense of importance. Our sense of importance has two basic sources. First, a Cosmic Source of Importance exists, which we can apprehend or intuit, more or less dimly. Our feeling that some things are important, and that some things are more important than others, is ultimately rooted in our intuition of the values inherent in this Cosmic Source of Importance. But this idea explains only why all people have a sense of importance and why *some* unanimity as to what things are important exists. To account for the great differences among peoples in this respect, we need to appeal to a second source of importance, which is the stories by which we live. We can point to individual life stories, the stories of particular communities, and the stories of the larger communities in which these are embedded. All these levels are important, but the most important, in the long run, is the *story of the universe* that a culture accepts.

This cosmic story forms the more or less unspoken background for the more particular stories. This most encompassing story embodies a culture's worldview. A *worldview* indicates which factors in our experience are the most important factors in reality as a whole: which things are eternal and permanent, not transitory; which things are the primary causal powers, not secondary and derivative. Our worldview tells us what should be of ultimate concern to us by showing what is of ultimate importance in the very nature of things.

Ultimate concern was Paul Tillich's term for religion and its object. Whatever is of ultimate concern or importance to you is in effect your deity. The beliefs, emotions, attitudes, and practices oriented around this ultimate concern constitute your real religious life—regardless of the religious institution to which you may or may not belong.

The ultimate basis for every religion is a worldview, and every worldview suggests a religion. Why is this? Why should a view of the universe tend to evoke religious reactions within us? Because it is important to us to be in step with the universe. It is important to us to orient our lives around that which is truly important in the ultimate nature of things. The devout Jew, Christian, or Moslem wants to be in harmony with the eternal God, creator of heaven and earth, whose nature and purpose were revealed decisively through Moses and the history of Israel, or through these and Jesus of Nazareth, or through all these and Mohammed. The Vedantist wants to be in harmony with, in fact to realize his or her oneness with, eternal Brahman. The Taoist wants to be in harmony with the eternal Tao, which, without coercion and without effort, is the most effective force in the world. The "scientific" Marxist wants to get in step with the dialectical process of history which is inevitably, omnipotently, leading us to the classless society. The Social Darwinist wants to be in harmony with the evolutionary process, which entails the survival of the fittest and the ruthless elimination of the weak in the competitive struggle for existence.

Each of these religious orientations has a different vision of the ultimately important reality. But the basic desire is the same in all: the desire to be in harmony with that which is most important in the nature of things—that which is eternal, that which is most powerful. For "most powerful'' we sometimes say "omnipotent." But most powerful need not mean omnipotent in the usual sense of that term; the power in question only needs to be primal, nonderivative, and ultimately most effective.

With this in mind, let us look, in broadest terms, at the transition from the medieval to the modern worldview. In this transition, the importance of being human was reduced drastically.

II. THE TRANSITION FROM THE MEDIEVAL TO THE MODERN WORLDVIEW

Three features crucial for the importance of being human were involved in the transition from the medieval to the modern worldview. First, in the medieval worldview, the world was created by a personal God. Personal qualities—the kinds of qualities human beings embody—were thereby regarded as eternal, primordial, and foundational. Personal qualities made things happen: the ultimate power of the universe was a personal being.

Second, human beings were said to have a privileged place in the scheme of things: we were the crown of the creation on earth, and only "a little lower than the angels." We were created in the very image of God. We were near the top of a great chain of being. While we exemplified creaturely qualities more perfectly than did other earthly creatures, these qualities were for the most part the *same* qualities, meaning that we human beings both belonged *and* were special.

Third, our life on earth was not the end, but only the beginning, of our existence. However horrible we may consider the traditional doctrine of heaven and hell, it did make what we do in this life, what kind of persons we become, extremely important!

In the modern worldview, all three of these elements have been denied. First, in the neo-Darwinian view of evolution, the world as we know it, with its various forms of life, including human life, is not in any sense the creation of a personal God, but is the result of purely impersonal forces ("chance and necessity"). The eternal and omnipotent powers of the universe are impersonal in nature. In the atheistic worldview of modernity, furthermore, no omniscient, personal being "looks on the heart," in the biblical phrase. That is, what we really are, deep inside, is not known by anyone; so how can it be important?

Second, the human being is no longer the chief exemplification of the general qualities of the universe. Atheism, of course, entails that we are not created in the image of God. But the modern worldview goes even further in belittling the importance of being human. Beginning in the seventeenth century, it divided qualities into primary, secondary, and tertiary. The *primary* qualities are those considered really real. These are qualities such as size, shape, and mass—in other words, purely objective, quantitative, impersonal qualities.

Labelled as *secondary* are the sensory qualities of color, sound, smell, taste, heat, and so on. These are secondary because they are thought to refer to nothing really "out there" in the objective world, apart from human subjectivity. For example, the rose is not *really* red, it is *really* comprised of colorless atoms that vibrate at a particular frequency. When those vibrations reach our eyes and our optic nerve, which are also devoid of color, something occurs that results in the perception of red. How this miracle takes place has never been understood, but the idea has been widely accepted, and its message is clear: all these sensory qualities, which are so central to human experience—especially to human beings who take aesthetic experience to be of extreme importance—are secondary and derivative in the nature of things. Matter, with its size, shape, and mass, is real; but the sound of music, and the colors, aromas, and tastes of nature, are less real, less important. Human beings wanting to be in step with the ultimate scheme of things can ignore them.

Finally, *tertiary* qualities include all those qualities of consciousness that, unlike secondary qualities, do not even appear to qualify nature but are clearly features of consciousness itself. Included under tertiary qualities are purpose, emotion, and virtue, and judgments of good and evil, true and false, ugly and beautiful. The idea that "beauty is in the eye of the beholder" does not simply mean that people disagree about such judgments. It means that there is, really, no such thing as beauty, that no things are inherently beautiful. Beauty is a purely tertiary quality, not pointing to anything of ultimate importance in the nature of things.

The same is also true of virtues and vices, which had been at the center of the medieval worldview. People thought then in terms of the "seven deadly sins," the "four cardinal virtues," and the "three theological virtues." But in the modern worldview, which began emerging in the seventeenth century, all these qualities are said to be tertiary in the nature of things. Developing virtues and overcoming vices is no longer a way to be in step with those dimensions of reality that are ultimately important. The way to do this is to use power to possess and control the really real thing: matter. *Having* becomes more important than *being*.

This relegation of human beings with their distinctively personal qualities to an insignificant status was completed by the theory of evolution, insofar as it is interpreted atheistically. This theory implies that beings with personal qualities are entirely accidental products of a blind, impersonal process. Beings with moral, aesthetic, intellectual, and religious interests were in no sense "intended." This modern doctrine of creation implies that the cultivation of moral, aesthetic, intellectual, and religious feelings can no longer be regarded as important. The protests against the theory of evolution, taken in this sense, are not necessarily merely the outcries of know-nothing dogmatists.

The third feature of the medieval worldview that made the cultivation of human qualities seem important was the belief in life beyond bodily death. This idea, of course, has also been denied by the materialistic worldview. People living within the medieval worldview were like children of very strict parents, living in constant "fear and trembling" of punishment for disapproved behavior. People living within the modern worldview have been like children whose parents "don't give a damn" about what they do. Neither situation is desirable; but is the latter not even more horrible?

With this threefold denial of the medieval basis for the importance of being human, the modern worldview has cast its inhabitants into a cosmos that is a meaningless void, and in which they are aliens. As Martin Heidegger put it, we are beings who care, who experience ourselves as having been thrown into a world that does not care. In other words, we have concerns, we think some things are important; yet the universe in which we find ourselves seems to have no sense of importance. How can our concerns be ultimately important if they are not somehow important to the whole? We are aliens.

III. LIVING IN TERMS OF THE MODERN WORLDVIEW

How could sensitive human beings make a go of human life in this context? Many, of course, have not made a go of it, becoming alcoholics, drug addicts, war addicts, mental patients, or suicides. Others have lived lives of quieter desperation. I have heard that one leading scientist, when asked how he copes with the utter meaninglessness implied by his viewpoint, said: "Whenever I allow myself to ask that question, I lock myself in a room for several days of utter despair—until I get over it."

The meaninglessness of the universe has provided the backdrop for that type of philosophy usually called *existentialism*. Jean-Paul Sartre entitled one of his books *Nausea* to name the experience evoked in him by contemplating the meaninglessness of being. The absurdity of the universe was portrayed so effectively by Franz Kafka that the term *Kafkaesque* has become an adjective for the grotesquely absurd. The existentialists give what advice they can as to how to live a human life in an inhuman world. Paul Tillich, in his well-known book *The Courage to Be*, makes central to his philosophy the courage to affirm life in spite of its objective meaninglessness.[2] Albert Camus, in *The Rebel*, advocates that we live a life of rebellion against the absurdity of the universe, even though there is no one in charge against whom to rebel. The term *existentialism* is usually taken to refer to the claim that existence precedes essence: no essence is to be found in the nature of things with which human beings should live in harmony. No natural law, no divine purpose, no objective importance, no hierarchy of values is inherent in the nature of things, to which we should conform. Rather, in the very act of existing we must create our own values, realizing all the while that they only seem important because we have chosen to make them so.

One of the best-known and most eloquent statements of the existentialist position was presented by one who is seldom considered an existentialist, Bertrand Russell. In "A Free Man's Worship" he described the meaningless world he believed to be entailed by modern science:

> That Man is the product of causes which had no prevision of the end they were achieving; that his origin, his growth, his hopes and fears, his loves and his beliefs, are but the outcome of accidental collocations of atoms; that no fire, no heroism, no intensity of thought and feeling, can preserve an individual life beyond the grave; that all the labours of the ages, all the devotion, all the inspiration, all the noonday brightness of human genius, are destined to extinction in the vast death of the solar system, and that the whole temple of Man's achievement must inevitably be buried beneath the debris of a universe in ruins—all these things, if not quite beyond dispute, are yet so nearly certain, that no philosophy which rejects them can hope to stand.[3]

Russell next remarks upon the place of human beings in this world:

> A strange mystery it is that Nature, omnipotent but blind, . . . has brought forth at last a child, subject still to her power, but gifted with sight, with knowledge of good and evil, with the capacity of judging all the works of his unthinking Mother. . . .[4]

Russell then asks how there can be any place in such a universe for our ideals. He first says that ideals make a claim upon us, but then makes clear that these ideals are created by us: we worship "our own ideals," and hence a god who is "the creation of our own conscience."[5] Better to worship a god of our own creation, which can be good, than to worship the ultimate reality of the universe, he says, for this is omnipotent matter, which is not good. To worship it would be to succumb to power-worship. This line of thought leads to Russell's famous final paragraph:

> Brief and powerless is Man's life; on him and all his race the slow, sure doom falls pitiless and dark. Blind to good and evil, reckless of destruction, *omnipotent matter* rolls on its relentless way; for Man, condemned today to lose his dearest, tomorrow himself to pass through the gate of darkness, it remains only to cherish, ere yet the blow fall, the lofty thoughts that ennoble his little day; disdaining the coward terrors of the slave of Fate, to worship at the shrine that his own hands have built; . . . proudly defiant of the irresistible forces that tolerate, for a moment, his knowledge and his condemnation,

to sustain along, a weary but unyielding Atlas, the world that his own ideals have fashioned despite the trampling march of unconscious power.[6]

Although this existentialist advice is noble and courageous, it is, in the last resort, futile. Our religious drive gives us the desire to be in harmony with the ultimate nature of things, regardless of what it is like. If we think blind, amoral matter to be omnipotent, this is the god we will worship, willy-nilly. Joseph Wood Krutch, in his 1929 book *The Modern Temper*,[7] said that the deterministic worldview of modernity allows us only two possible responses: to fight it or to join it; that is, to live in existentialist opposition to the alien universe, or to use the techniques of indoctrination and sociological manipulation to produce well-adjusted citizens—the kind of option portrayed so well in Huxley's *Brave New World* and Orwell's *1984*. In the Preface to the reissue of his book in 1956, Krutch reported what had happened in the intervening three decades: "The modern temper itself has developed somewhat, especially in the direction of that attempted 'adjustment' to dismal assumptions which makes Social Engineering rather than Existentialist resignation the dominant religion of today."[8] In other words, the desire to be in harmony with the modern worldview had won out over the inclination to fight it.

What is the situation several more decades later, in our own time? On the one hand, a large portion of the population in European and North American countries lives in terms of the totally meaningless universe portrayed by Russell and the existentialists. At the same time, the development of nuclear arsenals has made it possible that human life will be extinguished within the next few decades. This possibility makes the question of meaning even more intense. Russell was talking about a world in which each individual would eventually die, but in which human society would go on for several more millions of years, until the planet became uninhabitable through natural causes. In that situation, you could see yourself as making contributions to human society which would outlast you for hundreds or thousands of years. You could still see your life as important—as long as you suppressed ultimate questions. But now, as Robert Jay Lifton has documented,[9] people have great difficulty seeing how their lives have any meaning at all, given the probability of a nuclear holocaust. Believing that no answer to the question of ultimate meaning exists, many people cope by means of what Lifton calls *psychic numbing*, in which all such questions are suppressed.

In the academic world, especially in artistic, literary, philosophical, and theological circles, the existentialist standpoint is today expressed in what is widely called a *postmodern mood*. This postmodernism, like the earlier atheistic existentialism, draws heavily upon Friedrich Nietzsche, especially his insight that the "death of God" implies nihilism. But, whereas the existentialist rebelled against the absurdity of the universe in the name of the authenticity of the self, the self has disappeared for the nihilistic postmodernist along with God and objective values. The idea of an autonomous, self-determining, centered self is regarded as an illusion to be "deconstructed." The so-called self is simply the product of impersonal forces, especially linguistic habits and conventions. Also, whereas existentialists affirmed the caring, value-realizing self in the face of the unhappy truth that the universe is objectively meaningless, the nihilistic postmodernists have rejected the very notion of truth. If all human ideas are simply products of forces passing through them, there is no basis for having more confidence in the modern worldview than in, say, astrological worldviews. This postmodernism, in rejecting the modern worldview, is not suggesting that it be replaced by a postmodern worldview. It offers instead what might be called an antiworldview, a therapy to prevent seduction by any and every worldview. In terms of my opening comments, this postmodern stance accepts no story of the universe in terms of which we could focus on those features of life that are of ultimate importance. This refusal is appropriate, of course, because this postmodernism denies that anything *is* of ultimate importance. Being human is therefore unimportant, and nothing that we do is important.

This nihilistic postmodernism has simply carried the basic philosophical premises of the modern worldview through to their logical conclusions, conclusions that were anticipated a century ago by Nietzsche and even another century earlier by David Hume. This stance is, therefore, more accurately called *ultramodernism*. The relativistic, nihilistic features of this ultramodernism are just those implications that some antimodernists had seen as dangers implicit in modern thought from the beginning.[10]

The most prevalent way to react against the modern worldview has been to return to some form of premodern worldview. This return is usually to some form of religious orthodoxy—or at least to a fundamentalism *assumed* to be orthodox. The rise of so-called creationist science in our time, in spite of the enormous amount of evidence supporting at least the most general features of the evolutionary story, is a testimony to the desperation of some people to regain a worldview in which human life again seems important. But the return to premodern outlooks is not limited to those who defend a literal interpretation of the creation story in the Hebrew scriptures. Many of those who are "turning East" and speaking of a "perennial philosophy" are essentially accepting a premodern worldview found in Hindu or Buddhist scriptures.[11]

But these two approaches—rejecting the modern worldview in the name of a premodern worldview or rejecting it in the name of an antiworldview stance—do not exhaust the ways of rejecting the modern worldview. A third possible approach combines features of the other two. With the nihilistic postmodernists, it sees the impossibility of any simple return to a premodern outlook. It sees the passage through modernity as irreversible, at least in many respects, but believes that we must pass beyond modernity. It also uses the term *postmodern*. But with those who advocate a return to a premodern worldview it sees the need for, and in fact the inevitability of, a worldview, some overarching view of the nature of reality in terms of which we understand our own place in the scheme of things. It therefore calls for a postmodern worldview—or, more accurately, it sees such a worldview to be emerging in our time, and seeks to call attention to, advance, and shape this emergence.

What *postmodern* means in this approach is very different from what it means in nihilistic postmodernism. In the first place, rather than carrying through the basic presuppositions of the modern world to their logical, antiworldview conclusions, this approach challenges and revises some of those basic presuppositions. In the second place, on this new basis many of the truths and values of premodern worldviews can be recovered. No simple return to a premodern worldview is involved, however, because many of the truths and values of the modern worldview are retained. It can be called "a return forward." To explain this notion, I must first complicate somewhat the highly schematic sketch given in the first section of the transition from the medieval to the modern worldview.

IV. THE TWO STAGES OF THE MODERN WORLDVIEW

To make the account of the emergence of the modern worldview more accurate, two major stages in its development must be distinguished. In the first stage, exemplified by Robert Boyle and Isaac Newton in England, and Fr. Marin Mersenne and René Descartes in France, the creation of the world by a personal God, the specialness of the human self, and continuing life beyond bodily death were not rejected. To the contrary, the mechanistic view of nature was adopted to buttress these beliefs. The world was said to be purely God's creation, having no creative power of its own. The personal God's absolute transcendence and power over the creation, including the supernatural power to intervene in the world's processes at will, were emphasized as strongly as possible.

By analogy, the human soul, as the image of God, was said to be absolutely different from the rest of nature. This doctrine is best known in terms of Descartes' absolute dualism between body and mind, but it was much more widespread. The human soul was no longer high on a chain of being that included the inanimate mineral world as well as plants and animals. An absolute gulf between the human soul and the rest of the creation below it was instead posited. The rest of the world was pure matter, with no consciousness, not even any unconscious feeling or striving. Physical matter and the conscious soul were absolutely different in kind. The aforementioned distinction between primary qualities, on the one hand, and secondary and tertiary ones, on the other, developed in this context.

Primary qualities, such as size, shape, and mass, were ones that could qualify insentient, unfeeling, uncaring matter. All those qualities that could not be conceived to exist apart from consciousness were labelled *secondary* or *tertiary* and lodged solely in the human mind.

In this first stage of the modern worldview, no intent existed to deny the ultimate reality of the human soul and the importance of its qualities. The dualistic doctrine asserted that the world was composed of two *equally* real things: souls and bodies, mind and matter. The motive of this dualism was to increase the importance of the human mind or soul, and to protect the plausibility of the claim that it survived the death of its body (even though the souls of [other] animals were not assumed to live on; the difficulty here was usually avoided by ignoring the question of animal souls or denying their existence outright).

The motive was one thing, however, the effect quite another. This supernaturalistic and dualistic view, with God absolutely transcendent over the world and the soul absolutely different from its body, could not long survive. The idea of God as an omnipotent personal being, totally determining the structure and events of the world, soon led to atheism, partly because of the problem of evil, partly because the idea that the world is a machine made God's action in it difficult to conceive. The idea of the human soul as an alien ghost in a machine soon led to mechanistic materialism, largely because of the problem of understanding how an immaterial, personal soul could interact with a material, impersonal, machine-like body. In this materialistic view, the mind or soul is said to be epiphenomenal. This doctrine means that the mind exercises no power. Only material things exert power; the so-called mind is merely a passive effect. Later versions of materialism do not even ascribe epiphenomenal reality to the mind, but regard it as somehow identical with the brain. This materialistic atheism, of course, entails the denial of life after death.

In this way, the first stage of the modern worldview led to the second stage (which I had earlier described simply as *the* modern worldview because it has become increasingly dominant in intellectual circles since the eighteenth century, and especially since the latter half of the nineteenth).

Knowledge of this historical development helps us understand the major basis for the widespread assumption that the atheistic-materialistic worldview is the only intellectually respectable view: this worldview seems better than the one it replaced, the supernaturalistic-dualistic view, with which advocates of the materialistic worldview still do battle. The materialistic-atheistic view did not win out in intellectual circles because scientific facts required it; they did not. It did not win out because it is free from problems; it is not. (In fact, it suffers from as many inadequacies as the dualistic-supernaturalistic view, a point that I discuss in chapters 3 and 6.)[12] Rather, it won out partly because it fit the spirit of the times and partly because it could easily point out the problems in dualistic supernaturalism, which it presumed to be the only serious alternative. Once we realize this, we become more free to challenge this reigning orthodoxy by presenting a third alternative.

This historical understanding also helps us identify those crucial assumptions in the first stage of the modern worldview that led to its overthrow and thereby to the antihumanism of the second stage of modernity. Identifying those crucial assumptions leads us to scrutinize them more closely.

With this background, I now give a sketch of a postmodern vision in which crucial assumptions of the modern worldview are rejected, and in which some truths and values lost in the modern interlude are recaptured. I give less attention to defending this new vision than to pointing out its implications for the importance of being human and preserving our most precious human qualities.

V. A POSTMODERN WORLDVIEW

A formal point to make about a postmodern vision is that it must be self-supporting; that is, its claim to truth cannot be based on some alleged revelation. There is nothing wrong with getting ideas through revelation, if one assumes, as I do, that revelation in some sense occurs.[13] But the claim that the ideas are true must be based upon their intrinsic convincingness: they must pass the usual tests of self-consistency and adequacy to all the facts of experience. This formal point distinguishes a postmodern worldview from most premodern ones. An acceptable postmodern vision must be self-consistent and must be adequate to the facts of science as well as to the moral, aesthetic, and religious dimensions of our experience. I now turn to the content of the postmodern vision I find most convincing.

The human self, with its personal qualities, is again seen as a natural part of the created world, as belonging to it. At the same time, the human self is again seen as the "crown of creation," as the chief exemplification, on our planet anyway, of the qualities that all creatures embody. This dual view provides a basis for rejecting anthropocentrism, according to which other creatures are emptied of all importance except their usefulness to human beings, while at the same time holding that human beings are intrinsically more important than other earthly creatures.[14]

Included in this position is *panenergism*, the idea that the world is exhaustively composed of things that embody energy. This idea has been widely accepted since the time of Einstein, whose formula declared energy and mass to be convertible. Following Whitehead, I would enlarge the notion of energy to *creativity* and extend it to living cells and to minds or souls. No dualism obtains between (internally) active minds and passive bodies, as in first-stage modernity, or between (externally) active bodies and passive, unreal minds, as in second-stage modernity. Minds and constituents of bodies both have (internal and external) energy, or creativity, and thereby the power to initiate activity. This universality of creativity is the theme of chapter 3.

A closely related element of this position is *panexperientialism*, the idea that all the individuals of which the world is composed are experiences. What we call matter is usually a large aggregate of individuals—billions of atoms exist in a rock, billions of cells in an animal's body. When we think of "matter," we are also thinking of such aggregates as viewed from without. But from within, the individuals are experiences—just as, from without I am merely matter, but from within I am experiences. This point is generalized to all individuals: apes, alligators, amoebae, and alpha particles.

Because everything has experience, everything has value or importance in and for itself. Nothing should be treated as a mere means to our ends. Everything deserves respect. With first-stage modernity, this postmodern vision exalts the human being. But it does so without denigrating everything else. This postmodern vision says that the human soul is really real, that it is actual and active. But this vision does not suffer from the mind-body problem that undermined first-stage modernity, the problem of how experiencing mind could interact with nonexperiencing matter. According to this postmodern view, the body itself is composed of experiencing individuals. The cells comprising the brain are different only in degree from the mind—*greatly* different in degree, to be sure, but different only in degree nonetheless. These cells themselves, considered from within, have experiences, or *are* experiences. The mutual influence of brain and mind is therefore not unintelligible: brain cells and the mind share feelings with each other.

The most important aspect of this position for our present topic is that experience and its qualities are regarded as primary in the nature of things. The qualities that modernity called primary—size, shape, and mass—are now considered secondary, even tertiary. The qualities that modernity called tertiary—the qualities of experience, such as purpose and emotion—are now considered primary. Being human is again important in the nature of things. The human soul is the chief exemplification of the type of reality that eternally exists and is the locus of all power in the universe. To focus on developing particular qualities of soul is to concern oneself with qualities of the ultimately real.

As a second point, the postmodern vision again sees the world as the creation of a personal deity. This deity is not, however, the God of medieval or of first-stage modern theism. That God had created the world out of absolute nothingness, which meant that the world had no inherent power of its own. God was omnipotent in the sense of essentially having all the power; the world was passive in relation to God. God was therefore totally responsible for all that went on in the world, and God could intervene at will to perform miracles and to provide infallibly inspired scriptures.

This idea of God was undermined by the problem of evil, by the historical discoveries which counted against the idea of infallibly inspired scriptures, and by various reasons for rejecting the idea of occasional miraculous interventions.

The postmodern God created our present world not by calling it into existence out of absolute nothingness, but by bringing order out of a chaotic realm of energetic events. This God neither controls all things nor interrupts the natural processes here and there. God does not coerce, but persuades. God does not create unilaterally, but inspires the creatures to create themselves by instilling new feelings of importance in them. This constant inspiration is a necessary part of the natural process, not an intervention into it. In this world, the vast amount of evil does not count against the reality and goodness of a divine creator, because all the creatures have some degree of power to act contrary to the purposes of the creator. The idea of an all-pervasive providential spirit is not contradicted by the evidence for extensive "chance and necessity" throughout the evolutionary process. This postmodern vision of a personal creation, if it becomes dominant, will therefore not be undermined by attention to empirical facts, as was the earlier vision.

Besides the fact that the qualities of personhood are again seen to be ultimate in the nature of things and that our high exemplification of personal qualities can be regarded as the *imago dei* in us, the universe again has an all-inclusive meaning, an all-inclusive meaningful story, in which our communal and individual stories can have their meanings. The all-inclusive story is what the Divine One is doing with the world: creating beauty. Beauty *is* in the mind of the beholder: beauty is what the Divine Beholder of all that occurs is seeking to create. At our level, the beauty sought is most importantly the beauty of our lives, which includes intellectual fineness and moral and religious beauty (the "beauty of holiness") as well as appreciation for and creation of beauty in the more usual sense of the term. In this sense, Whitehead says, truth, beauty and goodness provide "the final contentment for the [Divine] Eros of the Universe."[15] What we do in this regard, even in the inner recesses of our souls, is also important again, for it is known by the appreciative consciousness of the universe. The contribution we thereby make to the everlasting life of God is in fact the basis for the ultimate importance of our lives. Even if our lives do not continue beyond bodily death, they are of ultimate importance.

This question of continuing life is the third aspect of the various worldviews we have examined. In the materialistic worldview, evidence for life after death could not be taken seriously, because the human by definition is nothing except the physical body, all of which decays at death. In the postmodern vision, however, the reality of the soul and its distinctness from the physical body are again affirmed (even though the dualism of first-stage modernity is rejected). Accordingly, people who adopt this point of view are free to look at the evidence, such as that from parapsychology, for the idea that life goes on, and many who have looked at this evidence open-mindedly have been convinced.

This new conviction does not necessarily mean a return to premodern Western notions of life after death, because ideas from diverse traditions may have merit, and new ideas may be formed on the basis of new evidence, such as that provided by studies of near-death experiences. For example, a postmodern view would necessarily think of a continuing life in an evolutionary context, and see the state of the individual after bodily death as not unilaterally determined by God but as, like our present states of consciousness, partly determined by us. Furthermore, if human souls survive bodily death, while the souls of other animals do not, this fact could not be because human souls are absolutely different in kind from those of other animals, or that God created this whole universe for us alone, as a preparation for a future life. The human soul alone might survive bodily death because it developed the power to do so during the evolutionary process in response to divine promptings, just as it developed other fairly unique powers, such as the power of symbolism, rational thought, and reflexive consciousness. These issues are explored at much greater length in chapter 6.

For our present topic, however, the main point is that a postmodern worldview opens the way to considering the possibility that the human journey does not end with bodily death. If a continuing life is affirmed, the renewed sense of the importance of being human provided by the postmodern vision is reinforced. As we who had been moderns work our way into this new view, we will have a renewed sense of the importance of developing virtues in ourselves. We will also have a renewed sense of the importance of the lives of our fellow human beings, no matter how outwardly insignificant they may seem. People who look upon their fellow human beings as fellow travellers on a long journey to an all-inclusive commonwealth of love will be less likely to use them as mere means to their selfish ends, or to try to destroy the evil that is perceived to be in them by simply destroying them. This implication leads to a final point.

Although I have thus far used the language of "preserving" our most human qualities, nothing living can simply be preserved indefinitely in its present form. The law of life is: advance or decay. Our task is not simply to recover, or to preserve, the best way of being human developed in the past. Our task is to envisage, and incarnate, a still better way, a way that fulfills the human potential more fully, a way that more completely realizes the image of God in us.

I suggest that in our time, especially since the development of nuclear weapons, this task means learning to interact with each other in terms of persuasion, without resort to violent coercion. (I here touch briefly on the central theme of chapter 8.) The Divine One of the universe, in the postmodern vision, operates strictly in terms of persuasion. And the most unique thing about us, in comparison with the other creatures, is our capacity to persuade and to be persuaded. Should we not therefore say that this capacity constitutes the *imago dei* in us, which we should work to bring to fulfillment? This stance will, of course, take tremendous courage. Courage is one of our most important qualities—it has been called one of the four cardinal virtues. Perhaps with a vision of persuasion as the divine *modus operandi*, joined with a new vision of continuing life beyond bodily death, courage to live by persuasion alone will become one of the defining marks of a postmodern world.

3

CREATIVITY AND POSTMODERN RELIGION

The modern world arose through a clash of two spiritualities and has embodied a compromise between them. One was a spirituality of creativity originating in the scientific, philosophical, religious Renaissance which, coming after the literary and humanistic Renaissance of the fourteenth century, spread northward from its origins in Italy in the latter half of the fifteenth century. The other was a spirituality of obedience stemming from the Protestant Reformation of the sixteenth century. After defeating the previously dominant spirituality of Christian Aristotelianism, these two spiritualities in effect reached a compromise, with the spirituality of obedience dominant. The spirituality of creativity would inform only scientific and artistic life, while the spirituality of obedience would inform religious and moral life and also the *worldview* of the scientific as well as the religious communities.

In this chapter, I look at the transition from the premodern to the modern world in terms of the clash between these two spiritualities. I then describe a number of problems, both theoretical and practical, that have arisen because the spirituality of obedience became victorious in the worldviews of both the scientific and the religious communities. These problems, I suggest, along with developments within both the scientific and the religious communities, point toward a postmodern spirituality, in which the spirituality of creativity that was defeated at the outset of the modern age is recovered in a postmodern form. In contrast with most exaltations of creativity or vitality over law and order (some recent versions of which have even been called *postmodern*), this postmodern spirituality of creativity does not deny that the spirituality of obedience was also based upon a true intuition, as I explain later.

I. THE CONFLICT BETWEEN THE SPIRITUALITIES OF CREATIVITY AND OBEDIENCE

The giant of the later Italian Renaissance, which combined Hermetic and Cabalistic themes with a Christianized Neoplatonism, was Pico della Mirandola. As Frances Yates stresses, he was central in the transition in human self-understanding from passive contemplation to active operation, which many historians see as the crucial change from the medieval to the modern world. Pico said that our very relation to God, and hence our human dignity, consists in our creative power. Pico's view made it "dignified and important for man to operate" by making it a religious act, not something contrary to the will of God.[1]

Many schools of thought developed out of this Renaissance movement. Some were pantheistic, identifying the divine with the creativity in the world; others were more suggestive of what is now called *panentheism*, in which God and the world are distinguished though seen as mutually immanent. But in either case all things were usually seen as embodying creative power, and this power was regarded as divine or at least as rooted in and encouraged by the divine.

This wide movement is increasingly regarded by historians of science as the spiritual matrix out of which what we call *modern science* arose. And yet it was not to become the framework for the "scientific" interpretation of nature. It lost out to ideas rooted in the Reformation which were in turn based on the nominalistic-voluntaristic theologies of the preceding two centuries. According to this view, God has all the creativity, the world has none. The creative God is not present in the creatures, but is their external creator and controller. All of nature obeys God's laws. For humans to be religious means for them to be obedient.

Various sociological factors explain the defeat of the Renaissance views. One factor was related to the pantheistic or panentheistic form the Renaissance views often took, which was associated with "levelling" movements against the monarchy and the hierarchical church, and with belief in creative influence "at a distance" and therefore with witchcraft and naturalistic interpretations of miracles. Hostility to these implications by defenders of the hierarchical church and the monarchy led them to prefer a view of nature that denied to it any power of this sort. The Renaissance views are discussed more fully in chapters 2 and 6.

Quite consciously in opposition to all animistic views of nature, the formative thinkers of the modern worldview, especially Boyle and Newton in England and Mersenne and Descartes in France, portrayed natural entities in purely mechanistic, materialistic terms. As canonized in Newton's law of inertia, natural entities were said to have no power of self-movement; they remain as they are unless moved by an outside efficient cause. In exerting efficient causation on each other, they could operate only by contact, exerting no influence at a distance (which made the interpretation of gravitation and magnetism very difficult and controversial).[2] Natural entities were also said to be devoid of divinity and of intrinsic value of any sort, so that reverence for them would be "sentimental." Most important for our purposes, the laws of nature were said to be wholly imposed. Because natural entities in no way embodied divinity or any other self-moving power, the laws of nature could not be thought to reflect principles immanent in matter or in a "soul of nature." The laws of nature could not be regarded as merely descriptive laws, analogous to sociological laws—that is, as statements about the widespread habits of various species of being. They had to be regarded as prescriptive laws, imposed upon nature by its omnipotent, external creator.

This early modern view was dualistic. The human soul was said to be wholly unlike natural things. It not only had experience and hence intrinsic value; it also had a derivative form of creative power, which was delegated to it by God. It alone was created in the image of its creator.

This dualistic supernaturalism could support two types of human spirituality. On the one hand, believing that absolute laws for human behavior had been infallibly revealed by God (whether in the Bible, the teaching authority of the Roman Catholic Church, or in human conscience), humans could assume that their role in life was, like nature, to obey the divinely imposed laws. On the other hand, focusing upon the absolute difference between themselves and other creatures, they could believe that their role was to exercise their creativity.

II. Problems within Early Modernity

This early modern worldview, with its uncreative nature, its dualism, and its omnipotent, external deity, led to many problems. The most well-known problems are theoretical.

Evil had always been a problem for Christian theism, insofar as it stressed God's omnipotence and perfect goodness. But the problem became much more severe when the power of the creator was accentuated and the inherent power of the creation so explicitly denied, and when this new emphasis on omnipotence was advocated in the framework of a "natural religion" acceptable on the basis of experience and reason alone, without appeal to supernatural revelation or "mystery." If human beings have no inherent power *vis-à-vis* God, with which they could resist God's will, why do they sin? Or at least why does God allow their sin to cause such misery for other humans? Even if a "free-will defense" could handle these problems, the evil caused by natural events, such as the Lisbon earthquake, still remained unexplained.

A second problematic fact was that the Bible, purportedly the revelation of God, was shown through historical and literary criticism to have all the signs of human creativity. The idea that human beings have no inherent power with which to resist God's providential activity led people to expect God's inspired book to be free from all error and bias. But historical and literary criticism showed that the Bible contains many errors and contradictions, and that each author had a distinctive point of view. Many concluded that the category of "inspiration" was not applicable at all.

A third problematic fact was the rise of an evolutionary perspective. The idea of a sudden creation had fit with the idea that God inherently has all the power and that the creation was "out of nothing." If the world has no inherent power with which to resist God's creative activity, one would not expect the present state of our planet to have been several billion years in the making, or the physical structures of some species to be only imperfect adaptations of structures originally developed by earlier species. An omnipotent creator would not have had to resort to such compromises. The early modern view of the God-world relation forced a choice: either creation or evolution. This issue is discussed at length in chapter 5.

A fourth problem was the mind-body problem. How could the mind, with its creativity and experience, interact with a body, defined as having neither creativity nor experience? Although various answers were provided by Descartes, Malebranche, Berkeley, Reid, and others, they were all variations on a single theme: the omnipotence of God is needed to explain it. Without an omnipotent being for whom all things are possible, it was generally agreed, the apparent interaction of mind and body would be inexplicable.

Besides these well-known conflicts between theory and fact, the early modern worldview also created a serious practical conflict. Its portrayal of the God-world relation supported two conflicting spiritualities. On the one hand, it *explicitly* supported a spirituality of obedience by stressing the absolute omnipotence of God, and by emphasizing that this God had infallibly revealed absolute moral laws. The content of these laws was also generally interpreted in terms intended to suppress human creative energies in most areas of life—albeit not all, especially the domination of nature. On the other hand, this theology *implicitly* supported a spirituality of creativity. This point is based on the premise that the basic religious motivation of human beings is the *imitatio dei*. Because this theology portrayed God primarily as Creative Omnipotence, human beings were led by their desire to imitate deity to develop a spirituality not simply of creativity but of domination, even destructiveness. The implicit and explicit messages in fact coverged with regard to the domination of nature, in that the biblical injunction to "subdue" nature was given special prominence and the *imago dei* was defined in terms of our capacity to dominate the rest of the world.

The early modern worldview did not originate the conflict between the spiritualities of obedience and creativity. Nor did it inaugurate the fact that, insofar as creativity is supported, it tends to become domination, even destruction. These problems have been inherent within traditional theism, with its doctrine of coercive omnipotence, all along. But in the modern world the conflict became especially intense, because this vision of omnipotence was accentuated, and the support for domination and destruction became increasingly dangerous, due to the direction and advances of modern technology.

These points are illustrated by most fundamentalist Christians in the United States, who carry on the early modern worldview. (A person in our time with Isaac Newton's beliefs would be called a fundamentalist.) With regard to evolution and biblical authority, they exemplify a spirituality of obedience. They accept the infallibility of the Bible taken literally, and therefore the biblical account of creation taken literally, in spite of overwhelming evidence against both of these doctrines. At the same time, they show no willingness to modify the modern economic system, or to renounce militarism and nuclearism, in spite of the overwhelming evidence that these systems will soon destroy the very conditions of life. Although these fundamentalists would doubtless portray their allegiance to these systems wholly in terms of obedience, this allegiance seems also understandable as a manifestation of modernity's implicit spirituality of creativity, with its tendency toward domination and destruction.

III. Problems within Late Modernity

As discussed at some length in other chapters, the early modern worldview, with its dualism and supernaturalistic theism, evolved into the late modern worldview, which is materialistic and atheistic. This view is also plagued with many conflicts between theory and fact. For example, having rejected the soul, in which the early modern worldview had lodged all creativity and hence freedom, this late modern worldview cannot acknowledge the freedom that is presupposed by everyone in practice (even in the act of denying this freedom). Also, having accepted the view that all causal influence is by contact, but having rejected the omnipotent God who could explain apparent causal influence at a distance, the late modern worldview must dogmatically deny that any such influence occurs, even though there is much evidence for such influence. (This issue is discussed at greater length in chapter 6.) Finally, if early modernity had difficulty with disorder, as evidenced by its problems with evil, evolution, and biblical fallibility, late modernity has a problem with order. Having retained a materialistic view of nature, which rules out the view that nature's laws are its habits, it accepts the doctrine that nature obeys imposed laws, while explicitly rejecting an Imposing Lawgiver. It has to insist, also, that the evolutionary process reflects no teleological order, which strains credulity. And it must seek to explain those forms of human order called aesthetics and morality without appeal to any norms or principles rooted in a cosmic source of meaning and importance.

Besides having these well-known conflicts between theory and fact, late modernity, like early modernity, conveys an ambivalent message about spirituality. Here the ambivalence arises from the tension between the practice of the scientific community and the theory (the late modern worldview) that it promulgates. This community admires and rewards extraordinary exercises of creativity. And yet the worldview accepted by this community implies that creativity is an illusion. Those feats that appear to result from especially creative insight combined with extraordinary self-discipline are said, really, to result from purely deterministic causes. Nobel prizes should not be given to the people who make the breakthroughs, but to the molecules in their bodies; their "minds" are simply obeying, willy-nilly, the orders coming from some combination of DNA and environment. Of course, it would make no sense to reward the DNA molecules either; they are simply the products of deterministic causes lying further back. Ultimately, all Nobel prizes should be awarded posthumously to the Big Bang.

IV. RETHINKING THE NATURE
OF THE PHYSICAL

The conflicts within the early and late modern worldviews summarized above all result from the assumption that the fundamental units of the physical world are devoid of creativity. That assumption also is central to the conflicts between the spiritualities of obedience and creativity. A way beyond these conflicts might be found if the physical world were thought to have the inherent power to act that was denied it by early modernity for mainly theological and sociological reasons. This is the postmodern position to be explored in the remainder of this chapter.

The primary stimulus for rethinking the nature of "physical things" has come from physics and biology, especially those developments associated with Albert Einstein, Werner Heisenberg, Jean Baptiste Lamarck, and Charles Darwin.

One of the main reasons for thinking of nature as inherently passive or uncreative is the simple fact that most of the objects of our sight and touch appear to be passive. A rock just stays where it is unless moved by an external force. An absolute gulf seems to exist between active, self-moving things and passive, inert things. Because of this feature of the macroscopic objects of our ordinary experience, especially vision and touch, dualistic worldviews are widespread. But the drive toward a unified view of nature is strong. One way of achieving monism is the primitive animistic view that all things, including things such as rocks that show no signs of self-motion, have souls. A contrary way to overcome dualism is by the materialistic hypothesis that all things that appear to manifest creative action can be understood reductionistically as the outcome of noncreative things. Dualism, primitive animism, and materialism have, accordingly, been the three most widespread views.

Modern molecular or atomic theory opened up a fourth possibility, which can be called *postmodern animism.* Perhaps the passive objects of sensory experience are really composed of multitudes of self-moving entities. Perhaps the fundamental difference between a rock and a squirrel is that a squirrel has a dominant self-moving entity, a soul, which can coordinate the motions of its bodily members, while the rock does not, so that the movements of its millions of constituents simply cancel each other. Leibniz suggested this view, but did not develop it into a notion of universal creativity. Retaining the view that God has all the creative power, he said that all the motions of the "monads" making up the world were really programmed into them at the creation. And, in general, the atomic theory of matter did not lead to a fundamental challenge to the view of nature as passive. The molecules, then the atoms, and then the subatomic parts were imagined by analogy with objects of sense-experience. Atoms were pictured as if marbles were going around a billiard ball.

But twentieth-century physics, as symbolized in Einstein's formula $E = mc^2$, suggests a radically new way of thinking. Although the "m" in the formula stands for mass, not matter, the formula suggests that there may be no fundamental difference between matter and energy—that matter is "frozen energy." Subsequent empirical study has verified this intuition. Matter is being transformed into energy all the time, and energy into matter.

Traditional thought, at least in the West, had usually assumed that matter was one thing, energy or activity another. The "what" of a substance and its activity, if it had any, were distinguished. For example, Aristotle distinguished the material cause of a substance, what it was made of, from its final causation. This final causation could be intrinsic to it, but there was no thought of simply identifying the "stuff" of a substance with its activity. The "what," the material cause, was passive. Under the influence of traditional monotheism, the gap between matter and activity became even larger. Not only was the material cause of a material thing passive; the material thing in its entirety was devoid of activity, having no intrinsic final causality.

But the Einsteinian revolution opened up the possibility of regarding creative activity itself as the "material cause" of things, their very "whatness." The world could be seen as radically self-creative, with the evolutionary process bringing forth higher and higher forms of creative beings.

This view of the nature of physical things is fully consistant with quantum physics, for which Einstein's work is also fundamental. Whereas physics until then was supposed to support a deterministic philosophy of nature, quantum physicists such as Werner Heisenberg startled the scientific and philosophical world by speaking of an inherent indeterminacy. Some people interpret this "indeterminacy principle" in a merely epistemic way, so that it refers to nothing beyond the inability of the physicist to determine (in the sense of *ascertain*), say, the location and momentum of a particle at the same time. But the observational data are open to an ontic interpretation, according to which the principle points to an inherent lack of complete determinism in nature's elementary processes themselves. Heisenberg himself spoke of "potentiality" in nature. This ontic interpretation is compatible with the view that these processes are partly self-determining. Einstein rejected any such interpretation. Although the question as to which aspect of Niels Bohr's "Copenhagen interpretation" Einstein found most objectionable is complex, he clearly could countenance no suggestion that God "plays dice" with the world—that is, that nature harbors any principle of spontaneity and hence chance.

Einstein himself, therefore, did not accept the postmodern animism opened up by his own breakthroughs in relativity and quantum physics. He had long been captured by the Spinozistic vision of the Whole (God or Nature) as necessary. He could not accept the idea of genuine creativity in the world. In spite of the role played by creative insight in his own view of scientific discovery and his own creative efforts on behalf of peace—which make sense only if we have the freedom to do one thing instead of another—he was committed to the vision that everything happens as it must.

Similar to Einstein in this respect was Charles Darwin. It is Darwin above all with whom the idea of evolution is connected, and the idea of evolution is the other major basis within scientific theory for coming to think of nature as active and dynamic rather than passive and static. The idea of evolution has probably been more fundamental for this rethinking than twentieth-century physics, partly because it was developed earlier. But Darwin himself held to the idea of matter as essentially passive, devoid of any capacity for activity that is not rigidly determined by the past, that is, any capacity for genuinely creative activity. He thought that natural science required the assumption that there is no freedom in nature to do things that are unpredictable in principle.

In developing a theory of evolution on this basis, Darwin and his followers were rejecting a different view, developed by Jean Baptiste Lamarck, who was an earlier advocate for a gradualistic view of evolution, in which no supernatural intervention was needed to explain novelty. The basis for Lamarck's own theory was the idea of matter as having inherent spontaneity. The Darwinian idea that "natural selection" is the creative force of evolution is a denial not only of "divine selection" but also of the Lamarckian idea of creative, spontaneous matter.[3]

Darwin, like Einstein, is therefore associated with an idea that seemed to imply a dynamic notion of matter, yet himself rejected that dynamic notion. He may have done so largely because the physics of his time seemed to imply a fully deterministic picture of the elementary units of nature, and absolute predictability was at its height as an ideal for science. In any case, it was left to other thinkers to generalize the idea of creativity into the ultimate reality of which all things are composed, whether building on the notion of human creativity, biological evolution, physics, or a combination of these.

V. Creativity and Divinity: Bergson and Berdyaev

In the transition to the postmodern view, according to which all things are embodiments of creativity, Henri Bergson is of overwhelming importance. He spoke of evolution as "creative," to mean bringing forth something new, something that was not already implicit in the past. At first he was dualistic, limiting creativity to living things. But he later overcame this dualism, viewing even matter as creative. The traditional association of deity and creativity was retained. But now, rather than seeing God as creative, creativity was regarded as divine. Creativity was not in a being transcendent to nature, but was the very stuff of nature itself.[4]

One thinker influenced by Bergson was Nicolas Berdyaev, who put creativity at the heart of his thought and used it to reinterpret Christian theology. Berdyaev completely rejected the attribution of omnipotence to God and the notion of creation out of nothing. Rather, he saw "uncaused freedom"[5] as the fundamental reality out of which the world is formed. God should not be understood in terms of "power and might." Our relation to God should not be understood in terms of servile categories such as "dependence" (Schleiermacher) or "obedience" (Barth).[6] That kind of theology is guilty of sociomorphism, transferring to God categories from a particular form of human society. "What God expects from man is not servile submission, not obedience, not the fear of condemnation, but free creative acts. . . . Sin does not lie in disobedience to the commandments and prohibitions of God, but in slavery, in the loss of freedom. . . ." God finds expression in the world in freedom, not in domination. God is not a diminution of human freedom and activity but their very condition.[7] Christian ethics should be an "ethic of creativeness."

Berdyaev's theology of creativity is rich, exciting, and suggestive. But it is limited. He limits creativity or uncaused freedom to human existence, not seeing it as fundamental to all levels of creation. Perhaps his commitment to a Kantian dualism prevented the generalization of creativity to nature. He gives no explanation of the relation between creativity and causal determination, simply stating that "events which take place in the existential sphere lie outside any causal sequence." And, after rejecting traditional notions of God's all-controlling providence, he provides no positive way to understand the God-world relation: "The inconsistency and the paradoxical nature of the relation between the divine and the human is resolved only in the divine mystery about which no human words can express anything at all."[8]

Berdyaev's position also makes the goodness of God problematic. The problem arises because he, like Bergson, equated God with creativity. His position is thereby similar, as he himself pointed out,[9] to the Advaita Vedantist form of Hinduism, according to which our deepest self, or Atman, is identical with Brahman, the divine reality. If this is taken to mean that our own power of self-determination—our freedom or creativity—is simply divine, a serious problem results from the fact that we often exercise our creativity in evil ways. If the word *God* means the freedom or creativity exercised in the world, we cannot speak of God as unambiguously good, thereby worthy of worship without qualification. Creativity as such is, to be sure, the source of all good—of all life, all truth, all beauty, all moral goodness. But it is also the source of all evil—of all killing, all lies, all ugliness, all depravity. Creativity is both creator and destroyer; it is "beyond good and evil." Some forms of Hinduism and some other traditions have indeed used this language for the divine reality. But the religions arising out of the biblical tradition have usually insisted that the divine reality is perfectly good. The straightforward identification of God with creativity made it difficult for Berdyaev to articulate that intuition.

Another thinker heavily influenced by Bergson was Alfred North Whitehead. His position, along with the closely related position of Charles Hartshorne, does not restrict creativity to human life but makes it, as did Bergson, the central category for interpreting reality as a whole. Unlike Bergson and Berdyaev, however, Whitehead and Hartshorne do not simply equate God with creativity but regard creativity as the ultimate reality which is embodied by both God and all worldly individuals. In the remainder of the chapter I describe and employ this suggestion.

VI. WHITEHEAD AND THE ULTIMACY
OF CREATIVITY

For Whitehead, creativity is the ultimate reality of which all things are instances. This means that the basic things or entities are events, spatio-temporal processes of becoming. Whitehead's view not only generalized the Einsteinian notion of the convertibility of matter and energy, but also employed another basic Einsteinian notion, which is that space and time are inseparable. One cannot speak of space and time as separate, but only of space-time, or time-space. Whitehead's way of explaining this idea is that the things comprising the world are not essentially nontemporal things that just happen to be in time. They are essentially spatio-temporal events. They take—or make—time, as well as space, to occur. There is no "nature at an instant"—taking *instant* in the technical sense as having no duration or temporal extension. There are also no actualities devoid of spatial extension. All actualities are temporal-spatial events. Whitehead therefore says that all actual entities are "actual occasions." No actual things simply endure passively. Each real thing is a spatio-temporal happening.

These actual occasions or events can be extremely brief, with hundreds, thousands, millions, or even billions within a second. Things that endure, such as electrons, atoms, molecules, cells, and minds, are each comprised of a series of brief events.

Moments in the life-history of an electron, a cell, and a human being obviously differ immensely in terms of the forms they embody. But they all have one thing in common: each is an instance of creativity. Creativity is in this sense the ultimate reality, that which all actualities embody. All actual entities are thereby creative events.

The creativity of an event has two sides. One one side, the event creates itself out of its predecessors. This self-creative side has two moments. The first moment is the event as receptive, taking in influences from the past and repeating them. This is the event's *physical pole*. The second moment of the event's self-creative activity is its response to possibilities. The event thereby creates itself out of potentiality as well as actuality. This side of the event is called its *mental pole*, because it responds to ideality, not to physicality. Because of this response to ideal possibilities, the event is not totally determined by its past, although it is heavily conditioned by it.

The other side of the event's creativity is its creative influence upon the future. Once the event has completed its self-creative activity, it begins its career as an influence upon subsequent events. Just as it had used previous events as its own food, it now becomes food for later events. Much of an electronic event's immediate influence is received by the next event in that enduring society we call the electron. Much of my influence in this moment is taken up by the next moment of my experience, as I embody much the same character as did the previous moment and carry out its intentions. But obviously not all of the influence is limited to the next event in the enduring society. Much of the influence from my present experience is exerted upon the cells in my body in the next millisecond. The electron influences the other electrons in its atom, the events comprising the nucleons, the atom as a whole, neighboring atoms, and more remote ones (for example, by gravitational attraction).

I have already implied that various levels of creative events exist. All the creativity in the universe is *not* embodied in subatomic particles, with the creativity of the more complex things being reducible to the creativity of their constituents. The world instead contains various types of *compound individuals*, to use Hartshorne's term for organisms that have both complexity and individuality. The creativity of the atom is not simply the creativity of its subatomic parts added together. The atom as a whole has its own creativity. It responds to its environment—neighboring atomic events, the events of its own constituents, and the events of any larger society of which it is a part, such as a living cell; and it, in turn, influences subsequent events which find it in their environments. Likewise, the molecule as a whole can be thought to have its own level of creative activity, as can the cell as a whole. And the psyche of the multi-celled animal, especially one with a central nervous system, has its own level of creativity with which to create itself and then to influence others.

Whitehead and Hartshorne have generalized the Einsteinian notion of energy. The physicist's energy is an abstraction from the full-fledged creativity which is the ultimate reality of the universe, of which all individual things are instances. Saying that the reality pointed to by this larger notion is the "what" of all things implies that individuals at all levels are equally real. Against the reductionism of modern thought, this view says that living cells are not less real than their atoms and that souls are not less real than the brain cells with which they are associated.

Even to describe the ultimate reality as creativity is an abstraction. Creativity is always *creative experience*; that is, besides exercising creativity to some degree, every individual event enjoys experience of some sort. With this point brought out explicitly, all the elements needed for a solution of modernity's mind-body problem are provided. Because the soul or mind is not different in kind from the cells comprising the brain, interaction between mind and body is not unintelligible, as it was for modern dualism. Because dualism is overcome not by denying the reality of the mind or soul but by attributing creativity and experience to cells and their constituents, the freedom or creativity of the person is not denied, as it was by modern materialism. This postmodern position on the mind-body relation is described more fully elsewhere, especially chapter 6.

VII. CREATIVE EXPERIENCE AND THE GOD-WORLD RELATION

The idea that creativity is the ultimate reality also forms the basis for post-modern solutions to the problems that resulted in early modernity because of its portrayal of the God-world relation, and those that resulted in late modernity from its complete denial of a divine reality. These solutions all follow from a new understanding of the relation between creativity and divinity.

The idea that creativity is the ultimate reality in everything, combined with a positive view of the relation between creativity and the divine, could lead to their complete identification. The divine reality would therefore be not a distinct being but that creative energy surging through all things. As we saw in relation to Berdyaev, this view makes it impossible to insist that the divine reality is perfectly good, the source of good but not evil. Whitehead, while giving a highly positive evaluation of creativity, provides a way to hold to this insistence.

Whitehead at first followed Bergson in the equation of creativity (then called *substantial activity*) and the divine. But he soon distinguished between creativity and God, defining the latter as the principle of limitation and of rightness, which divides good from evil.[10] At this point, God was not an instance of creativity, but only an abstract principle qualifying it. Before long, however, Whitehead portrayed God as *embodying* creativity.[11] God not only exerts a creative influence on all other actual entities (God's "primordial nature"); God also exemplifies the receptive creativity characteristic of all other actual entities (God's "consequent nature"). God is said to be not the exception to the metaphysical principles applying to other actual entities, but their "chief exemplification."[12] Creativity is not God, but creativity is the ultimate reality, which God and the most trivial puff of existence in far-off space both exemplify.

John Cobb has suggested that we should think in terms of two ultimates.[13] The *ultimate reality*, which is called creativity by Whitehead, is similar to that which is called *Being* by Heidegger, *Emptiness* by Buddhists, and *Nirguna Brahman* by Vendatists. God, who is the source of all physical, aesthetic, and ethical principles, is the *ultimate actuality.* Whitehead differs from Advaita Vedantists and most Buddhists by not making this source of forms or principles subordinate to the ultimate reality. The ultimate reality and the ultimate actuality are equally primordial. God does not create creativity, but neither does creativity generate God. Each equally presupposes the other. Creativity that is uninfluenced by God's persuasion toward ordered beauty therefore never occurs. Nor could God exist alone as the only embodiment of creativity, the sole possessor of power.

This last point, which is crucial for the solution to the problem of evil, requires explanation. Given the notion of the ultimacy of creativity, a multiplicity of creative individuals must always exist. Why? Because it belongs to the very meaning of creativity that "the many become one, and are increased by one."[14] To be actual is to be an instance of creativity, which is to create oneself out of the many actualities which are given, and then to be added to that many as a creative influence out of which the next acts of creative synthesis will arise. To be a unity, an individual, is to be a creative synthesis out of a multiplicity. It would therefore be impossible by definition to be a one without a multiplicity, a one alone with itself.

The essential point is that creativity does not belong to God any more than it does to the world. As Hartshorne puts it, creativity must be embodied in both divine and nondivine instances of it.[15] That the finite embodiments exist is as essential as that the all-inclusive embodiment exists.

Given this notion of what it means to be an individual, the notion of creation *ex nihilo* is self-contradictory, if it means that once upon a time (or before time, whatever that might mean) God existed all alone, without any other actualities. Our world was created, to be sure. It is contingent. It arose historically. But it arose, according to this view, out of chaos, or, to use Berdyaev's term, out of *relative* nothingness, not out of absolute nothingness. It arose as the gradual development of order among actual occasions. Perhaps at one time all actual occasions occurred randomly, without even being ordered into very primitive enduring objects such as protons, electrons, or quarks. So-called empty space is perhaps comprised of such random events. The rise of quarks, protons, atoms, molecules, macromolecules, cells, and so on was the gradual rise of increasingly complex forms of order.

Because each actual occasion is affected by the creative influence of all previous occasions and also has its own inherent power of self-creation, God can never be the total cause of any event. God is a creative influence on all events, but never the sole creator of any, because each is partially created by its past world and by itself. God is uniquely the creator of our world, in that God is the one embodiment of creativity who is both everlasting and omnipresent. As such, God is the only enduring being who has influenced every event in the world directly. It is through the steady divine persuasion that order has been coaxed out of chaos and that the higher forms of existence, which make possible the higher forms of value, have come into being. But God is not and could not have been totally responsible for the details of the world.

The creative power of the creatures, their freedom in relation to God, is not a contingent matter. It is not that God could have created a world of actualities devoid of creativity but chose instead to make a world with self-creative creatures in it. Creativity does not belong essentially to God and only voluntarily, by gift, to the creatures. The embodiment of creativity in a plurality of individuals is the ultimate metaphysical truth (according to this hypothesis): any actual world would necessarily be composed of events with the twofold power of self-creation and creative influence on others. God's stimulation of the world to bring forth higher forms of creatures with greater embodiments of creativity, however, *can* be considered a voluntary matter. In *this* sense the creation of our world is due to divine volition. Our *high degree* of freedom is a gift of God. But that the worldly creatures have some degree of freedom is not due to divine choice.

Nor was it due to divine choice that higher creatures, with capacities for the higher forms of value experience, also have more power to create themselves and to affect other creatures. A world with more valuable creatures is therefore *necessarily* a more dangerous world, both because higher creatures can more radically deviate from the divine persuasion for them and because this deviation can create more havoc than the deviations of lesser creatures. A theology of universal creativity can in this way portray God as perfectly good while being consistent with the fact not only that the world has some evil in it but that it has *horrific* evils due to the presence of human beings.

From the point of view of a theology of universal creativity, the existence of chaos and evil is no surprise. They are to be expected, given a multiplicity of centers of creative power. The surprise is the existence of order and goodness. They beg for explanation in terms of an all-inclusive creative influence. Whereas starting with the concentration of all creativity in one divine being finally led to the denial of God, starting with many centers of creativity leads to the affirmation of God.

The postmodern God who is thereby affirmed is, of course, not the God that late modernity denied. With this new idea of God, we can explain the order reflected throughout nature, and the teleological order reflected in the directionality of the evolutionary process, without having our hypothesis contradicted by the vast disorder of the world. The compatibility between evolution and this idea of God is discussed in chapter 5.

With this position, we can also explain the order of the world in such a way that telepathy, psychokinesis, and other phenomena suggesting causal influence at a distance need neither be denied *a priori* nor regarded as supernatural interruptions of the order of nature. Once all events are seen to embody creative experience, it no longer seems obvious that action by contact, and therefore causality between contiguous events, must be the only kind of efficient causation that can occur naturally. Perhaps every event receives creative influence from, and exerts creative influence upon, noncontiguous as well as contiguous events. This idea is explored further in chapter 6.

Finally, this postmodern position allows for an idea of "inspiration" that overcomes the modern dichotomy between infallible inspiration and a complete denial of divine inspiration. Had the idea that all beings embody inherent creativity been presupposed, biblical criticism would not have played the negative, shocking role it has played in modern religion. The Bible would have been approached, like other books, with the expectation that the authors would express their own individualities, their own limited ideas, and their sin (for example, by projecting their desire for vengeance onto God), and that one author would often contradict another. With all of this expected, attention might have been focused on the amazing extent to which some of these writers, in some passages, transcend what we would normally expect from "all-too-human" writers. Without the preconception of infallibility, we might have marvelled more at the signs of genuine inspiration. We would have seen that this inspiration differs only in degree, not in kind, from the inspiration toward truth, beauty, and goodness that characterizes all human experience to some degree. Given this realistic account of divine inspiration, we would not have gone to the opposite extreme of denying divine inspiration altogether, which made late modernity unable to explain its own commitment to truth and the limited but real unanimity found in all cultures on aesthetic and moral values. By taking the universality of both creativity and divine inspiration seriously, we can be adequate to both the diversity and the commonality found in ideas of truth, beauty, and goodness.

Having dealt with the various conflicts between theory and fact that modernity created for itself by denying creativity to nature, I turn now to the topic of spirituality. I suggest that the position sketched above provides a spirituality and ethic that overcome the oppositions discussed earlier between obedience and creativity, between science and religion, and between worldview and practice.

VIII. A SPIRITUALITY AND ETHIC OF EXPERIENTIAL CREATIVITY

If the modern world had been based upon the universality of creative experience instead of its denial, modern spirituality would have led to a different ethic in several respects. First, no antithesis between "obedience" and "creativity" would have existed. The special *imago dei* in humans would have been regarded as the set of ways in which our capacity for creativity is quite unique. God's creative influence upon us would have been thought of as God's stimulation of our own creativity—in contrast to the early modern tendency to portray God's will in a way calculated to put a damper on most expressions of our creative energies. Rather than feeling an opposition between obedience and creativity, between ethics and aesthetics, people would have been taught that the Supremely Creative One is the source of their own desires to be creative, and that the divine call to ethical activity is simply part of the call to enlarge the scope of one's creative influence and to make its effects upon others truly creative instead of destructive. Had this been the prevailing view, the Church would have been perceived not as the opponent of the spirit of creativity admired in the sciences and the arts but as the chief witness to the Holy Spirit of Creativity of which science and art are two expressions. Had this been the case, incidentally, the Church would have been in position to give a critique of particular developments in science, technology, and the arts to which the culture might have paid heed.

This postmodern resolution of the modern conflict between the spiritualities of creativity and obedience in favor of the former does not mean that the latter was not based upon a true intuition. As religious beings, we naturally want to be in harmony with the ultimate reality of the universe and our own deepest nature, and "to be in harmony with" is the fundamental form of "obedience." We also want to be in harmony with the ultimate actuality of the universe, the Holy Power, which means "obeying" its "will," insofar as that language is deemed appropriate. The crucial distinction between the spirituality of obedience, as usually understood, and the spirituality of creativity is the way the ultimate reality and ultimate actuality of the universe are understood. If the ultimate reality and therefore our own deepest nature is creativity, then to "obey" it means not to give complete allegiance to any of creativity's past products, be they scientific ideas, religious dogmas, political institutions, or economic systems. Likewise, to "obey" the will of God for our lives is to become more rather than less creative. True obedience is therefore manifested in a life of maximal creativity.

Another dimension of the spirituality of obedience, traditionally understood, is a life lived according to divinely supported norms. This dimension is also not absent in a postmodern spirituality, as portrayed here. In contrast with the deconstructive or eliminative form of postmodernism, which is relativistic, this constructive or revisionary postmodernism affirms both the reality of, and the possibility of experiencing, divinely rooted norms. In contrast with most premodern and early modern spirituality, however, these norms are not felt to be in opposition to most expressions of creaturely creativity. The divine call is to exert our creative energies to the fullest in a wide variety of dimensions. The divine "no" is directed only against those expressions that are really destructive rather than creative, in that they cripple or destroy the creative capacities of others, including one's own future experiences.

A religion based upon the universality of creative experience would also lead to a different work ethic. The modern vision, in portraying worldly entities as essentially passive, has focused upon the possession of material goods as the prerequisite for the good life. In our economic theories, we have therefore concentrated upon the citizens as consumers, not upon their activity as producers. (Although this issue was central in the early writings of Karl Marx, which were not published until our century, it became peripheral in the writings of the older, more "scientific," more fully modern Marx, which were published during his lifetime, and which became definitive for "Marxism.") We devote much attention to the quality of the goods produced but very little to the quality of the worker's lives during their producing hours. A job is assumed to be a good one if it provides the worker with enough money to buy enough goods. And the main issue in the various "liberation" movements is widely assumed in our country to be equality of buying power. It has, therefore, been difficult for men and even many women to understand the motives behind the women's liberation movement in the United States except for the demand for equal pay for equal work.

Had we focused instead upon the creative nature of experience, regarding it as what is essential and common to all human experience and as what must be fulfilled if life is to be more satisfying than frustrating, we would have seen things much differently. Although Whitehead himself did not work out these categories, his analysis of creative experience suggests that there are three fundamental types of intrinsic value. Corresponding to the physical or receptive phase of experience are *receptive values*. The *essential* receptive values depend on conditions that must be provided by one's environment if one is simply to survive—adequate air, food, and water, absence of exploding nuclear warheads, and so on. These conditions allow for other receptive values that are not absolutely essential but do normally contribute to the goodness of experience—beautiful visual surroundings and music, stimulating educational resources, a satisfying sexual partner, labor-saving devices, luxurious items, and so on.

Corresponding to the mental or self-determining phase of experience are *self-actualizing* or *achievement values*. The satisfaction here comes from fulfilling one's own potentialities, doing something on one's own, or achieving a certain standard of excellence—for example, in writing a poem, building a house, raising a child, being a friend, leading a country, making a scientific discovery, teaching a course, growing a crop, feeding the poor, climbing a mountain.

Corresponding to the anticipation of making a creative contribution to future experiences are *contributory values*, which we enjoy in the present moment due to the anticipation that our current self-determining activity will make a creative contribution to future experience. When we plant a crop, build a house, write a book, get a law passed, cook a meal, raise a child, heal a patient, discover a vaccine, give an artistic performance, and so on, our sense of satisfaction comes not solely from doing the task well but also from the anticipation that this activity will contribute to satisfactions beyond the present experiences.

These self-actualizing and contributory values are *creative values*, in comparison with the receptive values, which are more passive. Once the essential receptive values are available on a regular basis, *these creative values are more important than an increase in the conditions for further receptive values*. If we Americans were predisposed by our worldview to recognize this fact, we would realize that our foreign aid should aim not at directly providing the conditions for receptive values (except in emergencies), but at increasing other people's ability to do things well on their own and to make their own contributions to the world. Instead of doing this, our efforts usually increase their sense of dependence upon us. (I refer here only to our "foreign aid" at its best, looking aside from the fact that it has all too often been used primarily to promote the American economy and/or to prop up repressive regimes.) We know from our own experience how important it is to be self-reliant, we who have a "declaration of independence" as a sacred document and place the "pioneer" and the "self-made man" high up in our symbolic pantheon, and yet we fail to generalize this knowledge to others. A religious outlook with creative experience at the center would lead us to place the issue of essential receptive goods within the larger human need—the need to satisfy the various dimensions of that creative urge which is of our essence.

An ethic based upon the ultimacy and universality of creative experience would, thirdly, lead to an ecological ethic. Modernity's dualism between experiencing, active human beings, and nonexperiencing, passive nature led to an ethic even more anthropocentric than that of traditional Judaism and Christianity. In the postmodern view, each individual being has an experience of value for itself which should be respected. While this ethic would be based on a reverence for life, it would not refuse to make discriminating judgments: some forms of experience would be recognized as intrinsically more important than others—for example, a human's more than a cat's, a cat's more than a microbe's. This is a complex issue, which can only be mentioned here.[16]

A religious outlook in which creative experience is primary would, fourthly, help dissolve the modern ethic of competitive individualism. Modernity's use of billiard balls for the paradigm of really real things has encouraged the notion that we are essentially self-enclosed individuals, whose relations to each other are purely external and more of a threat than a promise. When this notion was combined with the notion that our good consists largely in the possession of material goods, the interests of one person or nation came to be perceived as necessarily in conflict with the interests of another person or nation. The relations between persons, social groups, and nations came to be perceived largely in competitive terms. As is usually the case to the degree possible, the perception became the reality. In most of our relations, competition has become dominant over cooperation. Strategic thinking looks for a we win/they lose strategy based on antagonistic interests much more naturally than for a we win/they win strategy based on mutual interests.

The paradigm of creative experience orients us to the fact that experience lives upon experience—nothing else exists!—so that, far from being self-enclosed monads, we are in each moment receptive (to some degree) to all the experiences in our immediate and even more remote past. Although we always exercise some degree of self-creation, so that the quality of our experience is not totally a function of our environment, we are largely constituted by the experiences in our world. This fact is most obvious with regard to the experiences of our bodily parts and our own past. But those extraordinary moments in which we become conscious of a direct perception of another's experience, or a remote scene, so that we speak of telepathy or clairvoyance, suggest that influence from afar is streaming into our soul at the unconscious level all the time. Carl Jung's researches, which led him to speak of a collective unconscious, support this suggestion. If we come to see the world in this light, we will no longer assume that our good can be attained while defeating the interests of others, because the quality of everyone's experience contributes to the psychic atmosphere from which we all arise. We will realize that we are literally "members one of another" as St. Paul suggested, so that we can truly seek our own true good (which is not immoral in itself, and was certainly presupposed by Jesus and Gautama) only by seeking the good of all. A perception of universal creative experience leads to an ethic of universal cooperation.

This vision of reality as consisting of nothing but a vast society of creative experiences within the all-inclusive divine creative experience implies a fifth fundamental change in the human way of life. The modern visions, in conjunction with our religious desire to imitate the ultimate power of the universe, make coercive power the way to get things done in general and to defeat evil in particular. The early modern vision portrayed the ultimate power of the universe as an external, omnipotent deity, who controlled events from above and who would defeat evil in the last days with a cataclysm to end all wars. The late modern vision portrayed the ultimate power of the universe as blind, brute force, which brings about evolutionary progress through a ruthless competitive battle for survival in which the weak are eliminated. These visions have supported a ruthless capitalism, a ruthless socialism, and an unprecedented militarism. This point is discussed in much greater detail in chapter 8.

The portrayal of the world as a web of centers of creative experience leads to a quite different notion of holy power. No individual can be controlled. Control is not an ideal. Power is threefold. It is, first, the ability to receive the offerings of others creatively, which is receptive power. It is, second, the ability to transcend the power of others and to make a partially self-determining response (for example, forgiveness), which is self-creative power. It is, third, the ability to influence others creatively, so as to maximize their own creativity, which is the power of persuasion or evocation. This third form of power is the type of relational power God has. It is God's power over the creatures. But *over* is not the right term. It is God's power *in* them. God's power to influence us is just that—the power to *influence*, to enter into us, and thereby to evoke the highest receptive, self-creative, and persuasive power in us. If this notion of the ultimate power of the universe—which is the notion suggested by taking the nonviolent Jesus as the supreme incarnation and revelation of God's agency—had won out, the interactions of human beings wanting to imitate deity would have been quite different. If this idea wins out in our day, we may yet be saved from self-destruction. If we are converted to a postmodern religion, we may have a postmodern world.

4

GOD IN THE POSTMODERN WORLD

The widespread loss of belief in God in intellectual circles in the modern world has been due, in part, to a problem inherent in the traditional idea of God and, in part, to problems inherent in the modern worldview. Although the rejection of the traditional idea of God has been a gain, the negative consequences of the complete loss of belief in God in any sense outweigh this gain. Attempts to render God and the modern worldview compatible have been unsuccessful. The emerging postmodern worldview allows for the recovery of belief in God while eliminating the fatal problem inherent in the traditional idea of God. These four theses are developed in the four sections of this essay.

I. THE LOSS OF BELIEF IN GOD
IN THE MODERN WORLD

To discuss belief in the existence of God in the modern world requires definitions of *God* and *modern world*. Definitions are neither true nor false, but more or less helpful, given widespread usage.

Within Western civilization and within all cultures heavily shaped by Jewish, Islamic, and/or Christian thought, there is what can be called the *generic idea of God.* According to this generic idea or definition, the word *God* refers to a personal, purposive being, perfect in goodness and supreme in power, who created the world, acts providentially in it, is sometimes experienced by human beings, especially as the source of moral norms and religious experiences, is the ultimate ground of meaning and hope, and is thereby alone worthy of worship.

The *modern world* is defined in terms of the *modern worldview,* which is the worldview that arose in the seventeenth century through the thought of people such as Galileo, Descartes, Bacon, Boyle, and Newton, and was spread in the eighteenth century as the "Enlightenment." Although it underwent a radical change in the eighteenth and nineteenth centuries from its first to its second phase, as explained in chapter 2 and again below in terms of the issues of the present chapter, it can nevertheless be considered a single trajectory. The *modern world* refers to the world of human thought and practice insofar as it has been dominated by the modern worldview.

The thinking of the modern world, the distinctive features of which can be called *modernism,* has had two distinguishable marks: On the one hand, there is modernism's *formal commitment* to freedom. This commitment has entailed a rejection of all beliefs that seemed to curtail human freedom or to be based on authority instead of experience and reason. On the other hand, modern thought has also been characterized by the acceptance of a particular view of the world, according to which the basic units of nature are understood in a purely *mechanistic* way, and a particular view of human experience, according to which the perception of the world beyond the self is limited to *sense*-perception. These two ideas can be called the *substantive assumptions* of modernism.

The decline in belief in God in the modern world is due to many interwoven reasons. I discuss four of the most important.

Probably the most powerful reason for rejecting the existence of God has been the problem of evil. This problem is constituted by the apparent contradiction between the alleged goodness and power of God, on the one hand, and the experienced fact of evil, on the other. And not just a little evil, but overwhelming, horrendous, unspeakable evil—the rape of little girls; the enslavement or genocide of whole peoples; the starvation of millions; the destruction of life and property by floods, earthquakes, and hurricanes; the existence of viruses causing slow, debilitating, agonizing death; and on and on. Surely such features of our world contradict the doctrine of an all-good, omnipotent deity!

It should be noted that the word *omnipotent* is used here, whereas the generic definition described God as "supreme in power." The traditional idea of God, which modern thought in its first phase not only accepted but accentuated (as explained below), defined the supremacy of the divine power as omnipotence. This term has usually implied that God essentially has all the power. Any power possessed by creatures is not inherent to the world but is derived from a voluntary gift of God. That which has been arbitrarily given can be arbitrarily withdrawn. It has, accordingly, been held that God could interrupt or override the normal causal relations among the creatures at any time God chose to do so.

Closely related to this notion of divine omnipotence has been the view that the world was created *ex nihilo*. That is, God did not create our world out of some preexisting material which had some power of its own. Because the world was created out of absolutely nothing, it has no inherent power with which to defy or distort the divine purposes. God does not need to rely on persuasion, but can unilaterally control any and all happenings in the world. Divine "omnipotence" has meant that God could unilaterally bring about any state of affairs as long as no self-contradiction was involved: God could not create a round square, but could have created a world free of disease, drought, and daytime television.[1] This idea of God has led to the widespread conviction, in the second phase of modernity, that the existence of God is contradicted by the world's evils.

Although the problem of evil was not first noticed in the modern world, it became a source of widespread atheism only in the modern world for two reasons. First, while premodern thinkers had accepted the existence of omnipotent goodness, in spite of appearances to the contrary, on the basis of authority, moderns were committed to testing all beliefs against experience and reason. Before that tribunal, the God of the tradition appeared to be guilty of nonexistence. Second, the founding thinkers of the modern worldview, such as Descartes, Boyle, and Newton, like Luther and Calvin before them, were part of an Augustinian-voluntaristic tradition which stressed the absolute omnipotence of God far more than it had been emphasized by typical medieval theologians, such as Thomas Aquinas. These early modern thinkers, who defined modernism in its first phase, explicitly denied that the world had any inherent power with which to deviate from the divine will.[2] This denial made the clash between the dogma of divine goodness and the experienced fact of worldly evil all the more apparent.

A second basis for rejecting the existence of God in the modern world has been the perception that belief in God serves to thwart the drive to full human emancipation from the various types of oppression. The desire to have intellectual freedom of inquiry, so that all issues could be settled through reason and experience, clashed with the authoritarian approach to truth based on the acceptance of the Church and/or the Bible as an infallible, God-given source of truth. The clash between the Church and Galileo, while greatly exaggerated by later polemicists (Galileo's clash was more with Aristotelianism), has been paradigmatic for this issue. Much modern polemic against God has been motivated by the desire to undermine this theological authoritarianism.

The urge for social and political self-determination has clashed with sociopolitical systems said to be legitimated by God. The passage in Romans 13, in which St. Paul says that rulers are ordained by God, has been used to support the divine right of kings against democratic movements. More generally, the *status quo* has been sanctioned by appeal to the implication of the goodness and omnipotence of God: whatever is, is right. Against these deep-seated beliefs, progressive thinkers have attacked the existence of God in order to attack systems using God for self-legitimation.

These first two reasons for rejecting God involved a clash between the traditional idea of God and modernism's formal commitment to freedom. The next two reasons are based on modernism's substantive assumptions.

One of the major theoretical reasons for the modern loss of belief in God in intellectual circles is that the modern worldview simply has no natural place in it for God. The current, second form of the modern worldview is materialistic. The human mind is said to be not really real, but merely a by-product or aspect of the brain, devoid of power or agency. As such, it provides no analogical basis for thinking of a cosmic spiritual agent. Also, it is not readily intelligible how a personal, purposive, spiritual agent could act providentially in a wholly material world.

An ironic fact about the modern worldview, not yet widely appreciated, is that it was initiated by thinkers who wanted to forestall materialism and to protect a particular type of divine action. It has long been recognized that the central feature of the modern worldview, with which the rise of modern science has been associated, is its mechanistic account of nature. But it has not been so widely known that this account was directed not only against the Aristotelians, as the textbooks have it, but primarily against a Hermetic, Neoplatonic, holistic, "magical" view of nature.[3] In this holistic or magical view, the divine reality was immanent in nature, and those kinds of events traditionally called *miracles* (and now called *parapsychological phenomena*) were considered to be natural, if somewhat extraordinary, events (as they are by contemporary parapsychologists). That is, they were not miraculous interruptions of "laws of nature" requiring a supernatural explanation.

One motive of those who advocated the mechanistic view of nature, such as Fr. Marin Mersenne in Catholic France and Robert Boyle in Protestant England, was to defend the supernatural attestation to the unique truth of Christianity provided by the miracles of the New Testament.[4] Against the holistic magicians, they (and later Isaac Newton) insisted that God was totally transcendent, so that nature had no divine powers, and that in particular there was no possibility of action at a distance (Newton was a partial exception on this latter point).[5] Causal action could only occur by contact—an idea at the heart of the mechanistic view of nature. If any apparent action at a distance did occur, as in the New Testament healings, one therefore could infer a supernatural act of God (or a pseudo-supernatural act of Satan, if the apparent agent was a witch or some other pagan).

Another motive of the originators of the modern worldview was to protect the idea of the human soul and its immortality. Some of the holistic thinkers were "mortalists." The fact that the soul was a self-moving thing did not prove that it was immortal, they said, because the body is also composed of self-moving things and it is clearly mortal. In denying that the units of nature were self-moving things, mechanistic dualists such as Mersenne and Boyle were seeking to show the need for a soul that was different in kind from its mortal body and could therefore be presumed to be immortal.[6]

The first version of the modern worldview, with its mechanistic view of nature, was therefore originally adopted in part because it seemed to have soul-shaped and God-shaped holes of a particular kind in it. However, this theologically motivated attempt to save particular views of the human soul and of divine action soon backfired. The first version of the modern worldview was transmuted into a second version, in which God and the soul were lost altogether. The dualistic view of the human being created an insuperable mind-body problem. How could soul (or mind) and body, as totally different kinds of substances, interact? This problem led to a materialistic notion of human beings, in which there was no longer a soul to serve as an analogue for the divine existence. At the same time, the idea of miraculous interruptions of natural law lost credibility. The "God of the gaps," even the great Newton's version of it, was increasingly ridiculed. The deistic notion that the world was originally created by God, which Voltaire for one never relinquished, was retained for some time, by many members of the dominant culture, including Charles Darwin (as discussed in chapter 5). But by the twentieth century, even that remnant of the traditional idea of God was largely rejected in intellectual circles. The dominant worldview of modernity simply has no God-shaped hole.

A fourth reason for the death of God is that the modern worldview denies the possibility of an experience of God. Modernity's materialistic ontology has as its epistemological correlate the doctrine that all perceptual experience of the world must come through one's (material) sensory organs. In the first stage of the modern worldview, with its dualism, there was the possibility that the soul could have a direct perception of other worldly realities, both physical objects (clairvoyance) and other souls (telepathy). And indeed, some early moderns, such as Francis Bacon and Joseph Glanvill, accepted this viewpoint,[7] which provided an analogical basis for affirming a direct experience of God. However, there was a strong tendency, exemplified by John Locke, to equate perception exhaustively with sensory experience,[8] thereby making belief in God rest solely on rational inference from the order of the world as known through sensory experience. As the modern worldview became increasingly materialistic, identifying the "soul" or "mind" with a certain function of the brain (rather than as an entity distinct from it), the idea that there could be any nonsensory experience was ruled out *a priori*. Theories proliferated to explain how the idea of God ever arose in the first place, given the assumption that it could not have arisen from direct experience (Feuerbach, Marx, Comte, Freud, and Durkheim, among others).[9]

When taken together, as they usually are, these four arguments have provided a powerful presumption in favor of atheism in those circles in which the modern worldview has been directly or indirectly effective.

II. NEGATIVE CONSEQUENCES OF THE LOSS OF BELIEF IN GOD

In the eighteenth and nineteenth centuries, the leading thinkers characteristically considered atheism a good thing. Belief in God was thought on the whole to have been bad for the human race. In our own century, which Franklin Baumer has followed Arthur Koestler in calling the "age of longing,"[10] the leading thinkers are more prone to stress the negative consequences of the loss of belief in God. They have seen that Nietzsche's prophecy was correct: a world that has lost God altogether is worse than the world that believed in the God despised by Nietzsche and the rest of late modernity. Consideration of these negative consequences helps to make clear the importance of the question of divine existence. I will discuss five.

Dostoyevsky had one of his characters say, "If there is no God, then everything is permitted." This sentiment captures one of the consequences of the atheistic worldview of modernity, which is the relativism of all norms and values. The generic idea of God is in part the idea of a universal, personal, purposive being whose universal purpose provides a standard against which to measure the desires and purposes of finite beings. The divine will provides the locus for norms and values objective to the finite mind; human conscience at its best can be thought to be humanity's access to these objective standards. The "death of God," as Nietzsche and then Heidegger have stressed, means the death of all such transcendent norms.[11] Nothing can be said to be better than anything else, *really*. No form of behavior can be said to be wrong, *objectively*. All opinions about norms and values have to be regarded as purely subjective and therefore relative preferences, having no correspondence to anything in the nature of things. Modern thinkers had at first thought it a release and a relief to be freed from the supposition of objective standards. Now, in the midst of the "age of atrocity," as Hannah Arendt has called it, we are more aware of the need for a consensus on the objectivity of certain prescriptions and prohibitions.

A second consequence is nihilism. William James suggested that the pragmatic value of belief in God for most people is belief in their own immortality. God is the guarantor of their immortal existence.[12] It is easy to ridicule this egoistic and trivializing reduction of the meaning of the existence of God. But the connection between God and immortality can be generalized. One dimension of belief in God is the conviction that the world is not entirely meaningless, so that there is an overall meaning in which our individual lives have their particular meanings. We may not be able to conceptualize exactly how this is the case, but the conviction that our lives and those of others are not ultimately meaningless has been tied up in our tradition with belief in God. The denial of God has therefore generally implied the denial of any ultimate purpose behind the world and consequently of a context in which our lives could have meaning.[13] According to this nihilistic view, the way we lead our lives, including the way we treat others, does not finally matter. Human beings with this outlook and tremendous destructive power at their fingertips make for a very dangerous world.

Materialism is a third consequence. Human beings do not cease being religious simply because they lose faith in the traditional object of religious belief. The basic religious drive, which is to live in harmony with the ultimate reality or power of the universe, remains. Atheistic materialism simply means the replacement of one religious ultimate with another. In materialism, matter itself is thought to be the ultimate reality of the universe. It is the creator of all that exists, of all that we value. The religious motivation to be in harmony with the ultimate reality explains the transition from theoretical materialism to materialism as a religious way of life.

The most obvious form of this religious materialism is the insatiable desire to control and possess more and more material things. A less obvious form is the acceptance of Social Darwinism, according to which "survival of the fittest" is the only ethic. This ethic is based on the desire to conform to the method used by Omnipotent Matter (as Bertrand Russell at one period of his life called it),[14] which, according to Darwinism in its atheistic form, creates the world by ruthlessly eliminating those who cannot successfully compete. This ethic of unrestrained competition for the control of material resources describes much of the behavior of modern individuals, corporations, and nations.

A further consequence of atheistic materialism is militarism. The belief that we are purely physical beings, having only sensory experience, and that there are, in any case, no objective norms which could influence our behavior, implies that coercive power is the only way to influence the behavior of other individuals and nations. This is the presupposition of the Machiavellian *realpolitik* that has increasingly characterized the modern world. But there is also a religious dimension to modern militarism. The ability to control history through coercive power is felt to be a way of being in harmony with, of imitating, the ultimate power of the universe. The ultimate expression of this militarism is nuclearism. As Robert Jay Lifton and others have noted, there are unmistakably religious dimensions to the awe and trust that have been evoked by these weapons of mass destruction.[15]

It must be added here that nuclearism is not unique to materialistic atheists. Firm believers in divine omnipotence, especially some Christian fundamentalists, are as addicted as Social Darwinists to militarism and nuclearism. The connecting link is the common belief that the ultimate power of the universe exercises coercive, destructive power. Given the religious nature of human beings, either the theistic or the atheistic version of that belief promotes militarism and, in our day, nuclearism.

Neotribalism is a fifth negative consequence of the modern death of God. History amply reveals the tribalistic tendencies of human beings. Tribalism distinguishes between ''us'' and ''them'' and says that the moral norms that apply among *us* do not constrain our treatment of *them.*

Portraying a God who is the creator of all humankind has been one of the main ways in which human beings have sought to replace tribalism with universalism. This attempt has all too often backfired, as belief in God has been used to reinforce tribalistic identification rather than to transcend it. Indeed, one of the motives behind the humanistic championing of atheism was the conviction that theistic religion caused more division and warfare than it prevented. Even today we witness tragic conflicts between Jew and Moslem, Catholic and Protestant Christian, even Shi'ite and Sunni Moslem. Nevertheless, it can be maintained that nothing has done more to overcome the natural tribalism of human beings than the sense of kinship created by the belief that we all have a common divine source, live in the presence of a common divine reality, and have a common divine goal. Nazism and Stalinism serve as examples of the types of neotribalism that can be expected to emerge if the loss of belief in a divine source of human unity continues to recede. With the modern technologies of destruction at hand, this neopagan tribalism has been and will be far worse in its consequences than the premodern forms of tribalism.

Given the dual conviction that the modern worldview is incompatible with the traditional view of God, but that a humane form of life, at least in our context, is inextricably connected with talk of God, what is the philosopher or theologian to do? One possibility is to reaffirm a premodern worldview, as has been done by ''scientific creationists.'' This possibility will not be explored here because it ignores the undeniable gains of the modern worldview. A second possibility is to incorporate those gains within a postmodern worldview, which is the option advocated here. But first we should look at the most popular approach among philosophers of religion and liberal theologians, which has been to try to make talk of God compatible with the assumptions of modernity.

III. MODERN ATTEMPTS TO REAFFIRM THE REALITY OF GOD

The two major strategies of those who have tried to reconcile talk of God with the modern worldview have been to save God by redefinition and by insulation.

Saving God by redefinition means rejecting the generic idea of God, as given in Section I, and using the term *God* to apply to something else. Accordingly, even if this strategy "works" in some sense, it does not really save belief in *God*, insofar as God as generically defined in our culture is rejected. Rather, what is being saved is the *word* God and thereby *Godtalk*, as some put it.

Spinoza inaugurated in the seventeenth century one of the ways of making God compatible with the modern world by redefinition, which is to use the term *God* to refer to the universe as a whole. (There were some subtleties in Spinoza's own view, such as his distinction between *natur naturans* and *natur naturata*, which this simple statement, which applies to generic pantheism, obscures.) This pantheistic view of God removes the contradiction pointed out by the problem of evil, in that God is no longer understood as a personal, perfectly good being. God is instead "beyond good and evil," being indifferently the cause of both. Indeed, the very distinction between good and evil is regarded as a falsifying imposition of the unenlightened mind. Things are just what they (necessarily) are; no distinction between is and ought is possible.

The feature of traditional theism to which pantheism is most faithful is the doctrine of divine omnipotence; by equating God with the totality, pantheism obviously assigns all power to God. In fact, pantheists can well argue that their view simply carries out the logical implications of traditional theism: to say that God literally has and exercises all the power, as Augustine, Aquinas, Luther, and Calvin did, is implicitly to say that God is the only being (because, as Plato said, whatever has being has power). Spinoza made this argument, and a contemporary Calvinist, James Gustafson, has evidently found the move to explicit pantheism to be implied by the "radical monotheism" of Calvinism.[16]

The move to explicit pantheism has, however, generally been resisted in Jewish, Christian, and Islamic cultures, because it relinquishes certain ideas generally considered essential by those whose sensibilities have been formed in these cultures. The main problem with pantheism is its implication that no distinction can be made between what *is* and what *ought* to be. This notion, taken seriously, would undercut the ethical life altogether.

Closely related to pantheism is the doctrine developed by Paul Tillich that "God" refers not simply to everything but to the being (or isness) of everything.[17] Like pantheism, this view makes talk of God fully compatible with the modern worldview by not portraying God as a being distinct from the world who acts upon it. Because this God is neither a distinct agent nor a personal, purposive being to whom moral attributes could apply, the problem of evil does not contradict the reality of God. But this way of using the term *God* is even further removed than pantheism's from accepted usage. Talk of God is saved only by denying the existence of God in any intelligible sense.

Whereas Tillich's view equates God with, in Aristotelian language, the "material cause" of all things, some moderns have identified God with certain "formal causes," namely, ethical and aesthetic ideals. John Dewey in this country and recently Donald Cupitt in England have taken this route, as did Bertrand Russell in an earlier decade, at least in one of his most famous writings.[18] This view obviously avoids the problem of evil, because it does not regard God as omnipotent. And it sees God as unambiguously good, because God is equated with our best ideals. But few people can regard this as an acceptable way to use the term *God*. In denying that God is actual, it denies that God can in any sense act creatively or providentially in the world, because forms or ideals cannot be efficacious in and of themselves, but only insofar as they are entertained by actual beings. Without a cosmic actual being in which they can be located, furthermore, ideals must finally be regarded as our own creations, as Russell acknowledged.[19]

These and other examples which could be given[20] suggest that God must be redefined beyond recognition to be made compatible with the modern worldview.

Other philosophers and theologians have sought to have both the traditional idea of God and the modern worldview by insulating each from the other. The strategy of insulation declares science and religion to be two mutually autonomous spheres of discourse. Concepts in one sphere need not be modified in the light of those in the other. Belief in the existence of God is thereby intended to be insulated from the corrosive acids of modernity.

The first major exponent of this approach was Immanuel Kant. He distinguished between two fundamentally different functions of the human mind, the scientific (or theoretical) and the ethical (or practical). When functioning scientifically, the mind necessarily portrays the world as devoid of freedom and God. When functioning in a practical way, the mind necessarily presupposes freedom to act ethically, and the ethical life is said in turn to presuppose immortality and therefore God. Kant sought to show that this dual view of reality was not self-contradictory by means of an elaborate theory of perception and cognition. The scientific approach was said to give us mere appearance, the practical approach to put us into contact with reality.

This methodological dualism has been employed in modified form by many theologians to justify traditional theistic language without joining the fundamentalists' rejection of the modern worldview. Karl Barth distinguished between science and philosophy, on the one hand, and "faith," on the other. Faith with its object, the God of Calvinism, was said to be totally independent of all scientific and philosophical questions. There was no need to explain how or why God, who is as fully omnipotent as

Calvin said,[21] used a many-billion-year evolutionary process to create our world when it could have been created in one fell swoop.

Rudolph Bultmann modified Kant's position so as to distinguish between "theoretical" (or "objectifying") and "existential" perspectives. From the former perspective, there is no room for God to act in the world. But from the perspective of existential engagement, any event can become an act of God for the believer. The way divine and natural causation are related need not be explained. From one perspective, the event is fully explainable in terms of natural causes; from the other, it is praised as an act of God.[22]

Largely through the Austrian Ludwig Wittgenstein, this Kantian dualism of perspectives was transported to English and thereby American philosophy of religion. Wittgenstein was at least widely read as sanctioning the view that science and religion are two completely autonomous "language games."[23] This dualism was part of an antimetaphysical reaction in English-language philosophy, which paralleled the dominance of existentialism on the European Continent. Both approaches rejected the need for a metaphysical framework in which to reconcile the respective claims of science and religion.[24] The very idea of providing evidence or arguments for the existence of God, or even of showing it to be compatible with the presuppositions and discoveries of modern science, was ridiculed.

However, the human mind finally demands a unified, synoptic vision. It is now widely agreed that the attempt to protect belief in God by insulating it from the worldview associated with modern science does not work. As long as that worldview is accepted, there is pressure to redefine God beyond recognition, or to cease talking of God altogether. In either case, no basis is provided for resisting the relativistic, nihilistic, and materialistic implications of the modern worldview.

Modern theologians and philosophers of religion have failed with their central project, reconciling God and the modern worldview. But they cannot be faulted for this failure, because the task was impossible. The modern worldview simply is not compatible with an intelligible idea of God.

IV. A POSTMODERN WORLDVIEW AND THE RECOVERY OF BELIEF

Recovering belief in God, while retaining modernity's formal commitment to freedom, experience, and reason, is possible today only on the basis of a postmodern worldview that simultaneously overcomes modernity's substantive assumptions about nature and experience and traditional theism's assumption about divine power.

Given the incompatibility of God and modernity, the only way to speak intelligibly of God is to challenge the modern worldview. Many are challenging it today in terms of a premodern worldview. But for those of us who share modernity's commitment to freedom, experience and reason, the challenge must be based on a postmodern worldview, so that this commitment can be retained.

The rejection of modernity's substantive assumptions is not a sufficient basis for a recovery of belief, because the modern loss of belief was due in part to a problem inherent in the traditional idea of God itself. That idea of divine power put belief in God in opposition to the modern commitment to social and intellectual freedom. A theistic postmodernity, to be viable, must also challenge the idea of divine power traditionally associated with the generic idea of God.

Such a postmodern worldview is today gathering momentum. It makes belief in God possible again, even natural. But the feature of it that makes theism possible makes *traditional* theism impossible. This postmodern worldview also contains a fourfold critique of the substantive assumptions of modernity, involving pragmatic, philosophical, historical, and scientific arguments. I look first at this fourfold critique, than at the basis for affirming a modified version of the generic idea of God.

The *pragmatic argument* is implicit in the critique of the relativistic and nihilistic consequences of the modern worldview. The argument in brief is: The modern view of the world portrays it as devoid of all objective value and meaning; we human beings, who have been nurtured by this world and are integral parts of it, cannot live in terms of a completely relativistic and nihilistic worldview; therefore, there should be a presumption against the truth of the modern worldview.

The *philosophical argument* attacks the foundational belief of the modern worldview, which was that the fundamental units of the world (which modern physicists revealingly call "elementary *particles*") answer to the Cartesian and Newtonian notion of "matter." That is, they were said to be devoid of a "within," having no perception, no experience of any sort, no purpose, no self-determination, no inner activity of any sort. Given that starting point, one had to be either a dualist or a full-fledged materialist. The dualists said that the reality of one's own experience or mind, with its perceptions and purposes, was indubitable. They accordingly said that it was a reality different in kind from the material particles making up nature, including the human body. But this created the impossible task, as the materialists pointed out,[25] of explaining the way mind and body could interact.

The materialists avoided this problem by denying that the world is composed of two different kinds of things. The only really real things were said to be the bits of matter which make up material bodies. That which in ordinary language is called the "mind" was said to be not a really real thing but a mere by-product or aspect of a particular organization of bits of matter. This materialistic position, the dualists pointed out,[26] was paradoxical, if not outright self-contradictory. The materialists were claiming to be empiricists while denying the reality of that portion of the world which is given most immediately to our conscious experience, namely, our conscious experience itself! Even worse, they were implicitly affirming the validity of their own conscious experiences and reasoning processes that led them to affirm materialism, while the content of their affirmation denied that conscious experiences and reasoning have any reality.

This mutual annihilation of dualism and materialism provides a *reductio ad absurdum* of their common presupposition, the mechanistic view of nature, according to which its elementary units are insentient bits of matter.

The *historical argument* involves an attack upon a widely held twofold assumption about the emergence of the modern worldview. This assumption was that those advances generally identified with the "rise of modern science" both historically presupposed the mechanistic view of nature and provided empirical evidence for it. But recent studies have shown, as alluded to earlier, that the advances associated with the "rise of modern science" occurred within the context of a holistic, Neoplatonic, somewhat Hermetic worldview, which was decidedly nonmechanistic, and that the mechanistic worldview was later accepted more for theological and sociological than for empirical or scientific reasons.[27] The historical evidence therefore suggests that no logical or necessary connection exists between science as such and the modern, mechanistic view of nature.

The *scientific argument* consists of several developments within the natural sciences themselves that provide empirical evidence against the mechanistic view of nature with its idea of foundational matter. Physicists have led the way, as they have had to reflect upon the equation of mass and energy and the transformations of matter into energy and vice versa. Many physicists also now believe that good evidence exists for influence at a distance between so-called elementary particles, suggesting that they cannot be Cartesian or Newtonian bits of matter which can only be affected by contact.[28] Biologists point to the evidence for memory and decision in bacteria,[29] for "morphic causation" at a distance that cannot be understood in terms of ordinary physical fields,[30] and of the influence of the life of the planet as a whole upon its chemical processes.[31] These and related considerations have led to an increasing number of scientists to believe that the modern worldview, which was supposedly *based upon* the "hard" sciences, is not even adequate for *interpreting* these sciences.

This fourfold critique of the modern worldview is merely the negative aspect of the emerging postmodern worldview. This worldview fully accepts the achievements of modern science and modernism's commitment to freedom, experience, and reason. What it challenges is the mechanistic interpretation of nature and the sensationist epistemology, which constituted the substantive assumptions of modernism. The philosophers who have most fully developed this postmodern option are Henri Bergson,

William James, Charles Sanders Peirce, Teilhard de Chardin, Alfred North Whitehead, and Charles Hartshorne. My remaining comments are most consistent with the ideas of the latter two.

In this postmodern vision, the fundamental units of reality are experiential events. To say that they are "events" is to say that they exist only momentarily. To call them "experiential" is to say that they have an inner reality, which differs only in degree from our own inner reality, that is, our conscious awareness. Each event appropriates influences from beyond itself, which means that it has some form of nonsensory perception. Each event also has some elementary aim or purpose, in terms of which it creates itself. So-called elementary particles, such as electrons and protons, are enduring structures of momentary events in which the same form is repeated again and again. The human mind is also composed of a series of momentary experiences. A proton and a person are therefore not absolutely different in kind, only greatly different in degree.

At this point the modern mind boggles. It is incredible, it cries out, to think that protons have experiences! This cry shows how effective the modern worldview has been in conditioning us to reject any view but its own as absurd. I cannot take time here to provide evidence and arguments for this postmodern starting point, except to remind those who have been conditioned by modernity (which includes all of us) that accepting the modern starting point forces one into either dualism or materialism, both of which have insuperable difficulties. Assuming that this reply wins from the reader a provisional suspension of disbelief, I continue.

Besides saying that every momentary event has experience, the postmodern perspective says that each is an embodiment of creative power. There are three phases of each event's creative power. First, it creatively appropriates elements from its environment. (This is its nonsensory perception.) Second, it actualizes itself by creatively synthesizing these influences into an experiential unity. (Here its aim or purpose for itself is effective.) Third, it exercises a creative influence upon subsequent events. This threefold structure of appropriation, self-actualization, and efficient causation is thought to apply to all the individual events at every level of nature, from quarks, through electrons, atoms, molecules, and cells, to animal minds. (It does *not* apply to mere aggregates of individuals, such as rocks.)

God is the supreme, all-inclusive embodiment of creative power. As such, God both influences the world and is influenced by it. God differs from all other embodiments of creative power by being unlimited spatially and temporally and in knowledge and compassion.

God thus conceived exemplifies all the features of the generic idea of God (discussed in the first section). God's power and, therefore, God's creative and providential activity, however, are not understood as they were in traditional theism. Although God is the supreme power of the universe, God's creative and providential power to influence others is not unlimited.

*God does not have and could not have a monopoly on power and there-
fore cannot unilaterally determine the events in the world.* The reason for
this is that the creatures have their own inherent creative power to actualize themselves and to influence others, and this power cannot be
overridden.

God affects creatures, in this view, not be determining them from
without but by persuading them from within. All ideals or forms subsist
in God, by hypothesis, as potentials to be embodied by the creatures. God
acts in the world by presenting ideal aims to the creatures. God thereby
influences all creatures but totally determines none of them. What possibilities they actualize is finally up to them. The divine power is persuasive
not coercive.

This modification of the idea of divine power involves a revision of
the traditional idea of creation. Uncreated creativity has always, by
hypothesis, been embodied in some plurality of finite beings or other. The
creation of our universe therefore could not have been out of absolute
nothingness. Whatever point we designate as the beginning of our world
was created out of a previous state of events embodying creativity, perhaps a relatively chaotic state ("without form and void," as Genesis 1:1
put it). The creation of our world involved not the absolute beginning of
finite matter of fact but the constant evocation of increasingly complex
forms of order—which is indeed what the evolutionary picture suggests.
God creates the world by persuading it. This divine persuasion is, in the
long run, the most effective power in the universe. God can even be called
"all-powerful" if that is taken to mean "having all the power that it is possible for one being to have." But God is not omnipotent in the traditional
sense of actually or even potentially exercising all the power there is.

This postmodern theism overcomes the reasons within modern
thought for rejecting the existence of God. The first reason was that the
world's evil seemed to contradict the existence of a perfectly good, all-
powerful creator. The modification of the idea of God's power provides
the basis for a resolution of this problem. A world in which all beings have
some power of self-determination and some power to influence others, for
good or ill, is a world in which the possibility for evil is necessary. (Genuine
evil, carefully defined, is not necessary; but its possibility is.) God could
not create a world in which this possibility would not exist.

The second reason in modernity for rejecting God was that belief in
God seemed in tension with full human freedom. Belief in the postmodern
God could not be used to support an authoritarian approach to truth, because the possibility of God's infallible inspiration of a book or institution is denied. Likewise, no social or political arrangement can be justified
by the claim that it was ordained by God. In fact, far from being in tension with the freedom of the creatures, God thus conceived is the ground
of their freedom. Apart from God as the source of previously unrealized
possibilities, the creatures would be constrained to repeat the possibilities

that had been realized in the past. By providing novel possibilities, God allows the present to transcend the past.

The third reason for modernity's rejection of God was based on the assumption that the basic units of nature were insentient bits of matter. Just as it was difficult for dualists to understand the way the human mind could affect its bodily parts, it was difficult to understand the way God, as the universal mind, could influence nature. In the postmodern worldview, the units of the world are receptive events which appropriate influences from every level of reality. This view makes it natural again to think of God, the cosmic mind or soul, as immanently influential in every part of the world. God's pervasive influence throughout every level of the world is analogous to the mind's pervasive influence throughout its body.

Not only does this postmodern worldview allow talk of divine influence, it requires it. Because every event has some degree of freedom, a single, all-pervasive influence is necessary to account for the world's order, which is not perfect but nevertheless real. Also, the fact that novel forms or potentials have been realized occasionally in the evolutionary process requires an actuality in which these previously unrealized forms could be lodged and through whose agency their efficacy can be explained. In short, the postmodern worldview has a God-shaped hole in it.

The fourth argument against God was based upon modernity's assumption that sensory perception is our only means of receiving influence from the world beyond ourselves. In the postmodern vision, sensory perception is a sophisticated, derivative, lately evolved form of perception, not the basic form. All individuals, in appropriating data from the world about them, enjoy a more fundamental form of perception, which is nonsensory. Indeed, sensory perception presupposes this more basic form, as the neurons in (say) the optic nerve appropriate data emitted by firings in adjacent neurons.

Although God is not the kind of being who can be perceived through our sensory apparatus, we are, according to this view, apprehending God in a nonsensory way all the time. In those rare moments in which this constant apprehension of the divine reality rises to consciousness, we enjoy the "experience of the holy." Furthermore, our vague but insistent awareness of moral, aesthetic, and logical ideals that cannot be explained as the internalization of the norms of our society can be understood in terms of our direct prehension of those ideals as favored by God.[32] The inescapable objectivity of such ideals therefore provides another reason, within this framework, for affirming the existence of God.

CONCLUSION

The emerging postmodern worldview allows for the recovery of belief in God on the basis of experience and reason. The God thus recovered is similar to the traditional God, except for a modification of that feature of the traditional view most responsible for the rise of modern atheism, that is, the doctrine of divine power.

The postmodern worldview not only makes the recovery of belief possible; by having a God-shaped hole, it makes belief in God again natural. This worldview thereby makes it again natural to see the world as incarnating objective values and as manifesting an underlying purpose, so that relativism and nihilism are overcome. It also makes it natural to regard the world as an essentially spiritual matrix, so that our religious urge to be in harmony with the really real pulls us away from materialism. Its idea that the supreme power of the universe acts persuasively leads us to want to imitate this mode of acting and thereby to reject militarism, especially nuclearism. Finally, this worldview strengthens our sense of kinship with each other, portraying us all as having a common divine source, as living in the midst of a common divine reality, and as having a common divine goal. The divine reality of the universe dwells in us, and we in it, and our lives have immortal significance in it. We cannot violate the lives of our fellow creatures without thereby violating the divine origin and goal of our own existence.

5

EVOLUTION AND POSTMODERN THEISM

The issue of the compatibility of God and evolution is second to none in importance today. On the one hand, religion centers around the desire to be in harmony with the ultimate power of the universe, and in most religious traditions, especially those influenced by the Bible, the belief in God as creator has been an essential part of a theistic conception of the ultimate power of the universe. On the other hand, the idea that our world has come about through an evolutionary process is as well established as such a theory could be. Unless this evolutionary hypothesis is thought to be compatible with theism, the conviction that the supreme power of the universe is a personal, purposive, just and loving power will fade. The religious drive of people will lead them to bring their lives into harmony with a different kind of power.

A widespread conviction does in fact exist that God and evolution are incompatible, at least if we include "creator of our universe" in the meaning of "God." On the basis of this conviction, Creationists deny evolution, while Darwinians deny God. Modern liberal theologians *appear* to speak of God and evolution as compatible, but the idea of God as creator is in effect denied, as discussed in chapter 4. God is not described by these modern theologians as an agent who explains the direction of the evolutionary process. God is said, for example, to be "being itself" but not *a* being which can be a direction-giving cause. Or religion and science are said to constitute two autonomous perspectives, so that the affirmation of God as creator does not point to another cause distinct from the forces of physics and chemistry.

Seeing God and evolution as compatible requires a theistic evolutionism, which holds that the direction of the evolutionary process is rooted in a cosmic purposive agent. But Darwinism, especially neo-Darwinism, which has been the reigning evolutionary theory, excludes theistic influence in principle. The separation of theology and biology has in fact been the chief result of Darwinism.[1] And, as Stephen Toulmin has remarked, the modern injunction has been: "What Science hath put asunder let no mere Theologian seek to join together again!"[2] Theologians have for the most part obeyed this prohibition.

Any attempt to reunite theology and biology in a new form of theistic evolutionism faces four major obstacles. First, the traditional, *supernaturalistic idea of God* is incompatible with the facts and methods of science in general and of evolutionary theory in particular. Second, the *modern worldview*, which lies behind modern science in general and evolutionary theory in particular, is incompatible with any (not just the supernaturalistic) idea of divine influence in the world. Third, *modern science* in general is incompatible with any view of divine influence. Fourth, as just mentioned, *modern (Darwinian) evolutionary theory* in particular is hostile to any idea of divine influence in the evolutionary process. Accordingly, a credible theistic evolutionism requires revised views of God, the world, science, and evolution.

This fourfold revision does not, however, involve four unrelated tasks, because the four issues are closely interrelated. The modern ideals to which science in general and evolutionary theory in particular have conformed are largely functions of the modern worldview. The emergence of a new worldview will therefore bring with it new ideals of science and evolutionary theory. Also, the ideas of God and the world are closely intertwined: the modern worldview is largely if indirectly derivative from the supernaturalistic idea of God. A new concept of worldly entities will require a new understanding of God, and a new understanding of God will, in turn, promote a new conception of the world.

In the first section of this essay, I discuss the fourfold incompatibility of theism and evolution in modern thought. In the second section, I show the way a postmodern worldview makes theistic evolutionism possible.

I. The Incompatibility of Theism and Evolution in Modern Thought

The Incompatibility of Evolution and Supernaturalistic Theism

Inherent in the first stage of modernity, as represented by the thought of Descartes, Mersenne, Boyle, Newton, Locke, and Reid, was the traditional, supernaturalistic view of God. Supernaturalism denies that the relation of God to the world is a natural relation. It is, instead, a wholly voluntary relation, established unilaterally by a divine decision. The world was created *ex nihilo*, meaning out of absolute nothingness. It therefore in no sense exists eternally, not even in the sense of having been created out of an everlasting flux of finite events.

The first stage of modernity involved an intensification of the voluntarist, supernaturalist side of traditional theism. This intensification led to a purely mechanistic view of nature: taking seriously the absolute omnipotence of God meant insisting on the purely passive character of nature. To allow any spontaneity in matter would be to ascribe some divinity to it, it was thought, thereby compromising the absolute difference between the creator and the creatures. This antianimistic mentality also insisted that matter was devoid of any sentience, experience, or subjectivity, so as to prevent any suggestion of divine immanence in matter. The absolute transcendence of God meant that God could affect matter only by imposing laws and motion on it from without.

Because the human soul, with its experience, was not in this first phase of modernism denied activity and actuality, the antianimistic view of matter implied a strongly dualistic, anthropocentric view of the created world. Descartes' absolute distinction between extended and experiencing substances, with human souls being the only experiencing substances on earth, was the most explicit formulation of this absolute dualism. A wholly anthropocentric ethic followed: the nonhuman creation had no value in itself and no direct value for God. It was created to be of value to human beings.

This antianimistic view of nature also implied that divine influence could not be one causal influence among others in the normal course of events. Because nature was thought to be composed of insentient things ("hard, solid, massy, impenetrable," in Newton's words), wholly different from a mind, soul, or spirit, it was impossible to imagine how God as Holy Spirit could exert an influence as part of the normal causal interactions among these things. God's causal power on nature was, accordingly, increasingly restricted to two supernatural forms: (1) God had in the beginning created matter and imposed motion and laws of motion upon it; (2) God occasionally interrupted these "natural" laws with supernatural miracles.

This supernaturalistic, dualistic view of the universe is strongly disconfirmed by an evolutionary viewpoint. Although I will discuss this disconfirmation primarily in terms of Darwinism, supernaturalism is incompatible with the basic facts of the evolutionary picture, not merely with the Darwinian construal of those facts.

One of the main problems raised for Darwin by evolution was the problem of evil, because a wide range of evolutionary facts seemed inconsistent with Omnipotent Goodness.[3] But Darwin could reject neither the goodness nor the omnipotence of God. He therefore sought to solve the problem by restricting God's causality to the original creation of matter, at which time God imposed on it general laws plus the capacity for inheritance and reproduction. Darwin reconciled himself to the horrors of the evolutionary process by seeing them as following from a law—the survival of the fittest—that leads to increases in the general good.[4]

Darwin's deistic position provided no real solution. He separated theology and biology only by imposing a supernaturalistic theological interpretation on astronomy, physics, and chemistry which would not long be acceptable to scientists in these fields. His "solution" also simply moved the problem of evil back in time: a God truly omnipotent in the sense intended by Augustine, Occam, Calvin, Descartes, Newton, and Paley could have brought about all the good aspects of our world without the waste and horrors of the evolutionary process. Darwin himself did not ultimately find his own solution satisfactory.[5]

The second contradiction between supernaturalism and evolution is still at issue between evolutionists and creationists: the doctrine that all the present species were created *ex nihilo* by God is contradicted by the evidence that they have descended with modifications from earlier species. Darwin saw that "descent with modification" versus "creation *ex nihilo*" was the main issue in the arguments about design.[6] One can attempt to save the doctrine of creation *ex nihilo* as Darwin did, by allowing it to apply not to the various species but only to the original atoms. This view, that most of the present things have arisen through evolution from things that had been created *ex nihilo*, can be held without logical contradiction, but not without strong tensions. Why would a God having supernatural omnipotence have chosen to create our world in this way? Why wait so long before bringing forth the creatures with more freedom and value? Why design the process so that it is full of pain and waste? The fact that our world has come about through a long, slow, wasteful, painful evolutionary process strongly suggests that the supernaturalistic doctrine of a divine creator is false, even in its deistic guise.

The third tension between evolution and the supernaturalistic worldview of early modernity involves the latter's dualism and anthropocentrism. Evolution suggests continuity between humans and the other species, not an absolute difference in kind. Much of Darwin's work was, in fact, devoted to showing the similarity between humans and other higher animals.[7] He thereby opposed the supernaturalistic view that the human soul was created *ex nihilo* rather than being a fully natural product of the evolutionary process.

Anthropocentrism was undermined also by the difficulty of believing, in an evolutionary context, that everything else was created for human benefit. The supernaturalistic utilitarianism of William Paley, which Darwin opposed, had said not only that all the species were created directly by God but also that they were created for human utility.[8] To this day, Darwinians oppose the notion of cosmic design or teleology partly because they assume that all such notions support anthropocentrism.[9]

In summary: supernaturalistic theism is challenged by the evil, the evolutionary descent, the nondualism, and the nonanthropocentric implications of an evolutionary account of our world's creation. Evolutionism and supernaturalism can perhaps, by means of various *ad hoc* hypotheses, be shown not to be *logically* incompatible. But they certainly do not naturally fit together.

The Incompatibility of Theism and the
Modern Worldview

The second obstacle to theistic evolutionism is the fact that the modern worldview, in its present form, is incompatible with theism of any sort (not only with supernaturalistic theism). This currently dominant form of the modern worldview has in common with the supernaturalistic dualism of early modernity only the mechanistic, nonanimistic view of nature. In this second form of the modern worldview, supernaturalism and dualism have collapsed into atheism and materialism.

Supernaturalism turned into atheism for a variety of reasons. One was the problem of evil: The accentuation of God's omnipotence, combined with the modern commitment to base conclusions on experience and reason, made the inconsistency between God's alleged goodness and the world's obvious evil more intolerable than it had been in previous times. The problem raised for Darwin and others by evolution was simply part of this larger problem. The increasing rejection of miracles and of infallible inspiration of the Bible also removed two of the major reasons for believing in a providential God (understood supernaturalistically). The deistic removal of God to a temporally first cause prepared the way for doing without God altogether.

At the same time, dualism was turning into materialism. Dualists from the beginning had difficulty explaining how a spiritual, teleologically operating soul could interact with a material, mechanistically operating body. The only solution, finally, was to appeal to divine omnipotence—as did Descartes, Malebranche, Reid, and Locke. As this resort to supernatural solutions to natural problems lost its appeal, dualism increasingly seemed impossible. Darwin was merely one of a long line of thinkers who followed Hobbes in defining the mind or soul as simply a function or aspect of the brain.

The resulting worldview leaves no room for divine influence. Because of its materialism, divine influence cannot be part of the natural system of causal interaction. Any divine influence would have to be supernatural intervention, and that is ruled out by the rejection of the supernaturalistic God.

A third feature of the modern worldview, its sensate empiricism, makes the case against divine influence in the world seem even stronger. According to this sensate empiricism (or simply "sensationism"), all knowledge arises through perceptual experience, and all perception is through the physical senses. The physical senses are, by definition, capable of perceiving only physical or material things. Even if some nonphysical things exist, sensationists hold, we could not perceive them; they could therefore have no influence on our experience. Accordingly, even if God, understood as a spiritual being, exists, we could not be divinely influenced. The modern worldview thereby rules out divine influence not only in what we normally mean by "nature," that is, the nonhuman world, but also in human experience and hence "history."

The Incompatibility of Theism and Modern Science

A further obstacle to theistic evolutionism is the fact that the ideals of modern science forbid any notion of divine influence in the world. The main ideals in question are predictive determinism, reductionism, and scientism.

Darwin and his followers have believed that biology, to be a full-fledged science, must be as predictive as (nineteenth-century) physics. In the words of a contemporary Darwinian, to deny the ideal of predictive determinism "is to opt out of science altogether."[10] Complete prediction is a possible ideal only if the world is fully deterministic, so that knowledge of the "laws of nature" and of present conditions would give certain knowledge of the future. Darwin felt that any "caprice" in the world would make science impossible.[11] Accordingly, although Darwin and his followers speak of "chance," they mean by this word no absence of determining causes but only human ignorance of some of these causes.[12]

The ideal of predictive determinism provided a powerful motive for Darwin's turn to a materialistic view of human beings: a self-determining soul would make a science of human nature impossible. This ideal also provided a reason for his rejection of divine influence in the evolutionary process: such influence could insert something unpredictable into the process.[13]

The reductionistic ideal of modern science also counts against any acceptance of divine influence in the evolutionary process. The assumption that all wholes can in principle be reduced to (explained in terms of) their parts implies that all causation is upward, from the most elementary parts. If there were any "downward causation," from the whole to its parts, then reductionism would be a false ideal. This reductionistic ideal has militated against the idea that the human soul or mind has any autonomous power with which it can exert influence upon the body. All the more has this ideal forbidden any downward causation from God to the world.

Scientism is the belief, or the ideal, that there are no genuine explanations other than those of the natural sciences. Positively stated, scientism is the ideal that the explanations of science be in principle complete, not needing supplementation by philosophy or theology.[14] This ideal provides a strong incentive to deny the existence of causes except those with which natural science can deal, namely, *natural* causes. This dictum, applied to biology by Darwin, meant primarily that evolutionary theory could have no place for divine causation, because such causation was assumed by definition to be *super*natural.[15]

These three ideals of modern science, besides ruling out divine causation, also ruled out all teleological causation.[16] Teleological causation, in the sense of self-determination by an organism to reach some *telos* or goal, would obviously threaten the ideals of predictive determinism and of reducing wholes to their parts. It would also threaten scientism, because self-determination would be an inner, invisible type of causality not observable to the senses or to any scientific instruments designed to magnify them. Because divine causation has usually been closely related to teleological causation, this rejection of teleology provided a further defense against theistic evolutionism.

The Incompatibility of Theism and Darwinism

Theistic evolutionism is ruled out not only by modern science in general, but even more definitely by Darwinism in particular. The key notions here are that evolution is completely undirected and that natural selection is the only creative force in evolution. Stephen Jay Gould refers to the undirectedness of evolution as "the central Darwinian notion"[17] and says that the "essence of Darwinism is the creativity of natural selection."[18]

The Darwinian conviction that no direction is given to evolution except by natural selection is in part a denial that the direction of the process might be partly determined by the internal spontaneity of matter (which was the central notion of Lamarck, much more central to him than "inheritance of acquired characteristics," which neo-Lamarckians have stressed).[19] Matter for Darwinians is passive, being completely determined by the external forces upon it. In the words of Dobzhansky: there is "no principle of spontaneity inherent in living matter."[20] This feature of the Darwinian metaphysics is expressed by the doctrine that all evolutionary change comes about through natural selection operating upon random genetic mutations. The word *random* (or *chance*) means not that the genetic changes are not completely determined (as mentioned earlier), but that the mutations are not preferentially directed toward a feature that would be advantageous to the organism in its present environment.[21] This double denial—that mutations are not due to any principle of spontaneity and that they have no tendency to be advantageous—sums up the Darwinian denial that the evolutionary process is in any sense directed.

Darwinians, however, typically insinuate into the presentation an even stronger meaning to the assertion that all mutations are random. This stronger meaning is that mutations reflect no general trend in *any* sense (such as toward increased complexity and/or increased richness of experience). This stronger sense of "random"—which is often used interchangeably with the more precise sense, as if there were no significant difference between the two[22]—is not required by the letter of Darwinism, but it bolsters its spirit, which, in Gould's words, is that "selection is *the* creative force in evolution."[23] This stronger meaning of *random* rules out any possible theistic influence, however subtle, on the direction of evolution.

Accordingly, Darwinism in itself, and even more in its typical presentations, rules out any possibility of a theistic interpretation of evolution, not only through its endorsement of the ideals of modern science in general but also through its distinctive emphases. The fact that most biologists, philosophers, and even theologians in our century have been taught virtually to equate evolutionism itself with Darwinism has made it extremely difficult for theistic accounts of evolution to get a serious hearing.

II. The Compatibility of God and Evolution in Postmodern Thought

As Neal Gillespie points out, theistic evolution was never disproved; scientists and philosophers simply lost interest in it.[24] I reviewed in the previous section the main reason for this loss of interest: the premodern and early modern view of God, on the one hand, and the modern worldview, on the other, made "theistic evolution" seem like "round square."

Postmodern ideas of God, the world, science, and evolution, which make "theistic evolution" no longer seem self-contradictory, are emerging in our time. In my view, this postmodern movement can find its best philosophical guidance for rethinking the nature of the world, the divine, science, and evolution from the metaphysical cosmologies of Alfred North Whitehead and Charles Hartshorne.

I discuss first the way a postmodern theism is compatible with evolution and a postmodern worldview compatible with theistic influence.

Then I suggest a way in which a postmodern science and an evolutionary theory based thereon could include theistic influence.

The Compatibility of Evolution with Postmodernity's Naturalistic Theism

God need not be thought of as a supernatural being; theism need not be supernaturalism; *naturalistic theism* is not a contradiction in terms. Because this suggestion runs counter to such a widespread assumption on the part of theists and atheists alike, it is necessary to consider what we mean by the word *God*.

As I suggested at the outset of chapter 4, our civilization contains a "generic idea of God." This generic idea contains at least seven essential features. God is (1) the supreme power, (2) the personal, purposive creator of our world who is (3) perfectly good, (4) the source of moral norms, (5) the ultimate guarantee for the meaningfulness of human life, (6) the trustworthy ground for hope in the ultimate victory of good over evil, and (7) alone worthy of worship.[25] Most people would agree that the name *God* is rightly applied to any reality having these characteristics.

Both naturalistic theism (as conceived here) and supernaturalistic theism attribute these seven features to God; the two theisms differ only with regard to their interpretation of the first feature, which leads to different ways of conceiving the second and sixth features. As seen earlier, supernaturalism believes that God essentially has all the power in reality; its speculation that God created the world out of absolute nothingness is a denial that a realm of finitude, with power of its own, exists necessarily. Supernaturalism accordingly thinks of the normal God-world relationship as a voluntary contract on God's part which God can violate occasionally.

Naturalistic theism believes by contrast that the relation between God and the world is a natural relation, given in the nature of things. A world, in the sense of a realm of finite existents (which might sometimes exist in a state of chaos), exists as necessarily as does God. Put otherwise, what exists eternally is God-and-a-world, God and a plurality of finite existents. God is not the external creator of a wholly contingent world; God is essentially the soul of the universe. Because the normal causal relationship between God and finite beings is a natural, necessary relationship, it cannot be interrupted at will by God any more than by the creatures. Any divine causality on worldly beings would therefore have to be as fully a natural part of the process as any other causation. Divine causation could not be supernatural.

Because the things of the world have their own power which cannot be overridden or cancelled, God cannot unilaterally bring about any events in the world. All events occur through the cocreativity of God and the creatures. Divine causality is therefore always persuasion; it can never be manipulation or unilateral fiat.

The existence of God, so understood, is therefore not disproved by the kinds of things that disproved supernaturalistic theism. Neither the reality of evil, nor the fallibility of inspired writings, is evidence against the God of naturalistic theism, who only produces results with the cooperation of creatures.

By the same token, naturalistic theism's view of a divine creator is not embarrassed by the fact that the world evidently came about through a long, slow evolutionary process, filled with blind alleys and imperfections. Postmodern naturalistic theism in fact implies that God could have created a world only in this way. The creation had to be a step-by-step process: complex things could not have been created all at once. It had to take time: new developments could not be brought about until the environmental conditions made them possible and until the creatures in question made the requisite decisions. And the prevention of unfortunate, even grotesque, developments was impossible.

The Superiority of the Postmodern Worldview and Its Compatibility with Naturalistic Theism

No good reason can be found to continue holding the central tenet of the modern worldview, which is its mechanistic, nonanimistic view of nature. This view was not originally accepted for primarily scientific (empirical) reasons and is not required by any subsequent discoveries. Modernity's nonanimistic starting point, furthermore, according to which the elementary units of nature are devoid of both spontaneity and perceptual experience, forces a choice between dualism and materialism, both of which are inadequate. Dualism cannot explain the way mind and matter interact. Materialism cannot explain the way values, freedom, and downward causation are real, even though materialists cannot help presupposing that they are. And the sensate empiricism necessitated by materialism leads to a "solipsism of the present moment," because this form of empiricism cannot explain how we know the existence of causality, an external world, and the past. With all those weaknesses, the fact that this worldview has no room for divine existence and influence should not count heavily against the truth of every form of theism!

Postmodern animism provides a way to overcome all these weaknesses. According to this view, the world is composed exclusively of momentary units of partially self-creative perceptual experiences. Each unit of experience is partially spontaneous, or self-creative, and then exerts causal influence upon subsequent units. Because all units have some freedom, and higher experiences have more freedom, we can affirm our own freedom without getting involved in dualism. Because all levels of experience influence all other levels, we can speak of downward as well as upward causation, thereby avoiding reductionism. Because all sensory perception is derivative from a more basic nonsensory perception, we can adopt a "radical empiricism" (William James) in which we have a direct knowledge of other things, the past, and nonphysical values.

Besides showing that we can intelligibly affirm the past, the external world, causality, freedom, and values, this postmodern animism allows for divine influence as a natural feature of the world. Once we recognize that we have nonsensory perception, we can believe that we perceive God, which means that God influences our experience. Our knowledge of values such as truth, beauty, and justice can be understood as rooted in divine persuasion, through which God seeks to lure us to actualize these values. If all things in the world are, or are composed of, moments of experience, furthermore, we can understand how God, as the all-inclusive, omnipresent experience, can directly influence *all* beings. Although beings whose experience does not rise to the level of self-consciousness, or even consciousness, cannot reflect upon the meaning of truth, beauty, and justice, they can nonetheless be subject to divine persuasion in terms of ideal values that they are capable of actualizing. Divine influence upon human and nonhuman beings can thereby be regarded as similar in kind.

The Compatibility of Postmodern Science with Naturalistic Theism

A postmodern science will not have predictive determinism as an ideal. Because all individuals are assumed to embody some power of spontaneity or self-determination, predictive determinism is an ideal only for aggregates (such as rocks, planets, and computers), in which the individual spontaneities are cancelled out by the average effects of large numbers. All individuals are assumed to have some spontaneity, and higher-level individuals are assumed to have more than lower-level individuals. The idea of theistic influence therefore does not make science impossible by virtue of the unpredictable novelty that it allows to be introduced.

Postmodern science is not reductionistic. Many levels of genuine individuals exist, each with its own partial autonomy and its capacity causally to affect all other levels. Causal influence therefore goes not only sideways and upward but also downward, from the (relative) whole to the parts. Downward and upward causation can be assumed to be approximately equal in power, because the *greater number* of lower-grade individuals (for example, subatomic particles) is balanced by the *greater power* of higher-grade individuals (for example, macromolecules). The idea of theistic influence is accordingly not antithetical to science by virtue of the fact that it involves downward causation or even by virtue of the idea that God is the supreme power in the universe. In postmodern theism, which understands God as the all-inclusive soul of the universe, divine influence is the ultimate example of the influence of the whole upon its partially autonomous parts.

Postmodern science either is not scientistic, or else it expands the notion of "scientific explanation" to include types of causal influence associated with religious beliefs that were excluded in principle by modern science. As Stephen Toulmin states, "the disciplinary specialization of the natural sciences can no longer intimidate us into setting religious cosmology aside as 'unscientific'."[26] In this new context, the category of theistic influence can be used for causal explanations, as long as this theistic influence is naturalistic. Postmodern science does not insist that all causal explanations involve agents that can be observed through sensory means or that can be blocked out in controlled experiments. Postmodern science sets no such *a priori* standards (except for the exclusion of supernatural causes), but seeks to understand the various causal factors needed for a complete explanation of things.

The rejection of modern scientism also allows openness to the idea of teleological self-determination, according to which individuals partially create themselves in terms of values they choose to actualize. Although we cannot directly observe this type of causation in organisms other than ourselves, postmodern scientists do not hold that the behavior of all other organisms must be explained on the assumption that they exercise no such self-determination. Postmodern science thus allows that kind of creaturely causation with which theistic influence has usually been associated.

The Compatibility of Postmodern Evolutionary Theory with Naturalistic Theism

A wide range of thinkers are rejecting the panselectionist dogma that natural selection is the only creative force in evolution.[27]

A relaxation of the prohibition against downward causation in general,[28] and against an organism's influence upon its gene cells (or its DNA molecules) in particular, has also occurred. The previously heretical idea that an organism's purposive response to its environment could introduce inheritable changes is now discussed as possible and probable.[29]

A serious proposal has also been put forth that not all heredity should be identified with genetic inheritance, that there may be a type of influence of the more or less distant past upon the present that is not encoded in the genes.[30]

These ideas allow renewed discussion of the idea that the evolutionary process is somewhat directed and that this direction could reflect theistic influence. Not every conception of theistic causation is compatible with and illuminating of the facts, of course, but the naturalistic theism of the postmodern worldview seems to be.

Postmodern theism suggests that God, as the appetitive soul of the universe, lures the creatures to actualize values that will result in greater richness of experience. This greater richness of experience has a tendency to promote greater external attractiveness, which in general has a selectionist advantage. One writer has called this principle the "survival of the fanciest."[31]

Postmodern theism suggests the following partial explanation of the way this divine influence might work: First, God affects all beings directly but does not directly affect their outer demeanor, on which most selection works. The divine influence on this outer demeanor would be very indirect. God acts directly only on the inner, hidden aspects of events, by presenting a complex of forms (values, ideals, possibilities) to whet their appetites. Whether the creatures' appetites are whetted is partly up to them. Whether they actualize the new possibilities once their appetites are whetted is fully up to them. Once they have actualized them, their outer demeanor is different, and the question of their viability in the environment is raised. However, the environment in question may be only that of an animal's physiological system; the internal change may not yet have produced a change in the animal's external demeanor upon which the external environment would pass judgment. This view of theistic influence is therefore far removed from the sort that imagined God as directly shaping the observable forms of the various species.

Second, although God influences all levels of beings directly, God also influences every level indirectly, through the other levels. In particular, God affects the lower through the higher. For example, God (whether intentionally or not) could indirectly affect the genetic structure of an animal by influencing its purposes which then bring about an effect in its immune system.

Third, divine influence is a fully natural, ordinary part of the everlasting causal process. Every event is influenced by divine causation, and this divine causation is the same in form for all events—God never acts in an extraordinary, supernatural way. This stipulation does not entail that divine influence may not be more important in some events than in others. Although identical in form in all events, divine influence can differ vastly in content, that is, in the ideal forms it lures the creatures to actualize. These differences are not due to divine arbitrariness, because God always seeks to get actualized the best values possible in a situation. The differences are due to the differing contexts, which determine what possibilities in that time and place are best. Some contexts allow radically novel possibilities to emerge, such as life, consciousness, and symbolic language. Divine influence can also be more important in some situations than others because the creatures made it so by responding more fully to the divine impulse in them than to other influences.

Finally, the former three principles together imply that, whereas divine influence itself may be a regular feature of the evolutionary process, its observable effects may be quite irregular. A record suggesting "punctuated equilibrium" is therefore compatible with the supposition that divine influence is operating all the time, not spasmodically, and that it is all of the same type, with no novel forms occasionally inserted into the process supernaturally. For example, long periods of outer stasis could exist while the divine influence was whetting a species' appetite for a new form, and again after the appetite was whetted but not acted upon. The idea that evolutionary change involves revolutionary moments does not require that theism must be supernaturalistic to be illuminating of the facts.

SUMMARY AND CONCLUSION

Whereas theistic evolutionism was impossible both for supernaturalists and for moderns, it is possible in our time, given the emergence of a postmodern worldview with its naturalistic theism, and of new developments in natural science in general and evolutionary theory in particular.

Whether theistic evolution supplants the current impasse between creationists and nontheistic evolutionists will depend upon whether a postmodern vision of the world and science becomes dominant, and whether naturalistic theists can convincingly show divine influence to be a necessary, illuminating feature of the evolutionary process. If these things occur, the postmodern civilization will be one in which people's religious drive will lead them to bring their beliefs, attitudes, and actions into harmony with a supreme power that is personal, just, loving, and works by persuasion alone.

6

POSTMODERN ANIMISM
AND LIFE AFTER DEATH

In the modern world, it has been very difficult for intellectuals to believe in life after death. The modern worldview made life after death seem impossible, or at least extremely improbable; it made concern with the belief (except to refute it) seem suspect; and it discouraged attention to any positive evidence for the belief. The modern consensus has been that belief in life after death is metaphysically impossible, empirically groundless, and morally harmful. A postmodern outlook no longer rules out the belief on *a priori* grounds, and does not consider all forms of the belief harmful; it thereby encourages people to look at the available evidence for the belief open-mindedly, evidence which turns out to be convincing to many. These are the theses of this essay.

In the first section, I explain the way the modern worldview, which is an antianimistic worldview, rules out the possibility of life after death and of any evidence for it. In the second section, I lay out those aspects of a postmodern animism most germane to rethinking belief in life after death. In the third section, I look at the question of the possibility for life after death from the double standpoint of the metaphysics of postmodern animism and the indirect empirical evidence provided by parapsychology. The fourth section is devoted to the question of direct empirical evidence, while the final section examines moral objections to belief in life after death.

I. MODERN ANTIANIMISM AND THE *A PRIORI* REJECTION OF LIFE AFTER DEATH

Although it has conventionally been assumed that the modern worldview, which first emerged in the seventeenth century, was based on reason and experience and was inherently hostile to theology, the truth seems to be that it was originally based more upon theological and ecclesiastical than empirical considerations. This point, which has been introduced in previous chapters, is discussed more fully here, with particular attention to the topics of "miracles" and life after death.

Understood in context, the chief characteristic of the modern worldview, which was originally known as the "new mechanical philosophy," was that it was an antianimistic philosophy. It stood in opposition not only to Aristotelian animism (which made organisms paradigmatic, even regarding a falling stone as "seeking a state of rest") but even more emphatically to a wild mixture of Hermetic, Cabalistic and Neoplatonic "magical" Renaissance philosophies, some of which were strongly animistic.

In these animistic views, matter was understood to have both the power of self-motion and the power of perception. Each unit was often understood to be a microcosm, somehow reflecting the whole universe within itself. Action at a distance was widely understood to be a natural phenomenon: if all things are perceivers rather than blind bits of matter, no reason exists to suppose that all influence must be by contact. The "magical" or "miraculous" could therefore occur without supernatural intervention into the natural order of things. Also, the divine reality was understood more as the *anima mundi* than as an external, supernatural creator. Sometimes this divine "soul of the world" was understood pantheistically, sometimes more (to use a later term) panentheistically.[1]

The founders of the modern worldview and their ecclesiastical supporters did not like these tendencies. One of the major reasons was that the idea of self-moving matter could lead to mortalism, the doctrine that, when the human body dies, so does the human soul. (Or, in today's language, the so-called mind or soul would be identical with the body or at least the brain.) If the body is composed of self-moving parts and yet decays, the self-movement of the soul provides no evidence for its immortality. Against this mortalistic heresy (which threatened to undermine the authority of the Church, especially insofar as this authority rested on the "keys to the kingdom" and the correlative threat of hell), the new mechanical philosophy provided a defense. If the body is regarded as composed of inert, insentient corpuscles, argued Robert Boyle and others, it will be clear to people from their powers of perception and self-movement that they contain something that is qualitatively different from mortal matter. The mechanistic view of nature was therefore originally an integral part of a dualistic worldview accepted for largely theological reasons.[2]

The Renaissance animisms could also lead to atheism or, what was generally considered the same thing, pantheism. If matter is self-moving, the universe is perhaps self-organizing. If so, the order of our world provides no evidence for an external creator God. An atheistic philosophy was obviously seen as detrimental to the Church's authority. So was a pantheistic or panentheistic philosophy, insofar as it implied that God was immediately present to everyone, rather than being mediated only through a hierarchical church. Also, the Church could threaten the disobedient with hell no better in the name of a pantheistic or panentheistic deity than a nonexistent one. The mechanical, antianimistic philosophy was again seen as the answer. Newton was only the most prestigious person to argue that a natural world understood as composed of inert bits of matter demanded an external God who created matter, put it in motion, and imposed the laws of motion upon it. Newton also argued that neither the cohesion between the atoms in a rock not the apparent gravitational attraction between the stellar bodies could be inherent to matter itself. These phenomena therefore pointed to an external God who imposed the appearance of mutual attraction upon matter.[3] A mechanistic view of nature, far from being viewed as hostile to theistic belief, was regarded as the best defense for it.

The Renaissance animisms, because they allowed for action at a distance as a natural phenomenon, were threatening to the Church's belief in supernatural miracles. If events such as reading minds, healing by prayer, and moving physical objects by thought alone can occur without supernatural intervention, then the miracles of the Bible and the later history of the Church do not prove that God has designated Christianity as the one true religion. Because the "argument from miracles" was usually the chief pillar of the Church's evidence for its authority, this naturalization of the Church's "miracles" was a serious threat. Once again, the mechanistic philosophy seemed a godsend. Marin Mersenne, Descartes's predecessor in establishing the mechanistic philosophy in Catholic France, had at first used Aristotelianism in his battles against the Hermetic, animistic philosophers (such as Robert Fludd), because it disallowed action at a distance. When he learned of Galileo's mechanistic philosophy, he turned to it, partly because it made even clearer the impossibility of action at a distance—in a machine, all influence is by contact. Accordingly, when events occurred that could not be explained in terms of the principles of natural philosophy—and Mersenne and most other people in the seventeenth century had no doubt that such events did occur—then a supernatural agent had to be involved. The Christian miracles were thereby really *miraculous*, that is, supernaturally caused. The mechanistic philosophy, far from being opposed to belief in the miraculous, was originally adopted in part to support this belief.[4]

In sum, the mechanistic view of nature was adopted by the first philosophers of modernity for primarily theological reasons (which were closely related to sociological ones) and was part of a dualistic view of the creation and a supernaturalistic view of reality as a whole. This view was supernaturalistic in that God existed outside the world and could intervene in it at will, interrupting the normal causal relationships. This belief in supernatural miraculous intervention rested, in turn, upon the conviction that the world does not exist naturally or necessarily (as would be suggested by the idea that God is the soul of the world). Rather, the world exists contingently or arbitrarily, having been created *ex nihilo* on the basis of a divine decision. In other words, the basic God-world relation is not a natural, given feature of reality; equally unnatural are the normal causal relations between the creatures. God freely chooses how to act in relation to the world and therefore can choose to act in extraordinary ways from time to time; and because the normal causal patterns of the world were arbitrarily imposed on the world, they can be freely interrupted at will. This supernaturalistic view of the God-world relation can be and has been held without the mechanistic view of nature; but in the seventeenth century this mechanistic view of nature was seen as the best way to support belief in the supernatural God, a supernatural soul, and supernatural miracles.

This strategy backfired. Because of various problems inherent in supernatural dualism, it soon turned into an atheistic materialism, in which there could be no miracles and no life after death. I will mention several of these problems.

The dualistic view of a spiritual soul in a mechanistic body created an insoluble mind-body problem. How could there be any interaction between an experiencing soul and nonexperiencing, inanimate matter? The soul is not an impenetrable substance which can push against other things, but a spiritual reality which operates in terms of values and final causes. The body was said to be comprised of impenetrable, nonexperiencing things which can neither receive nor contribute values but which operate solely by pushing and being pushed. The seventeenth-century dualists, being supernaturalists, solved the problem by appeal to God: what is impossible for nature is possible for supernature. But that appeal became increasingly unacceptable to intellectuals in the eighteenth and nineteenth centuries, especially after the acceptance of the theory of evolution, according to which human beings evolved out of simpler species. Although a few people overcame dualism by adopting an idealistic position, saying that matter is not really real, the dominant solution was to declare mind not to be really real. It was said to be identical with the brain, or at best an epiphenomenal byproduct of the brain with no power of its own.

The supernaturalistic doctrine of God encountered several problems. The problem of evil led an increasing number of people to reject the idea of an omnipotent being who could intervene in the world at will. The growing rejection of the Bible as infallibly inspired removed one of the major bases for assuming the existence of a supernatural being who sometimes totally determines events in the world. The mind-body problem was paralleled by a God-world problem: If a finite mind cannot interact with insentient matter, how can a divine mind do so? It became difficult also to understand how the divine mind could influence the human mind and thereby be experienced by it. The seventeenth-century dualists had for the most part insisted on a sensationist view of perception, according to which we can perceive or experience things beyond ourselves only through our senses. This doctrine was held even more rigidly after mechanistic dualism collapsed into mechanistic materialism: If there is no soul distinct from the brain, then all perception *must* come through the central nervous system. Belief in the reality of God could therefore have no experiential basis. For these reasons, supernaturalism became agnosticism or outright atheism.

As the supernaturalistic God died, so did belief in miracles. The mechanistic view of nature implied that action at a distance could not occur *naturally*, especially after this mechanistic view was applied to the human being as a whole, so that a soul outside the mechanism was denied. The rejection of the supernatural God meant that events involving action at a distance could not happen *supernaturally* either. Because they could happen neither naturally nor supernaturally, it was simply concluded, *a priori*, that they could not happen *period*.

These three rejections—of the soul, God, and miracles—were mutually supportive. The denial of the soul as distinct from the body and acting upon it removed the primary analogue for thinking of God as distinct from the world and acting upon it. The denial of God, in turn, removed the only basis for explaining how spiritual soul and mechanistic body could relate to each other. And, just as the denial of a supernatural God removed the basis for understanding how miracles could happen, the denial of miracles removed one of the main bases for believing in such a God.

For our purposes here, the main point of this story is that every possible basis for believing in life after death was removed. The transition from dualism to materialism meant the denial of a soul which could survive the demise of the body naturally. The collapse of supernaturalism into atheism meant the denial of a God who could give us life after death through a supernatural resurrection of the body. And the *a priori* rejection of all phenomena traditionally called *miracles* meant that such phenomena could not provide credible evidence for life after death or against the worldview that ruled out its possibility.

The antianimistic view of nature, which was proposed and accepted in the first phase of modernity in part to buttress belief in life after death, thereby led to a worldview in the second phase of modernity that made life after death impossible. This second phase of the modern worldview is still the reigning worldview in most intellectual circles.

II. THE EMERGENCE OF A
POSTMODERN WORLDVIEW

Emerging in some circles, however, is a postmodern worldview, involving a new animism and a new theism, which again makes life after death *a priori* possible.

The new animism is emerging for many reasons. For example, once the idea of a supernaturalistic creation is fully overcome, the idea returns that the universe must be self-organizing and therefore composed of self-moving parts. Also, insofar as dualistic assumptions are fully overcome and human experience is accepted as fully natural, it begins to seem probable that something analogous to our experience and self-movement is a feature of every level of nature. Finally, twentieth-century developments in science support a new animism. Developments in physics have led to a world of energetic events which seem to be self-moving and to behave in unpredictable ways. And recent studies in biology seem to demonstrate that bacteria and macromolecules have elemental forms of perception, memory, choice, and self-motion.[5]

The most complete, and in my opinion the most coherent and adequate, form of postmodern animism has been provided by Alfred North Whitehead and Charles Hartshorne. Their viewpoint differs from typical premodern animisms in three ways. First, the power of perception and self-movement is not attributed to things such as rocks, lakes and suns. A distinction is made between individuals and aggregates of individuals. Only true individuals are self-moving, perceiving things. Most visible things therefore are not animate (although their constituents are). The only visible animate things (aside from the universe as a whole) would probably be animals, which, as their name implies, have an *anima* which gives the organism as a whole the power of perception and self-movement.

A second way in which this postmodern animism differs from most premodern forms is that radically different levels of *anima* are assumed. To have experience is not necessarily to have *conscious* experience, let alone *self-consciousness*. Most of the experiences in the universe are unconscious. Also, an organism's power of self-determination can be extremely limited; the organism can be almost totally determined by the past, so that its degree of self-determination is negligible for most purposes.

Third, whereas most premodern animisms (Buddhism was an exception) thought of the basic units of the world as enduring souls, postmodern animism takes the basic units to be momentary experiences. The ultimate units are "occasions of experience." This distinction is important with regard to the question of causal interaction. When the basic units were thought of as enduring souls, it was hard to understand how the within of things could affect the outer, perceivable world. Most animistic or panpsychist philosophies have affirmed parallelism, according to which the inside and outside of things move along parallel to each other, without influencing each other. Because our inner experience of free self-determination was therefore said not to influence the outer world, these philosophies were ultimately deterministic (for example, Leibniz, Bernard Rensch).[6] In postmodern animism, a unit is first an experiencing subject exercising self-determination, then an experienced object exercising efficient causation. What it *is* as an object depends on what it *became* as a subject. The efficient causation of individuals is thereby based upon some degree of self-determination. Also, the more power of self-determination exercised by an experience, the more efficient causation it exerts as an object on subsequent experiences.

Having differentiated postmodern animism from premodern, I must emphasize three more of its features before applying it to the issues of parapsychology and life after death. First, the human mind or soul is *numerically distinct* from the brain but *not ontologically different* from the cells making up the brain. *Nondualistic interactionism* is thus affirmed. Interactionism and dualism must be distinguished. In most discussions of interactionism, by both advocates and critics, it is *not* distinguished from dualism. This failure is due in part to the fact that the most well-known form of interactionism has been Cartesian dualism. Descartes said that the mind was not only numerically distinct from the brain (the brain was one thing, the mind was another) but also ontologically different (the brain was one *kind* of thing, the mind was *another kind*). The ontological dualism was what created problems for interactionism. The collapse of dualistic interactionism historically (as distinct from logically) led to nondualistic identism, in which the brain and mind are said not only to be ontologically similar (the same *kind* of things) but also numerically identical (the same *thing*). Its numerical identism makes this form of nondualism untenable.

Because modern thinkers have assumed that the basic units of nature were insentient, they, for the most part, have ignored a third, mediating position: nondualistic interactionism. Because the cells composing the brain are sentient, in this view, they are not ontologically different in kind from the soul or mind. But the mind is not numerically identical with the brain. The mind is one thing, while the brain is another thing—or, more precisely, a society of billions of things. The mind or soul is a series of very high-level occasions of experience, each of which unifies the myriad data received from the many brain cells into a subjective unity of experience. Each cell is a series of medium-level occasions of experience, doing the same thing on a lower level.

A second crucial feature of postmodern animism is its view that sensory perception is not the basic form of perception. Every individual, whether it has sensory organs or not, perceives its environment, in the sense of taking influences from other things into itself. Even *our* experience is not fundamentally sensory. For me to see the objects in front of my face presupposes that my soul has perceived my brain cells, thereby receiving the data from the outside world that have been transmitted through the optic nerve. I do not *see* my brain cells; that would involve a sensory perception of my sensory apparatus. But I must perceive them in a nonsensory way to receive the data they convey from the outside world. Those data have been transmitted up the optic nerve by a series of nonsensory perceptions from neuron to neuron. Sensory perception is a very high-level, specialized type of perception which may or may not occur and which presupposes the existence of nonsensory perception. Nonsensory perception occurs all the time in us and in all other individuals, from electrons to animal souls.

A third feature of postmodern animism especially relevant to our topic is its view that various *animas* or souls have various degrees of power. As indicated earlier, higher-level individuals have more power to determine themselves than do lower-level individuals, and more power to exert upon others. An amoeba has more power than an atom, a canine soul more power than an amoeba, and a human soul more than a canine. Some human beings evidently have more soul-power than others. Some people are, therefore, more transcendent over the power of the past and the contemporary environment than others. Some people also have more power than others to influence their bodies, for example, in bringing about psychosomatic illness and health. The epiphenomenalistic doctrine that the soul is a passive by-product of the body is therefore even less true for some human beings than for others.

The emergence of a postmodern worldview involves, besides this new animism, a new theism—a naturalistic theism. The naturalistic theism of postmodernity sets it apart from both the supernaturalistic theism of premodernity and early modernity and the naturalistic atheism of late modernity. According to this naturalistic theism, or panentheism, God is the soul of the universe, an all-inclusive unity of experience and agency which makes the universe a unity. Calling this theism *naturalistic* means that the fundamental relations between God and the world are natural features of reality, belonging to the very nature of things, not arbitrary features, based upon divine volition. The most general principles according to which the units of nature, including the units of human experience, operate are therefore not principles that can be arbitrarily suspended from time to time.

The crucial difference from premodern and early modern theism is that all creative power is not thought to belong to God alone. Creativity, or power in the most general sense (more general than the physicist's "energy"), belongs equally to God and to a realm of finite beings. God influences all finite events, but totally determines none of them, because they not only are influenced as well by all previous finite events but also have their own power of self-determination. The relative autonomy of the world from God is therefore not based upon a voluntary self-limitation on the part of divine omnipotence, which could be suspended now and then; it is an inherent feature of reality. If extraordinary events happen, they are not "miracles" in the sense of events in which the normal worldly causation is replaced by direct divine causation. *Extraordinary* cannot mean *supernatural.*

The reasons for the emergence of this new theism can be mentioned only briefly. First, once the supernatural God who unilaterally creates and orders nature is fully overcome, a cosmic source of order is still needed: the idea that trillions and trillions of self-moving things have organized themselves into their present order without some sort of overall guidance strains credulity as much as does the older idea of a single source of order. Second, once the idea that all things are ordered by Omnipotent Goodness is fully overcome, we see that the positive values of our experience point to a Noncoercive Cosmic Power that influences us in terms of the claims of truth, beauty, and goodness. (This point can be regarded as the specifically human version of the first point.) Third, the rejection of the sensationist doctrine of perception again makes it possible to understand the manner in which a cosmic mind could influence us. Fourth, the animistic idea that even the most elementary units of existence have some form of perceptual experience makes the influence of a universal soul upon *all* its constituents conceivable.

I turn now to the relevance of this postmodern worldview to the issue of life after death. The general question is: How does postmodern animism make life after death possible even though supernaturalism is rejected?

III. THE POSSIBILITY OF LIFE AFTER DEATH: POSTMODERN METAPHYSICS AND INDIRECT EMPIRICAL EVIDENCE

Whereas the modern worldview rules out a nonsupernaturalistic doctrine of life after death *a priori*, this *a priori* objection is overcome by postmodern animism, which makes life after death metaphysically possible. The idea that it might be *really* possible is supported by some indirect empirical evidence provided by parapsychology. Because of its differences from modern materialism and dualism, postmodern animism allows life after death to be affirmed on a naturalistic basis.

Because the soul is, *contra* materialism, not numerically identical with the brain, the soul can in principle be thought to live after the death of the body.

Because the soul is, *contra* dualism, not ontologically different in kind from the brain, that is, from the cells making up the brain, the numerical distinction between the brain and soul does not raise an insoluble problem of interaction. Animistic interactionism, unlike dualistic interactionism, is therefore not subject to collapse into materialistic identism.

Because the soul's perception of the world is not only or even primarily *sensory* perception, a soul separated from its physical body's sensory apparatus could still be capable of perception. While in the body, the soul's perception of the outside world by means of its bodily sensory organs presupposes the soul's perception of its body itself, especially its brain, and that perception is not sensory. Also, the present moment of the soul perceives its past moments, a type of perception that we call *memory*, and this perception is not sensory. The soul's direct perception of God, through which it learns of the reality of logical, moral, and aesthetic norms, as well as enjoying religious experience in the stricter sense, is not sensory experience.

These considerations suggest that a soul existing apart from its body could at least remember its past experiences and have new experiences of God. In a state freed from fresh stimulation from a physical body, the perception of both God and one's own past might be considerably more intense than it had normally been before. In this situation, reviewing its past in the light of a numinous experience of the Holy One, the soul might well transform itself quite radically. Indeed, reports of near-death experiences generally speak of a life-review and of being in the presence of a numinous reality, and these experiences seem to result in significant transformations.[7]

Postmodern animism also provides a basis for believing that a discarnate soul could continue to have fresh experiences of other finite beings. It suggests that we directly perceive all beings in our environment, not just those that are spatially contiguous with us. The soul, besides directly perceiving its own body, also directly perceives other bodies and other souls. This direct perception of realities outside the body usually does not rise to consciousness, being blocked out by our more intense perception of our own past, our own body, and the indirect data about the surrounding world supplied by the body's sensory organs. These other parts of the world are nevertheless always being directly perceived, by hypothesis, and no reason in principle exists why the soul could not become consciously aware of them. That exceptional type of perception to which the term *extrasensory* is usually applied is exceptional *not* because it involves nonsensory perception (which is ongoing), but because a person has become consciously aware of things that remain at the unconscious level most of the time.

The evidence from parapsychology supports this viewpoint.[8] Both controlled experiments and responsible reports of spontaneous phenomena over the past century provide evidence for the reality of extrasensory perception. The two major forms, *telepathy*, meaning the direct perception of the contents of another soul, and *clairvoyance*, meaning the nonsensory perception of other physical objects or situations, are about equally supported, both experimentally and spontaneously. (Technically, *clairvoyance* means having visual-like images of objects and is distinguished from, say, clairaudience; but *clairvoyance* is commonly used to refer to any knowledge of physical things acquired without sensory means.) Evidence also exists for the view that telepathy and clairvoyance are occurring all the time, and that only *conscious* extrasensory perception is extraordinary or para-normal.[9]

In a postincarnate state, the soul's extrasensory perceptions might take the place of sensory perceptions as the major source of knowledge about the surrounding world. Once the soul was not receiving sensory data from its body, its nonsensory perceptions might become much more conscious, regular, and reliable. (We may also have more than one "body," so that the soul's separation from its biological body would not necessarily leave it *completely* "disembodied." Another, subtler body might provide some means of perception. Whatever the merits of this view, it does not seem necessary to the possibility of perception apart from the biological body.)

Besides undermining the "sensationist" argument against disembodied perception, postmodern animism and parapsychology also provide an answer to the "muscularist" objection that a discarnate soul, even if it could exist and perceive, could not *act*, at least not so as to exert causal influence on anything beyond itself. In an animistic framework, "perception" and "causal influence" are simply two perspectives on the same event. What is causal influence from the perspective of the cause is perception from the perspective of the effect. The soul is able consciously to influence the body's muscular system only because the bodily cells of this system perceive the conscious aims of the soul for its bodily parts; the soul unconsciously affects the body insofar as the bodily cells perceive its unconscious feelings. The body likewise influences the soul insofar as the soul perceives the feelings of its various bodily cells. To be perceived *is* to exert causal influence. If it is possible for souls in a discarnate state to perceive each other, which was argued earlier, it is therefore by definition possible for them to influence each other.

This philosophical deduction from the animistic viewpoint is empirically supported by psychosomatic and parapsychological evidence. Psychosomatic studies show that the soul's influence on its body is not limited to the muscular system; the bodily cells in general seem to be responsive to the soul's aims and other feelings.[10] Phenomena such as stigmata show how strong the soul's influence on its "involuntary" system can be. Because we are inclined to take the soul's influence on its body for granted, however, seeing it as somehow built into the nature of things and in any case as an example of causation between contiguous things, the evidence for psychokinesis is more important. Psychokinesis is influence exerted by the soul (psyche) on material things outside the body without the mediation of the body. Because most of the founders of parapsychology (or, to use the original and more general term, psychical research) were dualists, psychokinesis has been radically distinguished from "thought-transference," which is simply telepathy from the perspective of the sender. From an animist (or panpsychist) standpoint, thought-transference and psychokinesis are not different in kind (so we do not have to worry, as some dualistic parapsychologists do, whether to refer to the influence of the human mind on plants as telepathy—as the term *plant perception* implies— or as psychokinesis; it is both).

In any case, well-documented evidence exists as to the ability of the human soul to exert influence on inanimate things, such as dice, geiger counters, photographic film, weighing scales, cloud chambers, and living organisms, such as bacteria and plants, as well as other human minds.[11] This evidence suggests that a soul existing apart from its physical body would be able to influence not only God and other souls, but also other things as well. (From an animist standpoint, any "other things," however different they might be from the objects of our present sensory experience, would likewise be composed of units of experience.)

Evidence for out-of-body experiences supports the above conclusion that the soul could perceive and act apart from its physical body *if* it can exist apart from it, and possibly the belief that it *can* exist apart from it. People report perceiving things from a perspective more or less removed from the standpoint of their bodies.[12] They also are sometimes perceived by others, animals as well as humans, as being there at the time that they themselves seemed to be there.[13] They therefore evidently can at least influence human and animal souls who are where they themselves seem to be, at some remove from their bodies. In some cases, they also seem to have brought about physical changes. The reality of their perceiving and being perceived from that out-of-body standpoint can be verified. What is notoriously difficult to ascertain is whether the soul is literally out of the body when it phenomenologically seems to itself to be so, or whether it simply is exercising clairvoyant and psychokinetic powers from afar while imagining that it is out of the body. In any case, out-of-body experiences provide evidence for the twofold capacity of the soul to perceive and act without employing its bodily organism, and *some* evidence, of a less conclusive nature, for the capacity of the soul to exist apart from that organism, at least temporarily.

The capacity of the soul to perceive without the body's mediation, and its capacity to exist without the body, are in a sense the same. To exist is to receive influences from other experiences, to make a self-actualizing response to those influences, and to contribute influence to subsequent experiences. Nothing else exists that is more basic or more real than this everlasting reception, self-creation, and contribution of experiences. The soul and its experiences are not "mental" things in distinction from "physical" things. That dualism between two different types of things is precisely what is rejected by postmodern animism. The distinction between physicality and mentality applies to each unit of which the world is comprised. Each momentary unit of experience, whether it be a moment in the life-history of a human soul or a living cell or a molecule, has a physical and a mental aspect. The physical aspect is its reception of influences from previous units of experience. The mental aspect is its self-determining response to its physical aspect. Because a moment of human experience has so much more capacity for free self-determination than does a moment of cellular or molecular experience, it has much more mentality. But it is not *fully* mental. In fact, there is a sense in which a moment of human experience is also more physical than are more lowly experiences, in that it is able to receive much more influence from other experiences into itself than can those more lowly experiences. This greater capacity to be significantly constituted by direct influences from a wider range of other experiences is indeed what raises the possibility that the soul could continue to exist after it is no longer receiving influences from its bodily source of experience. This wider range of influences can perhaps constitute the physical base needed for the soul's continued existence. Evidence for extrabodily influences on the soul is hence *ipso facto* evidence for the possibility of the soul's extrabodily survival.

Another dimension of postmodern animism supports the possibility of the survival of the human *anima* apart from its body. This viewpoint implies that the human soul not only has much more receptive power than other creatures, but that it has much more power, period. This greater power may allow human souls to survive in the universe apart from the body that was originally necessary to bring them about.

The idea that the human soul has the unique power to survive apart from the body that first allowed it to emerge does not imply dualism. The human soul is only different in degree, not different in kind, from the souls of other animals. But a difference in degree can bring about a radically new capacity, so radically new that it virtually amounts to a difference in kind. The human capacity for symbolic language constitutes such a difference. It *is* a difference in degree: the other higher animals are not devoid of a capacity for symbols (as distinct from mere signals), as had previously been thought. The human capacity for language has nonetheless been accompanied by an increase in self-actualizing and contributory power of such magnitude that the effect of human power on the planet has been qualitatively different from that of all other species. (The recent realization that this is a deeply ambiguous fact does not alter its truth.) In the same way, a difference in degree developed by the human soul some time in its evolutionary advance could have given it the unique capacity to survive separation from its body. In fact, I suggest that if the human soul has developed the power to survive apart from its body, this power, its unique degree of power to use language, and its power for self-consciousness all emerged at the same time—and in fact are one and the same power. If so, it would have been when human beings first asked, "If a human being dies, will he or she live again?" that it was first true.

Because this idea of life after death does not require an ontological dualism between the human *anima* and that of other animals, it does not require any supernatural act of God. The emergence of the human capacity for language, self-consciousness, and survival is simply one more radical emergence brought about by the persuasive, evocative activity of God, not different in kind from several previous divinely inspired emergences in the evolutionary process.

The two terms used most often in the West for life after death are *immortality* and *resurrection*. Many Christian theologians have set them in opposition. *Immortality* is denigrated as a pagan notion, because it is said to imply a dualism between soul and body and to imply that the soul has an inherent capacity to live on apart from a gift of new life from God. *Resurrection* is praised as the only authentically Christian notion, because it expresses the Hebrew sense of the soul-body unity of the human being and the Christian sense that our "life everlasting" is wholly dependent upon divine grace. This rejection of immortality in favor of resurrection was motivated, in part, by the more general desire of the Biblical Theology movement to make a strong contrast between Hebrew and Greek modes of thought and to expunge Christian theology of the latter. This contrast, while largely justified, was often overstated. The rejection of immortality was also motivated in part by the influence of the late modern worldview, according to which there is no soul or mind that could conceivably exist apart from the physical body. Insofar as the acceptance of this late modern worldview also involved the rejection of supernatural acts of God, the rejection of immortality in favor of resurrection really meant a rejection of life after death in any straightforward sense altogether, because it would obviously take a supernatural act of the most extreme sort to reassemble and instill life and consciousness back into a disintegrated physical body. *Resurrection* was being used by these modern theologians only as a symbol for the everlasting significance of our lives.

In postmodern theology, in any case, no strong contrast is drawn between immortality and resurrection. Each term, used in conjunction with the other, is found helpful. The term *resurrection* brings out the idea that the new life of the person beyond the body is rooted in God's creative activity—both God's past activity, in which the soul was sufficiently strengthened to make its postmortem continuation a real possibility, and God's present activity, in which new aims attract the soul into this new mode of existence. The term *immortality* brings out the idea that no supernatural divine action is involved, that the soul enters this new mode of existence on the basis of a fully natural, albeit divinely-rooted, capacity.

Each term also has its false connotations. It is difficult to disassociate the term *resurrection* from the idea of the resuscitation of the physical body, complete with its original cells, and atoms. (Which ones—those that constituted the body at age fifteen, age thirty, age sixty, or at death?) The term *immortality* suggests literally endless life—that we would continue as distinct centers of experience for not only millions or billions of years, but trillions and trillions, and that that would only be the beginning! Such a notion surely goes far beyond not only any evidence we have but also anything we can conceive or desire. I will return to this issue in the final section. For now, the main point is that, although the premodern terms *resurrection* and *immortality* are both misleading, they both connote an essential aspect of a postmodern belief in life after death. In particular, some of the connotations of "immortality" as to the status and power of the soul are essential to belief in life after death within a naturalistic framework.

IV. DIRECT EVIDENCE FOR LIFE AFTER DEATH

For those who will examine it with the presupposition that it might be genuine, impressive evidence exists for human survival of bodily death.[14] This topic, which needs a book-length treatment in itself, can only be touched on here with irresponsible brevity.

Some of the most impressive evidence comes from near-death experiences.[15] Besides their out-of-body feature, they often involve encounters with a "welcoming committee," which sometimes includes people of whose death the person did not previously know. Cross-cultural studies show that the series of experiences is very similar among people with vastly different cultural and religious beliefs, which suggests that this is a "natural" phenomenon.[16] Efforts to explain near-death experiences away pharmacologically or as an evolutionary adaptation have been unsuccessful.[17] When approached with the presupposition that the soul *might* continue after the death of its body, studies of these reported experiences provide reason to consider them authentic reports of what the first moments of that continuing journey is at least often like.

Apparitions of recently deceased persons are quite common.[18] They are especially impressive when information is learned through the apparition that can be independently verified and for which there had been no ordinary way of knowing—for example, that the person who appeared had died and how the death occurred. The possibility cannot be ruled out that the person to whom the apparition appeared had learned of the death of the other person through unconscious ESP and then produced a hallucination by which this knowledge could become conscious. (This explanation also cannot be ruled out in near-death experiences of the above-mentioned "welcoming committee.") Such explanations can, however, become so complex, especially in cases where the apparition appears to several people, as to lead one to conclude that a hypothesis based on survival is less implausible.[19] Furthermore, explanations requiring what is sometimes called "super ESP" presuppose that the soul has such extensive powers that its power also to survive apart from its body is supported.[20]

Cross-correspondences in mediumship material have provided some of the evidence most difficult to explain away.[21] In the most famous case, purportedly originating from the spirits of men who had been leading members of the Society for Psychical Research in turn-of-the-century England, several people were independently receiving material through automatic writing. None of them knew that the others were receiving material during the same period, yet the various messages only made sense after they were combined. The episode appears *prima facie* to have been the result of a plan formulated by clever souls who knew the ways in which most mediumistic phenomena could be explained away.

Although reincarnation-type phenomena had long been despised among psychical researchers in the West, Ian Stevenson has recently produced impeccable and extensive studies, based on evidence from a wide variety of cultures, which have provided impressive, although not undeniable, evidence for reincarnation.[22] The evidence consists not only of verifiable memories of the experiences of previously existing persons but also of physical phenomena correlating with the memories, such as birthmarks at the place on the body where the previous person had been shot or stabbed. Alternative explanations involving extraordinary psychosomatic, extrasensory, and psychokinetic powers are, of course, always possible. But if one has a philosophy that in principle allows for a reincarnational interpretation, then the data provide some evidence for reincarnation as a form of the soul's continuing journey that at least sometimes occurs.

These brief, abstract descriptions of some of the types of evidence available are presented here not as evidence that might be convincing in itself but only as a pointer to the kinds of evidence that some not uncritical minds have found impressive. Many sceptics assume, of course, that having a "not uncritical mind" implies having a "scientific" outlook that makes life after death impossible. People who look open-mindedly at the evidence are therefore *ipso facto* uncritical, and the fact that some of them find the evidence convincing is deemed irrelevant. That issue has already been addressed in previous sections in this chapter. But many modern people are prevented from looking at the evidence open-mindedly not only by the conviction that life after death is impossible but also by the feeling that believing in it is morally harmful. I turn now to this final issue.

V. RESPONSES TO MORAL OBJECTIONS TO BELIEF IN LIFE AFTER DEATH

Some readers may consider moral objections to belief in life after death irrelevant. "The issue should be resolved," one might argue, "solely in terms of metaphysical possibility and empirical evidence. Whether we think the belief harmful or healthy is irrelevant. We have to believe many things that we wish were not true. Those who consider belief in life after death desirable should be ready to reject it if the weight of philosophical argument and empirical evidence counts against it, and those who dislike the belief should be ready to accept it if argument and evidence show it to be probable." This position presents an austere ideal against which we should measure our practice. But it ignores the fact that most of us, most of the time, do not approximate this ideal.

In the first place, in spite of Karl Popper's claim that the effort to falsify our conjectures belongs to the core of the scientific method, we for the most part seek evidence *for* the ideas we want to believe, not evidence against them. In the second place, this psychological fact is bolstered by powerful sociological pressures against seeking evidence to support beliefs considered morally harmful. Strong taboos exist in the modern university against looking seriously at evidence supportive of life after death. While this taboo exists partly because life after death is rendered metaphysically impossible by the modern worldview, which is most fully incarnate in the university, it exists partly because of the widespread conviction within the academic community that belief in life after death is morally harmful and socially destructive. We can imagine the way most of us would react to the presentation of evidence by a biologist purporting to prove that Blacks are, as a rule, mentally inferior to other races. The biologist would likely be denied tenure, perhaps fired outright, perhaps shot. Few of us would look at the evidence with an open mind. This refusal would be based in part on our conviction that that issue has already been settled. But it would be partly based on our awareness that such claims have been used for horrible purposes in the past.

The question of the possible harmfulness of belief in life after death therefore cannot be ignored. Neither the metaphysical arguments for the possibility of life after death nor the empirical evidence for its possiblity and reality will receive an adequate hearing in intellectual circles unless the widespread assumption that the belief is necessarily harmful is overcome.

The issue of whether belief in life after death is morally helpful or harmful is a large and complex issue. I take here only a limited and negative approach, examining six reasons for considering the belief morally undesirable. I argue that, although they constitute valid objections to one or more forms of belief in life after death, they would not apply to all forms, and in particular to a postmodern doctrine of continuing life. I also indicate that one could propose counterarguments—that is, that lack of belief in life after death altogether is harmful and that belief in life after death conceived in certain ways would be healthy. I attempt, however, neither a positive portrayal from a postmodern perspective of what life after death might be like nor a comprehensive defense of the healthiness of belief in its reality. The discussion is limited to a response to some moral objections that seem especially influential in modern times.

The six moral objections to belief in life after death to be examined are: (1) the belief entails horrible doctrines of retribution; (2) it gives corrupt institutions power over people's consciences (and pocketbooks); (3) it is the opiate of the people, numbing them to social injustice here and now; (4) it prevents people from living life in the present to the fullest; (5) it produces complacency about the fate of the earth, which is exactly what we do not need in an age of pollution and nuclear weapons; (6) it is idol-atrous, encouraging us to think of ourselves, instead of God, as the ulti-mate recipient of value. I believe these to be the six most fundamental moral objections. In any case, an examination of them will illustrate the main points of my general response.

The association of belief in life after death with horrible doctrines of retribution is certainly well founded. Traditional Christian images of hell portray poor souls suffering eternal punishment for having offended the divine majesty. The example given to human rulers by this picture of vengeance and disproportionate punishment in the highest quarters was bad enough by itself; when this picture was combined with the doctrine of pre-destination, the apparent injustice of the universe was revolting. Even apart from these extreme doctrines, the idea of heavenly rewards and hellish pu-nishments is problematic. Given the grossly different circumstances with which people begin their lives, it cannot be fair to base their everlasting fate on the character they had attained in a few decades of earthly life. Some people are so psychologically abused in early childhood, for example, that it is extremely unlikely that they will ever (within this life) become trust-ing, loving individuals who can devote themselves to the good of others.

This objection to traditional Christian notions of life after death is important, especially in relation to those who are tempted to stem the acidic tides of modernity through a return to earlier forms of religious faith. But this objection does not apply to every doctrine of life after death. For one thing, we need not think of our lives as divided into two parts, this earthly life and our "eternal reward." Perhaps we should think instead of a long journey of the soul, of which the present life is simply one portion (many people have even assumed that it is not necessarily the first portion). Also, while the idea of "rewards" and "punishments" suggests that felicity or pain is imposed upon the individual by an external agent, the God of post-modern theism does not externally and unilaterally impose any state upon anyone. Because the current relation between God and the soul, in which God influences us by attracting us to better ideals, belongs to the very na-ture of things, this relation would necessarily obtain in any continuing life. God has not been holding back some awful coercive power that could be suddenly imposed upon us.

Finally, as horrible as the traditional Christian picture was, the mo-dern picture of the universe as an entirely meaningless place is probably even more horrible. Because human beings are meaning-demanding crea-tures, we can probably tolerate a horrible meaning better than no meaning at all. The point of this observation is not that we should return to the tra-ditional picture as the lesser of evils, but that we should rethink modernity's assumption that we can live happily and healthily apart from any and all beliefs in life after death.

Good reasons exist also for the second objection, that the belief in life after death is used by power-hungry religious institutions to gain control over people. One of the motives behind the advocacy of the dualistic view in the seventeenth century, as I mentioned earlier, was to bolster belief in immortality against those who were denying it to undermine the Church's authority.

Without the widespread perception that the Church possessed the "keys to the kingdom" through which is could consign the disobedient to hell, its power to support the ruling class against calls for political and economic change would have been greatly diminished, along with its power to protect its own temporal wealth. In our own day, we are aware of the power of fundamentalist evangelists on television to influence their viewers' voting and checkwriting hand, and all the regular viewers of these shows surely believe in life after death. Such examples of the way in which the common people's belief in life after death has been used to exploit them politically and economically, sometimes by rulers and preachers who do not themselves believe, lead modern minds to suspect that the very idea of life after death was invented by wicked priests and rulers precisely to attain and protect social power. These unsavory associations also evoke suspicions about anyone seeking to defend the idea.

The abuse of an idea, of course—we know in our rational moments—does not disprove its truth. Or, more precisely, the abuse of belief in life after death does not disprove the belief in general, although it might count against the particular form of belief that encourages the abuse. This particular form is the doctrine that some human organization has the "keys to the kingdom." An organization could have power over the postmortem state of human souls, presumably, only if this power had been delegated to it by the moral ruler of the universe. One reason the seventeenth-century defenders of the sociopolitical *status quo* objected to naturalistic ideas of deity (as well as to atheism) was that a divine power understood naturalistically would be equally accessible to all people. Only a deity conceived in a supernaturalistic, highly voluntaristic manner could have delegated the keys of the everlasting kingdom to the Christian Church—and to its hierarchy at that. Postmodern theology is based on a version of naturalistic theism. No doctrine of life after death compatible with it could maintain that the power to decide our ultimate destiny had been delegated to any earthly organization.

Finally, although it is true that a particular form of belief in life after death has enabled priests and affiliated political groups to exercise enormous social control, it is probably also true that the *absence* of belief in life after death leaves people even more subject to centralized control. Vital religious belief in a life beyond this world provides a standpoint from which people can resist the political power of the state, and it has probably functioned in this way at least as much as it has to bolster the state's power. After all, if we do not live on after this body's death, then the state, with its coercive power, does have the capacity to determine our ultimate destiny in a very strong sense. And in our century, the tyranny exercised over people by the modern secular state has been a much greater threat to human life than the control exercised by religious organizations. The modern sensibility now appears superficial. Whereas the moral concern to overcome tyrannical control once provided a motive to ridicule belief in life after death, this moral concern could in our time well lead us to reexamine the belief.

The third moral objection to belief in life after death is that it is the "opiate of the people." By promising that perfect justice will be brought about in heaven, the doctrine numbs people to the injustice on earth. (This is how the phrase is often used, even if it is not exactly what Marx himself meant by it.) In particular, the ideas that the present life is just a testing ground for the next, that one of the tests is our obedience to the rulers God has set over us, and that people's happiness in this brief life is a trivial matter compared with their condition in eternity, have served to legitimate the *status quo*, in which the masses are powerless and miserable while an elite minority enjoys power and luxury. The religious belief in immortality is an ideological opiate for both classes. It prevents the poor from becoming sufficiently motivated to improve their own lot while it salves the conscience of the ruling class, enabling them to believe that things are as they ought to be.

Again, so much truth is contained in this charge that one hesitates to say "Yes, but. . . ." A response is nevertheless in order. As before, this objection applies only to certain forms of belief in life after death. One need not, I have already pointed out, think in terms of this life and eternity, or of this life as a test and a future life as a reward. Within the context of naturalistic theism, furthermore, God cannot unilaterally bring about a state of justice, peace, and happiness. (One formulation of the problem of evil, valid against supernaturalistic theism, has been based on the ancient question: "How long, O Lord?" That is, if the Reign of God is someday to be ushered in by God alone, why not today—or long ago?) If a state of universal justice, peace, and happiness is ever to be realized, it will be the result of a transformation in the inner nature of the creatures and their internal relations to each other, and such a transformation cannot be imposed by God. It will be a development out of the present. From this perspective, no reason exists for delaying the attempt to create a better society in which healthy relationships and personal growth are encouraged. Every motive exists for encouraging creative transformations as rapidly as possible.

To provide a counterargument: the loss of belief in life after death does not necessarily increase concern for social justice in the present. Individuals freed from any anticipation of a future life may indeed become more aggressive, losing that "self-restraint" which comfortable conservatives wish they would practice. But their aggressive activity is more likely to be aimed at improving their own condition at the expense of others than at bringing about a better society. More generally, the decline in belief in life after death has led to a decline in the sense of the sacred importance of human life which lay behind most of the significant reforms in our civilization. Although the loss of belief in a transcendent destiny often releases moral energy for reformist activity in the first generation, the moral energy itself seems to disappear in subsequent generations. This phenomenon suggests a truth about human nature that modernity overlooked. In general, modernity assumed that human virtues were innate, not dependent upon contingent beliefs and social organizations. It accordingly assumed that the disappearance of supernaturalism would do nothing but improve human character and behavior. All the vices associated with supernaturalistic beliefs would disappear, while all the virtues that had been nurtured by supernaturalism would be retained—because the modern mind, with its superficial analysis, assumed they were not thus nurtured but innate. Given a deeper appreciation of human nature, might it not behoove us to distinguish between that particular doctrine of immortality we have rejected and the more general question of whether we may in some sense continue past bodily death?

The charge that the anticipation of a future life blocks the fulfillment of human potential in this life is not limited to the question of social justice. A related claim is that the expectation of a future life, in which all desires will be fulfilled, prevents people from living fully in the present. Belief in a future life promotes a dull, joyless life, lived in terms of a narrow, negative morality, in which few of the human capacities for play and aesthetic delight are realized. If we believed that "we only go around once in life," as the beer commercial puts it, we would do everything with "gusto."

Again there is truth to the charge, but it is limited to the view that regards life after death as an extrinsic reward for the virtue exercised (or at least the vice resisted!) in the present life, and that assumes that one will be suddenly transformed into a person capable of eternal delight. The charge would not apply to a conception of life after death appropriate to a naturalistic theism, according to which one's postbodily life would be a natural continuation of the journey travelled during one's earthly life. The next phase of the journey would be carried on with the virtues and talents that had been developed thus far. From my own observation, people who have this kind of expectation live the fullest form of life. In particular, they seem much more likely to develop new interests and talents late in life than both those with a supernaturalistic belief and those with no belief at all. Furthermore, although those with no belief may outwardly live with more "gusto," at least temporarily, the life lived for immediate gratification with no future reference seems generally to be experienced as less intrinsically fulfilling than even the parodied puritanical life. If this is so, the concern that people live fully in the present, which motivated many people in the modern period to consider arguments and evidence against the supernatural doctrine of life after death, should motivate people now to consider arguments and evidence for belief in a continuing life naturalistically conceived.

The most contemporary form of the moral objection to belief in life after death is the fifth claim—that belief in life after death creates complacency about the fate of the earth, a complacency we can ill afford in this age of environmental pollution and nuclear arsenals. If human souls can live without bodies, at least biological bodies, runs this objection, then they can live without the planet. The destruction of the planet's capacity to support life would therefore be no ultimate tragedy. The complacency produced by this belief is increased by those apocalyptic visions according to which our everlasting life will be preceded by the foreordained destruction of the earth (through nuclear war, many Christians believe), followed by the creation of a new earth. But even without this extreme doctrine, it is felt, belief in life after death prevents that intense passion to save the earth which is now needed. If we are to be motivated to engage in the almost superhuman task of ridding the planet of nuclear weapons, Jonathan Schell seems to believe, [23] we must be convinced that the destruction of the planet's life would be the ultimate tragedy—the very death of meaning— and this it cannot be if billions of human souls live on in some other realm. This objection, unlike the former ones, does not apply only to a supernaturalistic understanding of life after death. Of course, the apocalyptic vision of the destruction and instantaneous re-creation of the world is supernaturalistic to the extreme degree. But the more general charge applies to all views of life after death, insofar as they lead us to think that the planet's death, however tragic, would not be the very death of meaning.

As a first response, I think Schell is simply wrong on this issue (even if he is right on most others). That is, he is wrong in thinking that the nuclear destruction of the planet would be the death of meaning and also in thinking that this is a motivating belief. If the anticipation that the planet's life will be destroyed makes life meaningless, then it is already meaningless. The planet's life *will* eventually disappear, whether within 50 years or 50 billion years. If its eventual disappearance would make all previous life meaningless, then all life would already be meaningless. That conclusion would not provide good motivation for saving the earth; whether we save it or let it be destroyed would make no ultimate difference. [24]

Furthermore, if the one thing human beings cannot face is the lack of meaning, then the claim that nuclear annihilation would destroy all meaning is not a good way to encourage people to think about the nuclear problem. People who accept that view are more likely to try to avoid thinking about the nuclear problem than to spend much of their time reading, thinking, writing and speaking about it. The fact that belief in life after death would keep us from thinking of the destruction of our planet through nuclear holocaust (or more gradual ecological deterioration) as the end of meaning is therefore actually a point in its favor.

"Fair enough," a critic could reply, "but you must admit that belief in life after death can provide a doctrine of ultimate meaningfulness that makes people too cavalier about the preservation of the planet. How would a postmodern doctrine guard against this?" No satisfactory answer could be given without developing a full-scale doctrine, which cannot be done here. But a couple of points can be made. First, even if we believe in life after death, *much* of our sense of meaning comes from our conviction that life on this planet will continue indefinitely. The meaningfulness of our lives would be greatly reduced, even if not totally destroyed, by the anticipation of the imminent end of planetary life. Insofar as Jonathan Schell's book dramatically makes this point, it is invaluable.

Second, a naturalistic theist assumes not only that the creation of life on our planet took the creator many billions of years, but also that it *had* to take this amount of time. The cosmic source of order, novelty, and life, using the power of persuasion on partially self-determining entities, could create life only through a long, slow process of astronomical, geological, and biological evolution filled with chance and uncertainty. A planet capable of sustaining life may also be a very rare phenomenon. In any case, we have to assume that our planet is extremely precious to its creator. The continuation of the planet's life for its natural duration is surely essential to the complete fulfillment of the creator's purpose. Its premature destruction through human carelessness or brinkmanship would certainly be the greatest imaginable tragedy and a manifestation of the greatest conceivable human sin. All this would be true even apart from some central role the planet might play, perhaps beyond our capacity to fathom, in the continuing journey of human souls.

Beyond not weakening motivation to save the planet, belief in life after death might strengthen it. Insofar as this belief supports people's sense that the world is an essentially spiritual place—that it is ultimately good, fair, and God's—and thereby intensifies their orientation to spiritual concerns, their commitment to God's purposes will be strengthened. Within the context of postmodern naturalistic theism, this commitment will entail resolve to save the planet.

Overcoming the objections to belief in life after death on the part of morally sensitive people would require much more than this brief response. A new conception of a continuing journey would eventually have to replace the hitherto dominant image. But I hope that my response, inadequate as it is, is enough to suggest that the modern objections to premodern conceptions of life after death would not necessarily apply to a postmodern conception, and also that the modern assumption, which is that people can live perfectly healthy lives without any belief in life after death, needs to be reconsidered.

Before concluding, I must deal with a sixth objection, which is based on different assumptions. This sixth objection is that belief in life after death reinforces our tendency to think of ourselves, instead of God, as the ultimate recipients of value. While the first five objections are compatible with atheism, and are often made in the name of it, this sixth objection is made in the name of theism. It has, in fact, been made most strongly by Charles Hartshorne in the name of the naturalistic theism, or panentheism, on which postmodern theology is based.

Central to Hartshorne's theistic vision is the conviction that the ultimate meaning of our lives consists in our "objective immortality" in the one everlasting center of experience. As the sympathetic soul of the universe, God feels and is in fact partly constituted by the contributions of all creatures, and is enriched or pained by them, depending upon their qualities. We can serve God, therefore, primarily by serving our fellow creatures. What we do for our descendents will, for example, continue to enrich God long after we die. Besides answering the question of the ultimate meaning of our lives, this vision of ourselves and all other creatures as objectively immortal in God pulls us beyond our natural egoism, with its ethic of enlightened self-interest, towards an ethic in which we evaluate all actions in terms of their contribution to the good of the whole.

This theistic vision has led Hartshorne strongly to reject personal immortality, according to which we have infinite careers of new experiences after bodily death. This belief, he holds, provides transcendental justification for the ethic of enlightened self-interest, according to which the meaning of all things is to serve our egos. This belief often leads us to reduce the meaning of God's existence to that of the provider of our immortality, rather than realizing that the meaning of our lives lies in serving God. Hartshorne therefore says: "To clear the way to the idea of God we need to get rid of all rivals to Him as the ultimate recipient of the fruits of our labors."[25] Closely related to this moral objection is Hartshorne's contention that the idea of personal immortality involves ascribing to us an attribute, temporal infinity, that belongs to God alone. Unlike the One who exists necessarily, we are not infinite in knowledge, goodness, or spatial extensiveness; why would we, once created, be infinite in temporal duration?

In expressing his objection to the idea of personal immortality, Hartshorne has sometimes written as if the idea of life after death itself were objectionable.[26] And certainly many people have read him as rejecting life after death altogether. He has made clear in careful formulations, however, that his objections are not to the idea that there will be further chapters to our lives beyond bodily death, but only to the idea that "there will never be any end, that the chapters will be infinite."[27] It is only the latter idea that he considers impossible and objectionable. He has no objection to the idea of life after death, as long as it is not thought to be literally everlasting.

Can we have a meaningful idea of life after death if we reject immortality in the sense of a literally everlasting life as a distinct individual? Actually, although much popular thinking has tended to equate these two ideas, most philosophical and theological conceptions, worked out by people who have thought long and hard about the idea, have not. They have not promised (or threatened) that our individual lives would continue for billions times billions of years. Although Christian creeds speak of "life everlasting," most Christian theologians have spoken of "eternal life," meaning a mode of existence in which time, at least in the ordinary sense, does not occur. Hindu and Buddhist discussions often use the metaphor of a drop being reabsorbed in the ocean. The cycle of birth, death, and rebirth is thought to continue for a long period, but not endlessly. Salvation is, in fact, generally understood as involving the cessation of individual existence, through overcoming the karmic form of life that endlessly perpetuates the cycle.

Perhaps this latter idea provides a clue to the truth. A karmic life is a desiring, attached form of life. Perhaps we continue to exist as distinct individuals as long as we desire at a deep level to do so, that is, as long as we have unfulfilled desires. This idea is fully consistent with postmodern animism, according to which enduring individuals are serially ordered societies of momentary experiences. Each experience inherits the emotions, desires, and purposes from prior members of that society. The continued endurance of an individual depends not only upon a favorable environment but also upon the appetite of the momentary experiences to continue that mode of existence.

It is not my intention to develop and defend a conception of life after death in this chapter, and certainly not with any hint of certainty. Here, more than with most issues, we see in a glass darkly, if at all. But it is important to see that a meaningful idea of life after death does not necessarily include the problematic notion that life after death would be literally unending. By making this distinction, we retain the insight of Whitehead and Hartshorne that the ultimate meaning of life consists in our contribution to God.

At the same time, we can make this prospect of objective immortality in God seem more important and more appealing. We can believe that the universe does not frustrate this unsatiated, if not insatiable, desire most of us seem to have for more life. We can perhaps even believe that we will continue to have more life until we ourselves decide we have had enough. We can suppose that the great inequalities of the present life will be overcome, so that all people will have had a chance to fulfill their potentialities and to have made a contribution to the divine experience about which they can feel good. In this way, we can overcome the feeling that the doctrine that we are immortal only in God is an elitist doctrine, comforting only to those happy few who have been fortunate enough to make what they can consider a significant and positive contribution to the universe.

Through these two notions, that inequalities will be overcome and that desires and potentialities will not be left unfulfilled, the goodness of the universe and therefore of God is more obvious and our desire to live in terms of God's will is thereby made more intense. Furthermore, belief in life after death generally leads people to a more spiritual vision of the universe, and therefore to take spiritual issues more seriously. Such people are more likely to live in terms of the good of the whole than in terms of narrow self-interest. For these reasons, belief in life after death in a postmodern framework, far from undermining a theist's devotion for God, should actually strengthen it.

SUMMARY

The modern denial of life after death has been based less on evidence, or the lack thereof, than on the *a priori* convictions that it is impossible and that belief in it is harmful. The conviction as to harmfulness resulted from the confrontation of premodern conceptions of life after death, which *are* objectionable, by a modern sensibility, which was superficial. The conviction as to impossibility followed from the antianimistic starting point of the modern worldview. Although originally part of a supernaturalistic dualism, this antianimistic view of nature eventuated in an atheistic materialism. The materialism of this worldview forbad nonsensory perception, influence at a distance, and a mind or soul distinct from the material body. Life after death could therefore conceivably occur only through a supernatural act, but the atheism of this worldview ruled out that possibility. Because life after death could occur neither naturally nor supernaturally, no evidence for it needed to be examined, because no alleged evidence could possibly be genuine.

Postmodern animism changes everything. Life after death is conceivable apart from supernaturalism. Nonsensory perception and other forms of influence at a distance, which can provide evidence for the possibility and reality of life after death, are not ruled out. The mind or soul is distinct from the brain, yet without an ontological dualism requiring a supernatural deity to render the interaction of mind and brain intelligible. Although the soul of human beings is not ontologically different from that of other animals, it can be thought to have developed naturally, through its evolutionary interaction with the divine source of novel order, the unique capacity to survive apart from its biological body. A postmodern conception of life after death would, furthermore, not be subject to modernity's moral objections to premodern conceptions, and a postmodern sensibility opens one to the possibility that the moral harmfulness of a supernaturalistic belief in life after death may be surpassed by the lack of belief altogether. Finally, a postmodern belief in life after death would not detract from devotion to God and therefore the good of the whole, but would strengthen it.

7

SPIRITUAL DISCIPLINE IN THE MEDIEVAL, MODERN, AND POSTMODERN WORLDS

Theology is a practical as well as theoretical enterprise. Besides seeking to answer intellectual questions for their own sake, that is, for the sake of discovering truth, theology supports various forms of practice, such as ethical activity, public worship, and spiritual discipline. Whereas the prior essays in this volume were primarily concerned with truth for its own sake (although the ethical side of spirituality was discussed in chapter 3), these final two essays are concerned with practice. The present essay is oriented primarily to that form of practice which is widely called *spiritual discipline*. So as not to be misleading, I should say immediately that the focus is not on spiritual discipline as such, for example on methods. The essay is as fully theoretical as the others. But the focus is on the way various theories about the nature of reality (theologies or antitheologies) support or fail to support spiritual discipline.

The other three words in the title—*medieval, modern,* and *postmodern*—provide the outline for the three sections of this essay. In the first section, I suggest that spiritual discipline, which was prominent in medieval life, was supported by the dominant theoretical framework of the middle ages, the theology of St. Augustine. But I suggest that this Augustinian theology supported spiritual discipline only ambivalently, because aspects of it undermined the concern for spiritual discipline. In the second section, I suggest that spiritual discipline has waned in the modern period not only because the undermining aspects of Augustinian theology became more prominent in postmedieval theology, but more importantly because the modern worldview has *completely* undermined any basis for spiritual discipline. In the third section, I suggest that we are now moving into a postmodern period, one feature of which is a recovery of the concern for spiritual discipline. I suggest further that Whiteheadian theology has the capacity to provide the overarching framework for this postmodern spirituality and that it overcomes those aspects of both the Augustinian and the modern worldviews that undermined spiritual discipline.

I. AUGUSTINIAN THEOLOGY AND SPIRITUAL DISCIPLINE

The desire to support spiritual discipline was at the heart of Augustine's Christian theology. One of the central features of his life and theology was his rejection of Manichean dualism, which he had once accepted. Peter Brown has argued that Augustine's major criticism of Manicheanism was based not on its dualism *per se* but on the fact that this dualism made the good passive and impotent, leaving only the evil as active and aggressive.[1] This doctrine implied that the soul was on the defensive, simply trying to ward off the potentially evil influences of the body and the surrounding material world. Neoplatonism, by helping Augustine see evil not as an active, substantial force but only a privation of the good, provided the basis for putting good on the attack. In his Neoplatonic Christian perspective, all substances are intrinsically good: there is only the one God, who is totally good, and the substances created by this God.

If this interpretation of Augustine is correct, his ability to affirm monotheism over cosmic dualism was above all the affirmation of a view that supported spiritual discipline. Even his later stress on predestination, which to the Pelagians and the monks seemed to undercut self-discipline, was in Augustine's mind a support for continuing the battle against evil: the doctrine of predestination gave the guarantee to Augustine and his fellow Christians that their efforts would be effective. It was the ultimate expression of monotheism's meaning, that the good is active and powerful and will be ultimately victorious, so that the battle against the *apparently* superior forces of evil is not in vain. In his later years, Augustine was not as optimistic as he had been in his early years as a Christian about the degree to which the passions of the flesh and other effects of original sin can be overcome in this life. But he never abandoned the belief that one should work toward that end. Augustine would have been very unhappy to think that his theology would in part undermine, rather than completely promote, a life of spiritual discipline.

Some aspects of Augustine's theology, however, do seem to have undermined concern with spiritual discipline within the Christian tradition. It is important to understand this fact. Preachers and theologians have long been blaming the growing lack of interest in Christianity, especially among the educated, on the materialistic assumptions of modern thought. There is much truth in this charge, which will be examined in the next section. But it must not be the whole truth, because the growing interest in things spiritual during the past two decades within one portion of our culture has not usually meant a revival of interest in Christian thought and practices. (The apparent revival that has occurred comes from other portions of the culture.) Rather, the thirst for spiritual discipline has largely meant a turn to Eastern forms of spirituality. Christianity is assumed to have little to offer. This assumption is based in part on the fact that most Christian theologians and ministers do not speak much about spiritual discipline and in part on the public *image* of Christian priests and ministers. Seldom are they looked upon as spiritual giants. To find a spiritual guide usually means finding a guru, which means someone who has attained wisdom from the East. Christians in general who participate actively in the Church are not perceived as attaining much spiritual growth.

To some extent, these perceptions reflect the tendency to see only the weaknesses of the old, familiar, home-country religion and only the best in the religions of exotic countries. But to a great extent these perceptions correspond to reality, and this reality reflects the influence of Augustinian theology. I will discuss two Augustinian doctrines that have undermined concern for spiritual development. The first concerns the Donatist controversy; the second, the Pelagian controversy.

While the Donatist controversy involved a complex mixture of social, political, and theological issues, at the center, theologically, was the question whether a priest's lack of virtue affected the validity of the sacraments he administered. The Donatists said Yes, sacraments received from a wicked priest might not be efficacious for salvation. Augustine said No, the efficacy of the sacraments ordained by God through Christ is not dependent upon the subjective moral and spiritual qualities of the priest administering them.

While Augustine had a number of personal and political motives for rejecting the Donatist position, his argument was rooted theologically in the omnipotence of God.[2] To say that the priest's lack of virtue could prevent God's grace from being effective through the sacraments would imply that "heretics had the power to pollute" what belongs to God,[3] that is, that human power could distort God's intended effect. Augustine argues specifically against the Donatist attempt "to show that the man who is baptized is made to partake of the character of him by whom he is baptized."⁴ Augustine's view triumphed and became orthodoxy.

Although Augustine was speaking only about the mediation of grace through the sacraments, not about whether the character of a priest has an influence in general upon the lives of his parishioners, the anti-Donatist verdict of the Church has had the effect of minimizing the importance of the spiritual stature of Christian ministers. The generalized message of the verdict can be stated thus: God is omnipotent. The efficacy of God's grace is not dependent upon the quality of the human instruments through which it is mediated. The priest or minister therefore need not purify himself in order to perform his essential role. The ordained means for communicating God's grace work *ex opera operato*, from the very fact of doing the act (whether this be primarily administering the sacraments or, with the Protestants later, preaching the word).

This issue lies behind a common generalization about the difference between East and West which, after all necessary qualifications, retains some validity. In the East, a person's philosophical-theological-psychological ideas are assumed to be unworthy of attention unless the person has attained a high degree of holiness; in the West, we take seriously the ideas of people whose lives have been major disaster areas. The East has in this respect been far more "pragmatic," assuming that one can be aided in spiritual matters only by a spiritual person. The West has officially held that the effectiveness of divine grace is independent of the human medium. In practice, we know this Western view to be largely false: we are often led either to experience divine grace or to turn away from things spiritual through the character of a particular believer.

There *is* an element of truth in the Augustinian position—how could it have been so influential otherwise? The challenge is to formulate this truth so as to retain also the element of truth in the Donatist position, that is, that God's transforming grace is mediated through others, and that it is colored, for good or ill, by the nature of the medium. This latter truth suggests that spiritual discipline may increase one's effectiveness as mediator of God's grace.

On the basis of his understanding of the omnipotence of divine grace, Augustine went from the Manichean position, that the power of good is on the defensive against the power of evil, to the other extreme, saying that the power of good not only is active but *encounters no real resistance*. This anti-Donatism is the first way in which Augustine's influence has undermined the concern for spiritual discipline within the Christian tradition. The second way involves Augustine's anti-Pelagianism.

On most of the issues involved in his controversy with the Pelagians, Augustine was much more profound than they. But they were absolutely right on one issue—the central issue for them: *human beings must have some freedom in relation to God or else the spiritual life is nonsense and God's fairness and hence absolute goodness must be denied.*

Although Augustine's early writings, before the Pelagian controversy arose, seemed to affirm human freedom—so clearly in fact that Pelagius was able to cite many of Augustine's statements for support—Augustine later rejected the Pelagian position totally, saying that *every* aspect of our relation to God is *totally* determined by God. If we have faith in God, that is totally God's gift. Even the first movement of our mind in that direction is due to God's irresistible grace. Our good works arising out of faith are themselves totally due to God. Being concerned to rule out the possibility of any human boasting or pride in achievement, Augustine never tired of repeating the rhetorical question from St. Paul, "What hast thou, that thou didst not receive?" (II Cor. 4:7), and several other proof-texts, such as: "It is God who worketh in you, even to will!" (Phil. 2:13), and "The will is prepared by the Lord" (Prov. 8:35). Neither our faith nor our work is *partly* due to God and *partly* to us: they are *totally* due to God. And yet Augustine maintained that he had not denied his earlier insistence on human freedom. In a late writing, *Grace and Free Will*, he stressed over and over that the exhortations in the Bible would be meaningless unless human freedom were presupposed. How could he say both things?

We can reconcile the apparent contradiction by distinguishing three aspects of human freedom: cosmological freedom, theological freedom, and axiological freedom. *Cosmological* freedom is freedom of the human soul in relation to other (finite) things in the cosmos, such as planets, angels, demons, and the human body. You believe in cosmological freedom if you believe that the human soul or mind has at least some power for self-determination over against all the finite forces in the cosmos acting on it, so that even all of them combined cannot fully determine the soul's states. *Theological* freedom is freedom of the human soul in relation to God. You believe in theological freedom if you believe that you have some power of self-determination in relation to divine power. *Axiological* freedom is the ability of the soul to actualize the ideals or values it consciously wants to actualize. You affirm that you are free in this sense if you believe that, by consciously deciding to live more fully in accord with the divine will (as you understand it), you can do so.

The debate between Augustine and the Pelagians is confused because these three meanings of "freedom" are not distinguished. By distinguishing them, we can agree with the consensus that Augustine won the debate while seeing that an element of truth in the Pelagian position got brushed aside in the confusion.

Both parties affirmed *cosmological* freedom. Augustine as much as the Pelagians agreed that our fates are not determined by heavenly bodies, demonic beings, or the passions of the body (although Augustine, at least, knew that the latter could be *very* strong). When Augustine affirms human freedom across the board, for elect and nonelect alike, he has in mind freedom in this cosmological sense.

Theological freedom was the main concern of the Pelagians. They believed as much as Augustine that God would condemn sinners to hell—they were not "liberals." They were in fact more rigorous than Augustine, limiting salvation to those who achieve perfect obedience to the Christian law. Given this assumption, they rightly saw that God would be unjust if God unilaterally decided (through predestination) who would and would not fulfill the law. The human soul must therefore be free in relation to God; whether we live a worthy life must be at least partly determined by our power, not by God's alone. Divine grace must provide only the context and preconditions for the good life, they held. It must not unilaterally provide our faith and good acts, as Augustine said.

With regard to *axiological* freedom, the Pelagian position was rather naive in comparison with Augustine's. The Pelagians had a less profound grasp of the Christian ideal, thinking of the Christian life primarily as a matter of external obedience to individual commandments. Augustine understood that the Christian ideal concerns the whole orientation of one's life, that this involves loving God and all other things in God, and that the capacity to fulfill this ideal is *not* under the simple control of our conscious wills—that myriad semiconscious and unconscious factors, long-ingrained habits, and influences from our physical and spiritual environments work against our loving the good of the whole instead of loving ourselves and other things selfishly. He understood that, when we are enabled genuinely to love, this enabling comes as a gift from first being loved. He understood that the healing of tendencies rooted in distorted love is usually a slow and partial process.

The Pelagians, by contrast, wanting to hold to both God's condemnation of sinners and God's absolute fairness, denied that the Christian life is too difficult for human volition to fulfill. "Ought" must imply "can" if one is to be justly condemned to everlasting torment for not fulfilling the oughts. Having a superficial understanding of the Christian ideal (as the external fulfillment of a set of laws), they spoke as if fulfilling the ideal were within the capacity of every person. No divine grace was needed beyond God's grace in giving the Christian law as a feasible means of salvation. Augustine was able easily to demolish the Pelagian position. He had only to point to St. Paul's writings and to his readers' own experience, that is, their experience in relation to the Christian ideal understood as perfect love of God and neighbor.

The tragedy of this discussion was that the two meanings of "freedom" at issue—theological freedom and axiological freedom—were not distinguished. It was, of course, to Augustine's advantage *not* to distinguish them. By writing as if only one meaning of "freedom" were at issue, or at least as if a refutation of the Pelagians' idea of axiological freedom carried with it a refutation of their claim about theological freedom, Augustine was able to gain a complete victory. In his anti-Pelagian writings, most of his argument is devoted to showing that their idea of axiological freedom is simple-minded and unbiblical. Having distinguished the two issues, *we* can entertain the possibility that while Augustine was more profound with regard to axiological freedom, the Pelagians were right about theological freedom (even if we may disagree with their way of protecting it—more on this below).

Much concern was expressed in Augustine's own time that his doctrine of absolute predestination and irresistible grace would undermine spiritual discipline and give support to sloth. This concern, along with that of protecting the fairness of God, was central to the Pelagians. The monks, who were dedicating their lives to the injunction "Be ye perfect," were likewise disturbed by Augustine's writings for this reason. They knew full well that sloth was at least as dangerous as pride, about which Augustine seemed one-sidedly concerned. In trying to prevent pride in the later stages of spiritual development (as they saw it), Augustine had undermined the great effort it takes simply to begin the spiritual path. If we can do *nothing* without God's grace, if God's grace *totally* effects every act of faith and love, and if a divine decree before our birth determined whether we are to receive this grace, self-denying effort seems senseless.

After much debate, with the irenic John Cassian taking up the case of the monks, an unstable compromise was reached in 529 at the Synod of Orange. The more horrible implications of Augustine's position, such as the predestination of the nonelect to hell, were rejected. The compromise was unstable, however, because the Synod only rejected some of the logical *implications* of the Augustinian position without challenging the basic doctrines from which these implications followed. (By analogy, I have not effectively challenged the conclusion "I am mortal" if I let stand both of the premises, "All humans are mortal," and "I am human.")

This unstable (semi-Pelagian or semi-Augustinian) compromise was maintained throughout the Middle Ages, with only occasional outbreaks of consistency. The Thomistic synthesis embodies this compromise fully, insisting explicitly on the reality of human freedom while maintaining a doctrine of God that makes theological freedom impossible.[5] This compromise was unmasked by the Protestant reformers, who stated even more openly than Augustine that we are not free in relation to God and that our eternal destiny is determined solely by God. (See Luther's *Bondage of the Will*, in which the philosophical points are articulated with utmost clarity. He may have been wrong, but he was logical.)[6] I cannot but believe that this doctrine has had a significant impact upon Protestant Christianity and therefore upon countries in which the ethos has been largely determined by Protestants. The logical implication of the Lutheran and Calvinistic theologies was that our fate is not at all in our hands. And, despite much evidence to the contrary, we *are* affected by logic.

The logic of this position worked itself out theologically in our century, in the so-called neo-Reformation theologians. "Christian faith" was contrasted with "religion." *Christian faith* humbly accepts what God has done for us, which we learn through revelation. *Religion*, on the other hand, is the prideful attempt to climb up to God. The idea of "cooperating" with God is treated as the worst sin, because it denies that God has already done everything for us.[7] The effect of these writings was to discourage spiritual discipline as un-Christian. Many Protestant ministers and seminary professors were educated in schools in which these neo-Reformation ideas were dominant. These ideas have also not been without effect in Catholic circles. In any case, this twentieth-century revival of Augustinianism, in conjunction with the effects of the Augustinianism of the Protestant reformers during the previous four centuries, helps explain why those who are today interested in spiritual discipline assume that they must turn to non-Christian sources for guidance. Most Christian theology in the West has implicitly opposed spiritual discipline, especially since the Reformation, and some of it has done so explicitly.

These factors also explain why many sensitive people, in both the East and the West, have assumed that spiritual discipline is in conflict with belief in God. As long as the word *God* conjures up the idea of an all-determining power, belief in God will be antagonistic to concern for spiritual discipline. St. Paul speaks paradoxically about these matters. He says, "I . . . , though it was not I, but the grace of God which is with me" (I Cor. 15:10, RSV), and "work out your own salvation with fear and trembling; for God is at work in you" (Phil. 2:12). Augustine resolved these Pauline paradoxes by denying theological freedom.

But perhaps another interpretation is possible. In fact, the philosophy of one of the giants of our century, Alfred North Whitehead, provides the basis for a postmodern interpretation of these statements that keeps both divine influence and human freedom. Before turning to the question of postmodern theology, however, we need to see what else, besides a resurgence of Augustinianism, accounts for the decline of spiritual discipline in the modern period.

II. The Antispirituality of Modernity

The modern worldview, especially in its second form, which is now dominant in intellectual circles, provides no basis whatsoever for spiritual discipline. It, in fact, promotes what can be called an *antispiritual spirituality*.

This expression is possible because "spirituality" can be used either in a broad or a strict sense. I have thus far been using the term in the strict sense, to refer to a stance in which one's life is oriented toward moral and religious (and perhaps aesthetic) values, as distinct from what are normally called physical or material values, such as the pleasures of the flesh and the possession of material goods. A spiritual person in this sense may, of course, be concerned about physical things selflessly, wanting everyone to have a fair share of a society's material wealth. But the spiritual person is less concerned, beyond a certain level, with his or her own physical possessions and pleasures than with the realization of other values. In this strict sense, spirituality is a matter of degree, and some people are hardly spiritual at all.

Everyone, however, embodies a spirituality in the broad sense of the term, because in this sense it means a person's fundamental convictions, values, attitudes, and habits, especially with regard to what he or she considers most important. To use Paul Tillich's term, one's spirituality embodies one's *ultimate concern*, which means what one takes to be holy, or of ultimate worth. A *materialistic spirituality* is therefore possible. Combining then the strict and the broad meanings of the term, we can speak of an antispiritual spirituality, which is a spirituality in the broad sense that discourages the development of spirituality in the strict sense.

The term *spiritual discipline* refers to any effort through which one seeks to become more spiritual (in the strict sense). One may pray, meditate, contemplate, do *t'ai chi,* develop lists of desired virtues (*a là* Ben Franklin), emulate admirable people, and so on. An antispiritual spirituality discourages a person from engaging in any of these forms of spiritual discipline by convincing her or him that spiritual discipline is impossible, unimportant, undesirable, or perhaps all three.

Augustinian theology promotes spiritual discipline, but only unstably. We can see why it does promote it. The basic motive of our spirituality (in the broad sense) is to be in harmony with that which is most real and important in the nature of things, and Augustinian theology portrayed God, the soul, and spiritual values as the most real, the most effective, and the most important realities. Spiritual discipline to bring the soul into harmony with the divine will, and thus to embody spiritual values, was thereby portrayed as important. The picture of heaven or hell as the goal of our earthly life increased this sense of importance considerably! The soul was portrayed as not only real but also free (in the cosmological sense), so that spiritual discipline was possible as well as important. At the same time, I have suggested, the anti-Donatist element in Augustinian theology tended to undermine the importance of spiritual discipline, while the anti-Pelagian element, in insisting that the soul is *not* free (theologically as well as axiologically), tended to undermine the possibility of spiritual discipline.

The modern worldview undermines the importance and possibility of spiritual discipline much more thoroughly. Whereas the spirituality-undermining features of Augustinianism occur within a context that overwhelmingly encourages spiritual discipline, the modern worldview is a context that overwhelmingly discourages it. I refer here to the second stage of modernity, which is atheistic and materialistic. The primal realities of the Augustinian vision—God, the soul, and spiritual values—are all said to be unreal. Only matter in motion is really real. Our spiritual (in the broad sense) drive therefore leads us to develop a materialistic spirituality, that is, an antispiritual spirituality. The virtues of this spirituality are those, such as competitiveness and greed, that help us to possess and control as much matter as possible. Spiritual discipline, through which one would cultivate attachment to nonmaterial values and disinterested love of others, is therefore not only unimportant but positively harmful. Because modern materialism is deterministic, it declares spiritual discipline also to be impossible. Matter in motion is said to interact deterministically, and the denial of a nonmaterial mind or soul implies that our convictions and values are wholly a product of deterministic interactions of the molecules of our bodies (now, in particular, our DNA molecules). There is no partially autonomous "self" to exercise self-discipline.

The first stage of the modern worldview had supported spiritual discipline, but only ambivalently and unstably. This first stage, which was articulated most influentially by Galileo, Descartes, Newton, Locke, and Reid, was supernaturalistic, dualistic, and sensationistic. The dualism portrayed nature and the human soul as equally real but absolutely different. The soul was a spiritual (nonmaterial) substance with the capacity to determine itself in accord with freely chosen values. It was thereby free, at least in the cosmological sense, and some early moderns gave it axiological and a few even theological freedom. The material world, by contrast, was fully material and mechanistic. It contained no sentience or freedom, and it possessed only the "primary qualities," which were really quantitative features, such as size, shape, and mass, which could be thought to exist in insentient matter. All qualities that are obviously mind-dependent, such as color and feeling, were called *secondary* or *tertiary* and said to exist only in the human mind.

This dualistic ontology was combined with a sensationistic epistemology, according to which influence (impressions, ideas, information) can enter into our spiritual soul only through our physical senses. This doctrine had obvious antispiritual implications, in that it said that the soul could have no direct commerce with nonmaterial beings, such as God and spiritual values. The concern for spirituality was protected, however, at least in intention, insofar as God, defined supernaturalistically, could communicate spiritual values to the soul in other ways. In particular, God could implant a "moral sense" in people at their birth (Francis Hutcheson), or could reveal spiritual truths and values through a supernatural revelation in people and documents, which could be known through the physical senses (John Locke).

The supernaturalism of this worldview was also essential to it in other ways. Because the mechanistic doctrine of matter meant that it was devoid of the power of self-motion, an appeal to God was necessary to explain why matter is in motion. Also, because the soul and the matter comprising the human body were said to be wholly unlike, as sentient and insentient, it seemed impossible that they could interact naturally; appeal was therefore necessary to God's supernatural power to explain their at least apparent interaction. Finally, the sensationist doctrine of perception depended upon an appeal to God to provide confidence that some correspondence exists between our ideas of the outer world and this world itself. The mechanistic view of nature, and hence the dualistic ontology, therefore depended upon belief in God. Belief in God was, accordingly, far from unimportant in the first formulation of the modern worldview. This belief in God, along with belief in the mind or soul, supported spiritual discipline as both possible and important.

This support, however, was both ambivalent and unstable. Whereas the dualistic view in principle declared soul (or mind) and matter to be equally real, various factors soon led matter to be regarded as more real. The doctrine that the qualities of matter were "primary" gave it a certain primacy. The doctrine that we can perceive reality only through our physical senses supported a tendency to regard only the objects of sensory perception as real. The dualistic view that made the human soul the great exception in an otherwise purely material, insentient, mechanistic nature (rather than, as in medieval views, a part of the great hierarchical chain of being) soon led to doubt about its reality. This movement toward materialism was fostered by a growing distaste toward the appeal to supernatural causation to explain the apparently natural relation of mind and body. The tendency of dualism to dissolve into an antispiritual materialism was perceived at the time by Bishop Berkeley, who sought to convince people that the instability of dualism pointed to the truth of personal idealism, in which only God and the human soul were fully real. But few were convinced. Modernity moved toward atheistic materialism.

A half-way house to full atheism was provided by deism, according to which God created the world, imposed motion and laws of motion upon it, but did not intervene subsequently. A spiritual life of a sort could still be supported by this vision. As mentioned above, an innate "moral sense" could be thought to have been implanted in the human soul by God at the creation (this was, of course, in preevolutionary times). This doctrine, developed most effectively by Francis Hutcheson, was crucial for such thinkers as Adam Smith and Thomas Jefferson. But this deistic view, as significant as it was in comparison with the full-fledged atheism that was to follow, did decrease the centrality of spiritual discipline. The human soul was no longer understood to have daily intercourse with God or transcendent moral values, and the Bible was no longer seen as a story of God's involvement in our history. Even before the collapse of the first stage of the modern worldview into the second, therefore, a considerable loss of support for habits of spiritual discipline had occurred, at least among modernity's cultural leaders.

Even though the support of early modernity for a spiritual life had been unstable and ambivalent, the emergence of the fully materialistic, atheistic form of modernity involved a spiritual sea-change. In this new world, there is no longer a spiritual divinity, meaning one who supports spiritual values. (Insofar as something is still taken in effect to be holy or divine, it is matter, or power, or perhaps sexual vitality.) No objective spiritual values exist in the universe, and we would have no way to know about them if they did. A soul, in the sense of a partially self-determining self which is not fully enmeshed in the deterministic process of nature, does not exist. And of course there is no immortality, except for what temporary fame one might achieve. For those living within such a context, the idea of spiritual discipline cannot arise, much less be taken seriously.

III. WHITEHEADIAN POSTMODERN SPIRITUALITY

Spiritual discipline will again become a pervasive feature of life, not just the practice of a minority dissenting from the prevailing culture, only if the antispiritual worldview of modernity is replaced by another dominant outlook. A new worldview does seem to be emerging in our time. This worldview can be called *postmodern*, in that it preserves many modern beliefs, values, and practices but places them in a larger framework, in which many premodern truths and values can be recovered. Closely connected with this emergence is the rise of a renewed interest in spiritual discipline. While this movement is very diverse, I believe that the best framework for articulating the new worldview and supporting the related postmodern spirituality is that of Alfred North Whitehead, although this position needs supplementation and modification from other sources.

In the remainder of this essay, I discuss this worldview in terms of its theological support for spiritual discipline, with particular attention to the issues central to the earlier discussion of Augustinian theology. Because the other essays in this volume have sufficiently contrasted this postmodern theology with the modern worldview, these two outlooks are compared here only in passing.

Whitehead agrees with Augustine in several ways. First, just as Augustine defended cosmological freedom against the Manicheans, Whitehead defends it against modern thought. Augustine's concern, we saw, was to portray the human soul not as an impotent, passive thing, hedged in by and on the defensive against the material world, but as a reality with power to shape itself and its environment. Whitehead rejects the claim of the modern worldview according to which only the most elementary physical entities or forces, such as electrons and atoms, have causal influence. He portrays instead a hierarchy of creative cosmological powers, with living cells above molecules, and psyches above cells. There is now increasing evidence for this view. The facts of psychosomatic studies and psychical research can be added to our own common experience to support the notion that the human soul, far from being an impotent spectator, is the most powerful of the earthly actors in the cosmic drama.

Whitehead provides a new basis for Augustine's concerns in a second way. Against the Pelagians, who affirmed God's grace only in the establishment of the basic conditions of human life, Augustine insisted that divine grace was present and effective in every moment. Modern thought, insofar as it has retained a transcendent deity at all, has been deistic, affirming divine influence with the Pelagians only "once upon a time." Whiteheadian postmodern theology affirms God's gracious influence in every moment of the world process, therefore in every moment of human experience. This theology can with Augustine summarize the position of Christian faith with the cry "Emmanuel!"—God is with us! When we come to the question of the *relation* between this divine activity and our own freedom, however, Whitehead parts company with Augustine, and precisely at the point at which Augustine's view of divine grace undermined the concern for spiritual discipline. Whitehead denies that our relation to God is unilaterally determined by God. A positive relation is instead due to our cooperating, our working together.[8]

While the idea of "cooperation" or "synergism" has always been anathema to Augustinians because of their denial of theological freedom, many other Christian thinkers have also been uncomfortable with it. The problem seems to arise from the fact that most theologies have portrayed divine and human power as competitive. On this model, the more efficacy God exerts in our lives, the less freedom we have; the more freedom we affirm for ourselves, the less we are influenced by God. Augustinian theology, fearing that the affirmation of genuine human freedom in relation to God would demean the sovereignty of God, denies theological freedom. In reaction, atheists usually assume that the affirmation of genuine human freedom requires the denial of divine efficacy in our lives. Doctrines called *synergistic* have usually been compromise positions within the competitive model. They limit the divine influence to make room for some human freedom. The reluctance to speak of divine-human cooperation in Western (as opposed to Eastern) Christianity, manifest even in Christian thinkers who affirm theological freedom, is due, I suspect, not only to Augustinian prohibitions but also to the belief that cooperation implies a diminution of divine efficacy.

But should the intuition of the radical otherness of God not lead us to consider a noncompetitive relation between God and the creatures, in which the *greater* efficacy of God in our lives might mean *more* rather than less freedom? This was surely Augustine's own deepest intuition: True freedom, he said, comes only through bondage to God; divine determinism does not conflict with human freedom. And yet his way of formulating this intuition did deny our freedom.

Some modern theologies have tried to overcome the competition between God and the creatures. Paul Tillich says that we must transcend the theistic God to the "God beyond God," which is Being Itself, if the affirmation of God is not to conflict with belief in human freedom. In Tillich's theology, however, this transcendence of the competitive model is achieved at the cost of denying individuality, hence personhood, hence causal influence, hence prevenient grace, to the divine reality. God is equated with what has been called in Aristotelian language the "material cause" of all things—the basic stuff (the "being itself") which all beings embody. Theologians have usually recognized that this idea of the holy reality is profoundly alien to the biblical vision.

Whiteheadian theology provides a noncompetitive understanding of the divine-human relation that does not deny personhood and hence causal influence to the divine reality. Prevenient grace consists in the provision of possibilities that free us from being simply determined by the past. Accordingly, it is precisely God's causal influence that provides us with both cosmological freedom and the possibility of axiological freedom. And yet this divine causal influence works in such a way that we also have theological freedom—freedom in relation to God.

I will try to explain this difficult idea briefly. According to Whitehead, our soul is not an enduring substance that is what it is, and has the powers it has, prior to its relations with other things. That notion of the soul as an independent substance is what leads to the competitive model: we must become less of ourselves if God is to become more in us. Whitehead has suggested that we think of our soul instead as a *series of momentary experiences.* Each experience is a synthesis of its relations to other things; each experience includes, in some sense, those other things into itself, making itself out of them. Given this understanding, I am not in competition with my environment; I need not shield it out to be authentically myself. Rather, the more of my environment I can take into myself, making it my own, the richer my experience is.

If our environment, however, were limited to everything we normally call our "environment"—our bodies, the things we experience through our physical senses, the ideas given to us thereby through books and other people—we would not be free, no matter how rich our experience might be. We would be condemned simply to take into ourselves the data that came our way according to the strength with which they forced themselves upon us. We would have no cosmological freedom. This would be the situation if our environment were limited to *actualities.*

But our environment includes something else: we find that *possibilities* as well as actualities are given. The given actualities can always be synthesized in various possible ways; possibilities must therefore also be given. This synthesis can thereby be a *creative* synthesis, rather than one that was determined by forces external to it. And we sometimes experience as given rather *novel* possibilities that allow us to transcend the actual past quite dramatically.

But how are possibilities given? As mere possibilities, they can hardly take the initiative to give themselves. Whiteheadian theology reformulates the medieval view that they are given by God. Our freedom is due to the fact that our environment includes God and thereby includes possibilities. God constantly calls us with these possibilities, calling us not simply to accept actuality but to respond creatively to it. God especially calls us to respond to our actual environment in terms of those possibilities through which truth, beauty, goodness, adventure, and peace will be embodied and promoted.

This divine lure to embody spiritual values is prevenient grace. It is always there, prior to every move on our part. But this grace is not wholly irresistible. We resist it to some degree in most moments of experience. Whiteheadian theology, while not being Pelagian, does agree with the protest of the Pelagians—and of countless persons through the ages—against the view that divine grace is incompatible with theological freedom. We are partly free, not only in relation to the stars above and the molecules below, but also in relation to the ubiquitous divine reality around us.

From the point of view of postmodern theology, therefore, St. Paul's paradox—we are to work out our own salvation, for it is God who works in us—does not involve a contradiction. God *is* working in us every moment, but this does not mean that *we* need not work. Although it is God who offers us freedom, we decide how and to what degree to respond to this offer. And how we respond to God's grace in one moment determines the nature of the gracious invitation that can be extended to us in the next moment. To the degree that we develop a habit of responding positively to the divine initiatives, higher divine possibilities can be presented in the future. Spiritual growth is possible.

Postmodern theology, in agreeing with Augustine against Pelagius that God is directly present to us, thereby transcends modern theology insofar as the latter has been deistic. Much modern theology, for example, in speaking of how we "encounter" God, has said that we do so only indirectly, through the neighbor. This approach, which is geared to foster an ethical as opposed to mystical form of faith, is ultimately self-defeating. If I never encounter God directly, the same must be true of my neighbor. But if my neighbor does not encounter God directly, then how do I encounter God through him or her? Presumably because he or she encountered God through someone else, but this answer leads to an infinite regress. Without a direct experience of God, which is at the heart of mysticism, the roots of the ethical side of spirituality will shrivel up. Postmodern theology provides a new basis for the Augustinian vision of a direct relation between the soul and God, but without the denial of theological freedom against which the Pelagians, and modern deists, protested.

I turn now from the issue between Augustine and the Pelagians to that between him and the Donatists. While the Pelagian controversy involved the issue of God's *direct* influence on us, the Donatist controversy involved God's *indirect* influence. From the postmodern viewpoint, the denial that God is only present to us indirectly does not mean that the indirect presence of God is unimportant.

Just as the indirect presence of God presupposes God's direct presence to us, so does the direct presence of the divine depend upon its indirect presence. God, in this postmodern vision, directly presents to us the best possibilities, including the highest spiritual values, that we are capable of incorporating. What is genuinely possible for us at any moment depends upon the kind of person we have become prior to that moment. And this depends, to a great extent, upon the nature of the traditions and institutions into which we are born and spend our formative years. What beliefs and values are incarnate in those traditions and institutions, and therefore in the people in which they are embodied, such as our parents, peer group, teachers, and cultural heroes? In theological terms: To what degree do these traditions, institutions, and people embody the divine spirit, and to what degree an antispiritual spirit? The kind of persons we become is determined to a great extent by these given realities which, to the degree that they are positive, can be regarded as indirectly mediating divine grace to us.

Not everything, however, is settled by these large-scale, long-term processes over which most of us have little control. Although the culture generally determines the average kind of persons it will produce, it does not determine the heights or the depths to which any particular individual may rise or fall. And we are shaped in our formative years not only by the general features of the culture, which are widely embodied, but also by the particularities of the crucial people in our lives. A parent, a friend, a teacher, a pastor, a priest, or a rabbi may exert a decisive influence, opening up possibilities that would have otherwise remained closed. In other words, the possibilities toward which we are *directly* called by the divine reality may be decisively influenced by an *indirect* encounter with divine grace through a fellow human being, due to some unique feature of that person which reflected his or her own spiritual development.

The theological point that distinguishes the Whiteheadian from the Augustinian position on this Donatist issue is finally the same as that distinguishing the two theologies on the Pelagian issue: (divine) grace does not destroy (human) nature. In the Pelagian issue, the point was that divine power does not override our power of self-determination. In this Donatist issue, the point is that divine power does not cancel the power of others to influence us, for good or ill. Augustinian supernaturalism held that the divine power to bring about effects in us could not be limited by the decisions of other persons. Whiteheadian naturalistic theism, while holding that the divine reality is distinct from the world and can present novel possibilities which transcend the options provided to us by the world, also holds that these novel possibilities through which God calls us beyond the past must be closely related to the possibilities that have already been achieved in that past. Einstein could not have been produced in the thirteenth century, Jesus in India, nor Gautama in Israel. What the divine grace can accomplish in the present moment is largely determined by the ways in which divine grace has been effective in the events prior to that moment. To personalize this issue: The kind of person you are, as a minister (whether professional or not) of God's grace to others, does make a difference to their relation to God. The Donatists were right insofar as they were making this point. The way God's grace can affect your neighbor is not independent of your relation to God. In fact, evidence from psychical research suggests that your soul affects others for good or ill not only through what you say and do bodily, but also directly, one soul to another. If this is true, it undermines the modern notion that our inner state is unimportant as long as our outer actions are proper. What we are will come through, in spite of our best efforts at hypocrisy. In any case, through the way we in our small way either raise or lower the general level of the culture, and through the dramatic effects we can have, for good or ill, on the lives of other individuals, our present responses to divine grace partly determine what divine grace will be able to achieve in the future.

8

IMPERIALISM, NUCLEARISM, AND POSTMODERN THEISM

The twofold task of the theologian is to speak the truth, and to speak the truth so as to set at liberty.[1] The departmentalization of Christian theology in modern times led to a division of labor: systematic and philosophical theologians were to deal with the truth of Christian faith, while theological and social ethicists were to apply this truth in a liberating way to practical matters. This division had unfortunate results. On the one hand, at best, the truths of the theologians were abstract and apparently irrelevant to most concrete evils; at worst, they provided implicit justifications of the *status quo*. On the other hand, the principles and strategies of the ethicists were sometimes disconnected from any theological vision, and even when the theological grounding was clear it often seemed outdated or otherwise inadequate to the theologians.

Liberation and political theologians have led the way in liberating Christian theologians from this disastrous dichotomy. It is increasingly recognized that an adequate theology requires both dimensions: the affirmation of truths intended to have universal validity, and a liberating engagement with concrete forms of evil.

127

Much of my theological study and reflection in recent years has been focused on the attempt to liberate the planet from nuclear weapons. This focus has seemed appropriate, in fact mandatory, for four reasons: (1) a nuclear holocaust would destroy all the values at the heart of the other liberation movements; (2) my own country has been the leader in developing, using and justifying nuclear weapons; (3) it seems likely that traditional Christian doctrines have had a causal role in leading to the current nuclear crisis; and (4) only a few theological ethicists and even fewer systematic theologians in the United States have been devoting major attention to this question.[2]

As I began this study, I assumed that the nuclear crisis was relatively distinct from other major problems, including that of social and economic justice for people in Third World countries. I assumed, therefore, the appropriateness of a division of labor on these concrete issues. And the fact that many more theologians (including theological ethicists) in the United States were working for socioeconomic liberation of oppressed peoples than for nuclear liberation seemed to provide an added reason for some of us to concentrate on this latter issue.

As my understanding of the actual role played by nuclear weapons in U. S. foreign policy increased, however, I learned that the nuclear issue and the concern by many peoples for liberation from the political and economic hegemony of the United States are closely interconnected. And I have come to see that both the global nuclear and social-justice crises, insofar as they are due to the imperialistic practices of primarily Christian countries—especially the United States in the present century—have causal roots in the supernaturalistic, extremely voluntaristic idea of God which has been particularly dominant in the United States.

At the same time, I have become more aware of the way in which the atheistic-materialistic worldview, which has become the dominant worldview of late modernity, has provided a framework at least equally conducive to imperialism, nuclearism, and economic exploitation. Indeed, the extreme supernaturalism with which the modern age began, and which still thrives in nonacademic circles (especially in the United States), and the atheistic materialism of late modernity, which replaced supernaturalism in academic circles, cooperate uncannily in these areas (however much their proponents may differ on other public policy issues, such as abortion, school prayer, and the teaching of evolution). This uncanny cooperation points to some basic assumptions on which they concur, in particular the type of power exercised by the supreme power of the universe.

In this essay, I focus on the way in which a postmodern theology, which transcends both the supernaturalism of the medieval and early modern worldviews and the atheism of the late modern worldview, provides the basis for a new attitude. Whereas premodern and early modern Western thought assumed that theism had to be supernaturalistic, late modern thought has assumed that naturalism must be atheistic. Postmodern theology, especially as inspired by the ideas of Alfred North Whitehead and Charles Hartshorne, presents a third option, naturalistic theism, which challenges the common premise of the previous views—that the supreme power of the universe, be it conceived as Omnipotent Lord or Omnipotent Matter, works coercively. Most of the essays in this book have focused primarily on the contrast of the postmodern worldview with the late modern worldview of materialistic atheism. The present essay, like the previous one, focuses primarily on the contrast with the supernaturalistic theism of medievalism, which early modernity intensified.

In the first two sections, I discuss this idea of God and its contribution to U. S. imperialism. In the third section, I describe postmodern theology's theism (or panentheism), which, with its understanding of God's power and love, overcomes the problematic features of supernaturalistic theism and which, if widely accepted, would contribute to different ways of being and relating.

I. THE SUPERNATURALISTIC IDEA OF GOD

By *supernaturalistic theism* I mean the idea that God essentially exists independently of this and any world, and that a realm of finite beings exists only through a decision of the divine will. Supernaturalism is hence *extreme voluntarism*, the view that the nature of God's relation to the world, including the fact that there is any relation at all, is entirely voluntary.[3]

This voluntaristic supernaturalism has to some extent characterized Christian theology from the beginning, but it has been more dominant in the modern world, especially in Calvinistic countries, such as the United States.

Western Christian thought and imagery have been heavily voluntaristic to a large extent because of the influence of Augustine, who insisted that God, having created the world *ex nihilo*, was absolutely free in relation to it. The distinctively modern version of supernaturalism arose largely out of the nominalistic-voluntaristic tradition, which developed in the fourteenth and fifteenth centuries and heavily influenced the Protestant Reformation. Because it also thereby influenced the movement that is usually called the "rise of modern science," especially as it occurred in primarily Protestant countries, the thought of Isaac Newton and other paradigmatic scientists helped spread this idea of God.[4] This voluntaristic tradition, which involved a revival of Augustinianism, also had its influence on the new science in Roman Catholic circles through, for example, Descartes and Pascal.

This voluntarism was concerned to protect and magnify the divine freedom. Thomas Aquinas had appeared to constrict the divine will by making it follow upon that which the divine reason had seen to be good and right. The voluntarists declared the divine will to be more fundamental.

Technically, this dispute was purely verbal, insofar as the doctrine of divine simplicity implied that the divine will and reason, like all the divine attributes, were strictly identical.[5] Rhetorically and imaginatively, however, the difference between voluntarism and intellectualism was tremendous. The voluntarists portrayed God as absolutely free to do as He pleased. (The male pronoun for deity is wholly appropriate for this tradition.)

This shift involved more than simply declaring the divine will more basic than the divine intellect. The doctrine of creation *ex nihilo* was made more central. In the Neoplatonic theologies, including even St. Thomas's more Aristotelian version, God had been described as being itself, and the creator-creature relation was described in terms of emanation and participation. This framework made the idea of creation out of absolute nothingness, in the sense that prior to this creative act there had been no realm of finitude at all, an unnatural idea. St. Thomas affirmed a beginning of the created world only because this doctrine seemed to be a revealed truth—reason alone would suggest an eternal creation, which could easily lead to the necessity of the created realm. The voluntarists, by contrast, portrayed God not as being itself, which was immanent throughout creation, but as *a* being, an individual, who existed outside the world. The world existed not through participation but through an external act of creation, which was entirely voluntary. The nature of the world's relation to God, and even the fact a world exists at all, were in no way natural or "given" features of reality.

Those standing in this tradition stressed, furthermore, that the world had no power of its own. All power belonged to God alone. Again, this emphasis involved no *conceptual* difference from Thomism. In spite of all that Thomas says about contingency, secondary causes, and freedom, a careful reading shows that everything happens just as it does because of God's primary causation. Rhetorically and imaginatively, however, the difference between Thomas, on the one hand, and Occam, Luther, Calvin, Boyle, Newton, and Descartes, on the other, is enormous. Their rhetoric about the freedom and omnipotence of God has meant that the image of God fermenting in the conscious and unconscious experience of modern men and women has been distinctive. This view has portrayed God as having a monopoly on power. (Luther spoke of the "sole efficacy of the divine will.")[6] Any power possessed, or seemingly possessed, by the creatures is at worst an illusion, at most a wholly gratuitous gift which could be withdrawn at any time. Nothing can happen except what God wills, or at least permits. According to this view, the world is essentially a *unilateral* world: it is possible and appropriate for it to be ruled from a single center of power.

At the same time, this doctrine of God's monopolistic omnipotence paradoxically increased the role of Satan, as God's mortal enemy, in the scheme of things. Reason's criterion of self-consistency by itself would have dictated the elimination of the notion of a demonic cosmic power working in opposition to the divine power, now that God was so emphatically said to have a monopoly on power. But reason's other criterion, adequacy to the facts of experience, made the doctrine of a Satanic power all the more necessary: If God is all-powerful, so that the creatures have no inherent power to resist the divine will, an outside explanation is needed for the world's evils, if the notion of God's goodness is to be preserved. Although the world is ultimately monopolar, it is *provisionally bipolar;*[7] its essentially monopolar nature will become evident only when Satan is defeated. This provisionally bipolar view of the world implies that world history is essentially a battle between good and evil.

This view raises the question of the method of battle. In particular, does God use the method of persuasion, through the attractiveness of love? Christians have never doubted this. But is this God's only method, or does God also use coercive, even violent and destructive, methods? On this question, Christians have differed. The biblical witness can be employed on either side. The image of God's incarnation in a man who rejected violent methods of overcoming foreign occupation, who preached love of enemies instead, and who brought salvation through self-sacrificial suffering, suggests that God uses the method of persuasive, suffering love to overcome evil.

Much of the biblical imagery, however, especially in the final book of the New Testament, suggests that the method of persuasive love is merely a temporary strategy, and that, when God becomes really serious about overcoming evil, unparalleled destructive power will be used. The voluntaristic idea of God has undergirded this second view. By stressing God's absolute freedom over the world, and the world's totally derivative status, it has said that the way God acts in the world is purely a matter of divine choice. The fact that God normally allows the world processes to go their own way without intervening does not mean that God's will is in any way limited by these worldly processes. God could, at will, unilaterally bring about the destruction of evil.

A second question is raised by this picture of the world as a battlefield: What is God's attitude toward those who are in the Enemy's camp? Does God love all people, as some of the Bible suggests? Or does God love only the good people while hating the evil, as other portions suggest? One theological view, based on the New Testament doctrine that God *is* love—that the word *love* is the best term we have to describe the divine essence—has said that God loves all creatures by nature, or naturally, therefore necessarily. God could no more not love than not exist.

The voluntaristic doctrine, however, has said that God's relation to the world is voluntary in all respects. Just as the way God exercises power on the world is not natural, or given in the nature of things, the way the world is regarded by God is in no way a natural or given feature of reality. God is free to hate, love, or be indifferent to the creatures. This doctrine provides a necessary support for the ethnocentric view that God, like humans, loves some beings (us), is indifferent to some others (those we exploit), and hates still others (our enemies).

Combined with the voluntaristic view of divine power, this voluntarism of the divine attitude has provided theological support for the bipolar view of the world as a battleground between the forces of good and the forces of evil. God hates those who have aligned themselves with evil and is ready to overcome the evil in them by destroying them in a cataclysmic act of violence. The fact that evildoers finally must be destroyed to destroy evil itself implies that divine love, with its lure to the vision of the good, is not sufficiently powerful to convert those who have been seduced by the Evil One. Evil can to some extent be deterred and contained by threats, but finally the incarnations of evil must themselves be destroyed if good is to reign supreme.

In summary, the supernaturalistic view of God often has the following characteristics (the first four are essential, the latter two are optional but prevalent):

1. The fact that the world exists, and the nature of the relations between it and God, are solely due to the omnipotent will of God.
2. God essentially has all the power; no power is inherent in the world and its members.
3. God can therefore exert unilateral, controlling power over the creatures.
4. If and when God loves the creatures, this is a free act; nothing prevents God's hating or being indifferent to the creatures.
5. God provisionally allows a cosmic power of evil to infect the world. We do not know why, but we know that God hates this Satanic power and those who are infected by it.
6. Although God has thus far primarily used persuasion in this cosmic battle, in the end God will unleash the full destructive capacity of the divine omnipotence to rid the world of evil.

II. SUPERNATURALISTIC THEISM AND MODERN IMPERIALISM

My historical thesis is that this supernaturalistic idea of God has contributed to modern imperialism in general and to nuclearism in particular. Given the complexity of human motivation, including its unconscious dimensions and the indefinitely complex ways in which causal factors are interwoven in the historical process, causal connections of this scope cannot be proven. Any effort to overcome the perpetuation of an evil nevertheless requires an analysis, however amateurish, of the causal sources of that evil. Without any attempt to offer convincing evidence, I simply state my conviction that the concept or image of God that has been dominant in modern times has contributed significantly to modern imperialism and nuclearism. (This historical thesis implies the formal thesis that ideas and images are not merely epiphenomenal by-products of the material conditions of historical existence in a particular era. I hold instead that ideal and material factors operate dialectically and conjointly.)

I maintain that the supernaturalistic idea of God has contibuted to these problems both directly and indirectly. I discuss first the direct connection.

The doctrine of divine omnipotence helps rationalize the acceptance of nuclear arsenals, in spite of their potential to destroy everything they are supposed to protect and much more besides, by contributing to complacency. Many theists simply believe it impossible that God would allow all human life to be destroyed. Their belief presupposes that God has the power unilaterally to prevent it. When confronted by the fact that God did not prevent previous unspeakable evils, such as the Jewish holocaust, they may admit the difficulty yet feel that the destruction of all life would be qualitatively different. Or, the real difference may be that this time God's *really* chosen people would be involved—Christians, especially American Christians. In any case, this complacent supernaturalism is a real problem in getting the Christian masses in America mobilized against nuclear weapons. This is simply the latest version of a complacency in the face of evil to which the supernaturalist doctrine of divine omnipotence has often contributed. The evil must not be intolerable, many theists have reasoned, otherwise God would (unilaterally) eliminate it.

An even worse type of complacency exists: the dual complacency of the Armageddon theologians, who hold not only that God's saints will be miraculously rescued before the destruction of the world, which will be initiated by a nuclear war, but also that God will simply re-create the world afterwards. As Hal Lindsey puts it in a discussion of II Peter 3:10-13 and Revelation 2:11 in *The Late Great Planet Earth*: "Christ is going 'to loose' the atoms of the galaxy in which we live. No wonder there will be a great roar and intense heat and fire. Then Christ will put the atoms back together to form a new heaven and earth. . . . ''[8] If a world can be created so easily, one wonders why God took some fifteen to twenty billion years to create this one. In any case, if God has that kind of power, then no reason exists to work to prevent a nuclear destruction of the planet. To the contrary, the sooner this world is destroyed, the sooner we can enjoy the next one. As Lindsey concludes: "That's where we want to be!"[9]

But, aside from those fundamentalists who look forward to Armageddon with anticipation and see nuclear weapons as the means to hasten its coming, how do we account for the behavior of Americans? The complacent conviction that God will not allow nuclear weapons to destroy civilization does not help explain why they were invented in the first place, and why they have been developed and expanded with such enthusiasm after their almost infinite destructive capacity has been understood.

I suggest that a significant portion of the answer lies in the nature of religion, combined with the supernaturalistic idea of God. At the root of the religious motivation of human beings is the desire to be in harmony with the divine power, as they understand it most deeply. The divine power is invariably identified with the ultimate, most effective power of the universe. Being in harmony with this power means, insofar as possible, imitating it. The basic religious motive, in other words, is the *imitatio dei*. Jesus' statement, "You shall be perfect [or merciful], as your heavenly father is perfect [or merciful]," is only a particular expression of this universal conviction, that we are to imitate the divine reality. The Taoist seeks to imitate the Tao, the "scientific" Marxist seeks alignment with the dialectical process of history, the Social Darwinist seeks to live in harmony with the law of the survival of the fittest, the Inca sun-worshipper seeks to exemplify the impartial generosity of the sun.

If this is the basic religious motivation, then the supernaturalistic idea of God is an extremely dangerous idea, for at least five reasons. First, true believers in this God would most likely feel that controlling the behavior of others through threats, and by the actual use of coercive power when the threats failed, was the divine way of doing things. The *imitatio dei* requires an omnipotent arsenal.

These true believers would, second, tend to believe that it is possible and appropriate for the world to be ruled from one center of power. And a particular people could see themselves as especially chosen by God to exercise this role. In imitating the divine power and freedom, they would not be greatly disturbed by the fact that their rule infringed upon the exercise of freedom by other peoples, because the freedom of self-determination is not inherent in the status of being a creature, and its exercise is not necessary for God's will to be done.

Third, anyone who stood in the way of the freedom of this chosen people to do as it wills would be understood as inherently evil, or as agents of the inherently evil empire. They would not, in other words, be understood as equal creatures with equal interests and equal rights to exercise their own freedom. That would be to understand the world as essentially pluralistic and multilateral. The provisionally bipolar view requires that their behavior be understood solely in terms of the evil desire of thwarting the freedom and righteous mission of the saints to save the world by dominating it.

Fourth, the use of coercive, destructive power, or at least its threat, would tend to be seen as the only way to do battle with this evil. That which is inherently evil cannot be converted; and to negotiate and compromise with evil would be betrayal. Also it does not work: any attempt at appeasement simply encourages evil to expand. Power is the only thing evil understands. It must be checked militarily at every place in order to be contained.

Fifth, however, the policy of containment cannot be ultimately satisfactory. Eventually a showdown must occur between the forces of good and those of evil. The world will be cleansed and redeemed by an unprecedented display of violence: a war to end all wars and to usher in a permanent era of peace.[10]

To hold that this mythic structure of belief has been influential upon American policy does not entail that those people whose views are reflected in the National Security Council completely accept this way of seeing the world. As far as I can tell, there seems to be in these elite circles a mixture, with varying proportions, of acceptance of this mythic worldview and cynical cultivation and exploitation of it in the masses. Richard Barnet in *The Roots of War* and *The Alliance*, Alan Wolfe in *The Rise and Fall of the Soviet Threat*, and Jerry Sanders in *Peddlers of Crisis* have shown how the "soviet threat" has been maintained since World War II and has been manipulatively increased from time to time to elicit approval for policies favored by an elite group.[11]

The fact that this manipulation of American opinion can be so effective is due in large part, I suggest, to the wide acceptance of the worldview based on the supernaturalistic idea of God.

One area in which a great discrepancy has obtained between the actual policy of the National Security Council and the declaratory policy designed to shape public opinion is the purpose of our nuclear arsenals. The declaratory policy has spoken of "deterrence," and by that has meant primarily deterring a Soviet first strike against America. A secondary meaning has referred to deterring a Soviet invasion of Western Europe by holding open the possibility of a first use of nuclear weapons by NATO in the event of such an invasion. Records show, however, that those who argued for the first-use option in Europe did not really believe a Soviet invasion to be a real probability. Ample evidence also exists that our government has never considered a Soviet attack on the United States a serious threat. Certainly the purpose of the Strategic Air Command from 1946 to 1949 (which was prior to the Soviet Union's development of an atomic bomb) was not for the purpose of deterring a Soviet atomic attack!

In the actual policy of the United States, nuclear weapons have been used to deter the Soviet Union and several Third World countries from doing things in various parts of the world that would run counter to American interests, primarily economic interests. Starting in 1946, just six months after the atomic bombing of Hiroshima and Nagasaki (at which time we gave the Soviets 48 hours to get out of Iran or else), the United States has threatened more or less directly to use nuclear weapons many times.[12]

Since 1962, when the Soviet Union was humiliated in Cuba, it has built up its nuclear arsenal to rough parity with that of the United States. (The U. S. government is therefore correct to speak of an unprecedented build-up of the Soviet military; but it is being less than truthful when it implies that our own build-up was not also unprecedented and speaks of our being "behind" and needing to catch up. The United States has consistently led in every category of the arms race, except for the meaningless one of "throw weight.")[13] This achievement of parity has evidently worked; the United States has been less inclined to threaten the Soviet Union recently. This inability to do so with impunity has apparently been a source of great frustration. The aim of recent administrations to achieve "escalation dominance" at every level seems to have been based on nostalgia for the days when our nuclear superiority could be converted into concrete political gains. The SDI ("Star Wars") program is fully consistent with this interpretation. (It could not be effective against a massive first strike, virtually everyone agrees; but it could be considered sufficiently effective against a small retaliatory strike to contribute to an effective bluff.)[14]

The voluntaristic idea of God, I suggest, has contributed directly to the fact of American imperialism. Although there is no absolute distinction to be drawn between the general public and the foreign policy elite, I suggest that the primary effect of the inherited idea of deity upon the general public has been in creating its readiness to accept both the bipolar worldview and the necessity of using overwhelming violence to contain and eventually destroy evil. The primary effect of this idea of deity on members of the foreign policy elite, I suggest, is the conviction that it is both possible and desirable for the world to be controlled from a single source of power. Given this conviction, they can use the worldview accepted by the masses to gain acceptance of policies designed to maintain or increase U. S. hegemony.

At the same time, the members of this elite are themselves not totally unaffected by the bipolar view of the world with its myth of America's selfless goodness and the enemy's essential wickedness. That is, they do not simply employ this myth cynically to manipulate public opinion for their own purposes. They do this to some extent. But the immanence of the Holy Spirit in people prevents them from working for goals that they regard as essentially evil. They must believe that, however cynical this or that tactic is, their overall strategy is morally justifiable. This is the chief function of ideology. Even the members of the foreign policy elite, who know better than most of us the actual policies of the U. S. government and the real motives behind them, accept the bipolar view of the world to some extent.

Likewise, although the U. S. public would not support many of the actual policies of its government if it fully understood them (at least the governmental leaders must not think so, or why do they lie to us?), the people of the United States in general are not completely innocent of the idea that it is both possible and appropriate for the world to be controlled by American power.

When the meaning of *deterrence* is understood in the actual nuclear policy of the United States, the close connection between the nuclear crisis and the problem of global economic injustice is evident. The failure of most Americans to understand this connection is due to the success of the U. S. government in disguising its actual offensive policy behind the rhetoric of a policy of defensive deterrence. This distortion of the truth could be so successful because of the extent to which the American people have accepted the bipolar view of the world. Those who attempt to reveal the truth, thereby challenging the basic tenet of the American state religion, as Noam Chomsky calls it, that America only does good, can be easily dismissed as agents, witting or unwitting, of the Satanic empire.

Likewise, because the American mind accepts the notion that evil can only be overcome if the good have more destructive power at their disposal than do the evil, the public and the U. S. Congress regularly consent to increases and "improvements" in the nuclear arsenal that clearly have no justification from a standpoint of defensive deterrence. Because of the twofold commitment of Americans to nuclearism and the bipolar worldview, the administration can sell as defensive necessities weapons systems whose only conceivable use is offensive.

Besides affecting the American psyche directly, the supernaturalistic idea of God has also had an indirect effect upon American imperialism. It has achieved this indirect effect by being offensive and incredible to modern thinkers, with the result that the theistic worldview was replaced by an atheistic one interpreted in Darwinian and Social Darwinian categories.

The supernaturalistic idea of God was offensive primarily because of the social implications of its view of divine power. The idea that God can unilaterally control human affairs was used to support the *status quo*. For example, the divine right of kings was supported by appealing to this idea of God in conjunction with Romans 13. The modern urge for free inquiry was curtailed on the basis of an authoritarian approach that presupposed God's infallible inspiration of the Church and/or the Bible. Many of the philosophical arguments against the existence of God were formulated by reformers who sought to undermine the authority of those who were using appeals to God—appeals that presupposed the notion of divine omnipotence—to support the *status quo*.

Much atheism has resulted from the fact that the modern mind has found the dominant idea of God incredible. I have discussed in previous chapters the ways in which theism was undermined by the problem of evil, by historical-critical study of the Bible, and by evidence for evolution because the idea of divine omnipotence led to unrealistic expectations. The conflict between omnipotence and evolution is most relevant to the present topic. The rejection of the doctrine of God's special creation of each species out of nothing led to a deistic or totally atheistic interpretation of evolution in terms of the "survival of the fittest" and the "elimination of the unfit" through competition and pure power relations. The categories of ideals, cooperation, final causes, and divine influence are excluded. The world is thought to be the product of Omnipotent Matter alone.[15] This Darwinian interpretation of nature led to a Social Darwinian interpretation of history and international relations (a result not in conflict with Darwin's own intentions).[16] This result is an example of the effect of the religious motivation to be in harmony with the ultimate nature of things. The belief that nature achieved its progress through ruthless competition supported the notion that we ought to live accordingly. The language of Social Darwinism is often heard in the utterances of U. S. policymakers.

In sum: while the supernaturalistic idea of God has directly supported imperialism, militarism, and nuclearism by portraying the universe as ruled by coercive power, the offensiveness and incredibility of this idea of God led to an atheistic version of the same belief. Whether they be atheists or theists, therefore, modern human beings are led by the dynamic of the *imitatio dei* to want to control the world through the use of coercive power. Of course, it can be maintained that this is a natural desire, which would exist even without a supporting worldview. To whatever extent that is true, it remains the case that modern religion, both in its theistic and atheistic forms, reinforces that desire rather than mitigating it.

III. POSTMODERN THEOLOGY'S NATURALISTIC THEISM

Postmodern theology rejects the extreme voluntarism of supernaturalistic theism and the atheistic naturalism of modernity, replacing both with a naturalistic form of theism. This naturalistic theism is not a disguised rejection of theism: it is as distinguishable from atheistic naturalism as from theistic supernaturalism. God is understood as a personal being, distinct from the world, active in it, and responsive to it. Nor does the rejection of extreme voluntarism mean that the notions of purpose and freedom cannot be applied to God. What is rejected is rather the notion that the basic God-world relationship is itself an arbitrary feature of reality, determined by divine volition. In Whitehead's words, "The relationships of God to the world should lie beyond the accidents of will."[17] Postmodern theology rejects with Whitehead the idea that the way God acts in the world (by persuasion), and the way God responds to the world (with compassion), are matters of divine volition. Rather, these relationships are "founded upon the necessities of the nature of God and the nature of the world."[18]

The voluntarism of supernaturalistic theism presupposed the doctrine of *creatio ex nihilo*, in the sense that the creation of our world was the beginning of finite beings altogether. Postmodern theology follows Whitehead in rejecting this doctrine in favor of a version of creation out of chaos. In contrast to the theory endorsed by Newton, of "a wholly transcendent God creating out of nothing an accidental universe," Whitehead suggests that "the creation of the world is the incoming of a type of order establishing a cosmic epoch. It is not the beginning of matter of fact, but the incoming of a certain type of social order."[19]

This alternative view is not an arbitrary preference on Whitehead's part but is implied by his entire worldview. The actual units of the world are creative events. Each event creates itself by unifying influences it has received from other events. It then exerts a creative influence upon subsequent events. In each such creative event, "The many become one, and are increased by one."[20] If the very nature of actuality involves the creative synthesis of a many into a unity, it does not make sense to talk about a time when there was not a multiplicity of beings, a time when God existed all alone.

Postmodern naturalistic theism thinks of uncreated creative power as the ultimate reality. In this regard, it agrees with supernaturalism. Both views hold that the power of creativity has always existed. But supernaturalism believes that it exists inherently in God alone; whether a world of finite beings with creative power exists depends on God's volition. Naturalistic theism holds instead that creativity inherently belongs to both God *and* a realm of finite beings. Although Whitehead thought of God as the creator of our world, in the sense of having evoked its present order out of a chaotic state of very primitive entities, he was nervous about referring to God as creator because "the phrase is apt to be misleading by its suggestion that the ultimate creativity of the universe is to be ascribed to God's volition."[21] That is, God is the creator of our world in a very strong sense; but God did *not* create creativity itself, even the creativity of the realm of finite beings.

From this discussion it follows that God's relation to the world is a natural rather than an arbitrary feature of reality in a threefold sense. (I discuss the first two here, coming to the third sense on page 142.) First, a world of some sort must exist. *Our particular* world, with its electrons, protons, neutrons, atoms, molecules, cells, plants, and animals is, to be sure, contingent, and reflects the divine decision (as well as the decisions of trillions of creatures over the past fifteen billion years or so). But *a* world, meaning a multiplicity of finite beings embodying creativity, exists necessarily. The existence of a world is, like God's own existence, fully natural or necessary.

Second, the way God acts in relation to the world is also natural, being part of the very nature of things. God's action in the world is persuasive rather than coercive. In Whitehead's words, "the divine element in the world is to be conceived as a persuasive agency and not as a coercive agency. . . . The alternative doctrine, prevalent then and now, sees either in the many gods or in the one God, the final coercive forces wielding the thunder . . . , the supreme agency of compulsion. . . . "[22] When *coercion* or *compulsion* is used in this context,[23] it refers to the kind of efficient causation that unilaterally determines the outcome, such as when one billiard ball strikes another. *Persuasion*, by contrast, refers to causal power that does not unilaterally determine the outcome, but only influences it, leaving the outcome to be partly decided by the individual upon which the persuasion has been exerted.

Given this distinction between persuasive and coercive activity, many supernaturalistic theists would agree that God uses persuasion, at least for the most part, and especially in relation to human beings, to whom God has given free-will. The fact that God does not coerce human beings, at least usually, is thought to be due to a voluntary self-limitation. Postmodern theology, by contrast, holds that God uses persuasion in relation to *all* individuals, from quarks (if such there be) to angels (if such there be), because all individuals have some power of self-determination. (Individuals are distinguished from mere aggregates of individuals, such as rocks, which as such have no creative power. All the creative power of the rock resides in its individual constituents, that is, its molecules, atoms, and subatomic individuals. God's activity on the rock is understood in relation to its individual constituents.) Because the world's creativity is *inherent* to it, God's use of persuasion is not based on a voluntary self-limitation. God could not choose, from time to time, to intervene coercively here and there in the world. This point is at the heart of the difference between postmodern theology's naturalistic theism and the voluntarism of supernaturalistic theism.

In his most explicit criticism of traditional theology on this point, Whitehead, after expressing appreciation of the early Greek theologians, points out what he considers their unfortunate presupposition:

> The nature of God was exempted from all the metaphysical categories which apply to the individual things in this temporal world. The concept of him was a sublimation from its barbaric origin. He stood in the same relation to the whole World as early Egyptian or Mesopotamian kings stood to their subject populations. Also the moral characters were very analogous.[24]

Whitehead's statement of his own contrasting naturalistic position is one of his most quoted statements: "God is not to be treated as an exception to all metaphysical principles. . . . He is their chief exemplification."[25] With regard to the question of causal power, this principle means that God does not exist outside the universal order of causal interaction with the freedom to violate this order at will. Rather, the whole complex, God-and-a-world, exists naturally or necessarily, with those basic principles that are called metaphysical because they could not be otherwise. These principles belong to the very nature of God and of the world, that is, of the total natural complex, God-and-a-world.

Naturalistic theists, of course, cannot prove that this view of what exists naturally, or necessarily, is true, any more than supernaturalistic theists can prove *their* metaphysical assumption that only God, apart from any realm of finite beings, exists necessarily. A Christian's choice between the two views must be made on the basis of three questions. Which view's implications are more credible? Which view's implications are more helpful or liberating? Which view allows Christian faith to be interpreted more authentically?

Among the reasons for considering naturalistic theism more credible than supernaturalism is the fact, discussed in previous chapters, that it is fully compatible with the facts of evil, evolution, and biblical criticism, all of which constitute extreme difficulties for supernaturalism.

Besides being commendable as true, naturalistic theism can also be commended as liberating truth, which is the main point to which the discussion thus far has been devoted. I now summarize three ways in which it is a liberating truth, at least in relation to a people enslaved to an imperialistic ideology. First, this theology provides no grounds for complacency before the nuclear threat. God may succeed in persuading us to avoid a nuclear holocaust, but God cannot unilaterally prevent it, nor can God unilaterally reverse the destruction of a created order that has been billions of years in the making.

This theology is liberating, second, in portraying the world as essentially pluralistic. The world inherently and necessarily has a multiplicity of centers of power. No center of power, not even the divine center, can unilaterally control the world. People nurtured on such a worldview would not have dreams of controlling the rest of the world. They would know it to be impossible. And their desire to imitate the divine reality would not lead them to desire this control. To the contrary, the *imitatio dei* would lead them to want to stimulate other centers of power to develop their own creative freedom to the greatest possible extent.

In the third place, the desire to imitate deity would lead them not to develop technologies of coercion and destruction with which to threaten and destroy others, but to reduce the use of force to the absolute minimum necessary.

This application of Whiteheadian naturalistic theism is not alien to Whitehead's own intentions. For example, in speaking of the idea of God portrayed in some of the *Psalms*, he says:

> This worship of glory arising from power is dangerous. . . . I suppose that even the world itself could not contain the bones of those slaughtered because of men intoxicated by its attraction.[26]

Whitehead published that passage in 1926, having no idea of the nuclearism that would be the ultimate expression of this intoxication with an omnipotent deity. Another passage makes equally clear his awareness of the connection between the doctrines of a religion and the behavior of its devotees:

> [T]he doctrine of [a] . . . transcendent creator, at whose fiat the world came into being, and whose imposed will it obeys, is the fallacy which

has infused tragedy into the histories of Christianity and of Mahometanism.[27]

In the light of these passages, we can appreciate the antimilitaristic intentions of his own description of God:

> God's role is not the combat of . . . destructive force with destructive force; . . . he is the poet of the world, with tender patience leading it by his vision of truth, beauty, and goodness.[28]

A civilization that had been nurtured on this vision of the divine reality of the universe would not use its best minds and the lion's share of its wealth for developing ways to kill, but for ways to increase the beauty, justice, and peace of the world.

The third question for a Christian deciding between the two theisms is, Which one expresses Christian faith more authentically? Although postmodern theology is a philosophical theology, it also, in its specifically Christian form, can be seen as a development of a strand within the biblical writings that is more authentically Christian than the strand developed by supernaturalistic theism. Many parts of the Bible obviously suggest supernaturalism and overwhelming divine power (even if *creatio ex nihilo* is seldom if ever clearly articulated, and divine omnipotence in the Augustinian sense is not in view). But to take Jesus as the supreme incarnation and decisive revelation of God, given the nature of Jesus' teachings, life, and death, implies a critique of the image of God as overwhelming power. St. Paul, in First Corinthians, refers to the word of the cross as the "power of God," and to Christ crucified as the "wisdom of God," in contrast with the "wisdom of the world." Should we not see these contrasting ideas of wisdom as related to contrasting ideas of power? What is more fundamental to the wisdom of the world, with its *realpolitik*, than to believe that the only kind of power to which we can entrust our security is coercive power—the power to control, to threaten, and to destroy? But Paul, reflecting on the idea that God was most fully manifest in the crucified Jesus, said that the "foolishness of God is wiser than men, and the weakness of God is stronger than men." Does this not imply that an authentically Christian view of divine power, the most effective power in the universe, sees it as a kind of power that the wisdom of this world considers "weakness"?

I come now to the third sense in which God's relation to the world is a natural rather than a voluntary feature of reality. While the second sense applied to God's action in the world, the third sense involves the way in which God responds to the world. (The supernaturalistic theism of the traditional theologians said that God is impassible and hence does not "respond" to the world at all. But this notion, so at odds with the biblical picture, has seldom been affirmed in popular Christianity.) This side of naturalistic theism implies that God loves all creatures naturally. God *could not* hate, or be indifferent to, any creature. It belongs to the very nature of God to respond to each creature with sympathy, or compassion.

The idea that God is necessarily good has not been the dominant view in departments of philosophy (as well as in popular Christianity, Judaism, and Islam). Philosopher P. H. Nowell-Smith says, "There is nothing in the idea of an omnipotent, omniscient creator which, by itself, entails his goodness. . . . " Henry David Aiken puts it more bluntly, saying "there is no reason why an almighty and omniscient being might not be a perfect stinker."[29] Postmodern theologians, by contrast, hold that God's omniscience, or perfect knowledge of the world, entails God's perfect love for it, God's perfect sympathy for all its creatures.

The basis for this latter view is the Whiteheadian-Hartshornean view of perception. Divine knowledge is to be thought of not as indirect, inferential knowledge, but direct "knowledge by acquaintance," or perceptual knowledge. A basic point is that the most fundamental type of perception is not sense-perception. Sense-perception presupposes a more fundamental relationship, which Whitehead called *prehension*. The reception by the soul of sensory information about external objects from its body's sensory channels presupposes the soul's relation to and knowledge of its body. The soul's relation to its body is a prehensive relation. Its knowledge of its body is prehensive knowledge, which is "knowledge by acquaintance," direct perceptual knowledge. This form of perception involves a direct transfer of feeling—in short, sympathy. In Whitehead's words: "The primitive form of physical experience is . . . *sympathy*, that is, feeling the feeling in another and feeling conformally *with* another."[30] In sense-perception, by contrast, the relation between the perceiver and the object is so indirect and mediated that the values or emotions of the object are virtually lost. If we see nails pounded in the hands of another, we do not perceive the pain in the hands; but if the hands are our own, we are directly aware of their pain. We sympathize with their pain, literally feeling it with them.

Charles Hartshorne stresses that we should take this mind-body relation as the basis for understanding unmediated perceptual knowledge, and that we should use this type of perceptual knowledge as a model for thinking of God's omniscience.[31] On this basis, it follows from God's omniscience that God is naturally motivated by the interests of others, because they are in a sense God's own interests.[32] Hartshorne suggests the following thought-experiment: "suppose all 'others' were within the body, as its members; then, since the need of the body is for the flourishing of its own parts or members, bodily desire and altruism would be coincident."[33] If all creatures are within God, as Hartshorne's panentheism holds, then divine omniscience would entail a "certain and absolute coincidence of other-interest and self-interest."[34] Does this lack of freedom to hate or be indifferent to the welfare of others imply that we cannot speak of God as ethically good? It would, Hartshorne replies, *if* to be ethical necessarily meant to resist temptation. "But," he continues,

> if it means being motivated by concern for the interests of others, then God alone is absolutely ethical; for to know interests, fully and concretely, and to share them are indistinguishable. The "simplicity" of God has here its true meaning, that there can be no duality of understanding and motivation in a being in which either understanding or motivation is perfect. Both come down to love pure and simple and indivisible. To fully sympathize with and to fully know the feelings of others are the same relationship, separable in our human case only because there the "fully" never applies. . . . [35]

Contrary to the views of P. H. Nowell-Smith, David Aiken, and most other modern philosophers, therefore, divine omniscience does imply divine goodness. The idea that God directly knows the world fully, combined with the insight that direct knowledge is sympathy or compassion, implies that God naturally sympathizes with the feelings of all creatures. For God to love us, now that we exist, is as fully natural to God as to exist, or to know all that is knowable. To assume that God could hate or be indifferent to creatures is to think of divine knowledge by analogy with sense-perception, in which there can be knowledge without sympathy, or to apply to God our finite inability to know more than a small portion of reality with any directness and fulness.

This doctrine of God's impartial love does not imply that God is not unhappy with much that is going on in the world and does not prefer the actions of some people to those of others. It does not mean that God supports the aims of all indifferently. What this doctrine of God's impartial love implies is that God's unhappiness with some people's lives does not involve hate. It implies that we cannot translate our hatred into divine hatred and thereby justify and reinforce it. It implies that, when we find ourselves fighting against other people, we are fighting against people whom God loves as much as us. It implies that we cannot justify and reinforce our own indifference to some people's welfare by assuming divine indifference. In brief, it implies that there can be no divine sanction for the typical bipolar, imperialistic viewpoint, which divides the world into the favored saints and the hated enemy, with the rest of the world being a matter of indifference except insofar as it figures into the bipolar battle.

Similarly to postmodern theology's doctrine of divine power, this doctrine of the divine attitude portrays an essentially pluralistic, multilateral world. It says that *every* center of experience is loved for its own sake. No center of experience is hated, and none is viewed as having only instrumental value. This view takes literally the New Testament suggestion that, in doing something to the (in the world's eyes) "least of these," we have done it unto the Divine One.

Given our human tendency to imitate deity as we most deeply conceive and imagine it, the widespread appropriation of postmodern theism at a deep level by our culture would do much to overcome our penchant for imperialism and nuclearism.

NOTES

CHAPTER 1
INTRODUCTION: POSTMODERN THEOLOGY

1. Although Richard Rorty's views on some topics are eccentric, he surely articulates the majority sentiment among intellectuals when he refers to a period in our background "when religious intuitions were weeded out from among the intellectually respectable candidates for Philosophical articulation" (*Consequences of Pragmatism* [Minneapolis: University of Minnesota Press, 1982], xxxviii).

2. Stephen Jay Gould, *The Panda's Thumb: More Reflections in Natural History* (New York: W. W. Norton & Co., 1982), 225.

3. I do not mean to deny that a Buddhist could use the Whiteheadian conceptuality to formulate a Buddhist vision with its valuations. (See Takao Tanaka's discussion of a Whiteheadian Buddhist natural theology in "From a Buddhist Point of View," *John Cobb's Theology in Process*, David Ray Griffin and Thomas J. J. Altizer, eds. [Philadelphia: Westminster Press, 1977], 99-111.) I am only saying that the writings of Whitehead and Hartshorne as they stand express a vision and valuations that are fundamentally Christian. See Ryusei Takeda and John B. Cobb, Jr., "'Mosa-Dharma and Prehension: Nagarjuna and Whitehead Compared,'" *Process Studies* 4/1 (Spring 1974), 24-36.

4. See the discussion by John B. Cobb, Jr., in the final chapter of *A Christian Natural Theology: Based on the Thought of Alfred North Whitehead* (Philadelphia: Westminster Press, 1965).

5. Because use of the term *postmodern* may seem somewhat faddish, I will review my own use of the term within the context of its use within the Whiteheadian tradition. I first used it in an essay "Post-Modern Theology for a New Christian Existence," which was written in 1972 as the introduction to a volume on John Cobb's theology, although it did not appear until five years later (*John Cobb's Theology in Process*, David Ray Griffin and Thomas J. J. Altizer, eds.

[Westminster Press, 1977]). I took the term from Cobb's article, "From Crisis Theology to the Post-Modern World," which was first published in 1964 (*Centennial Review* 8 [Spring 1984], 209-20). I next used the term in a paper calling for a postmodern christology presented at Cambridge University in Fall 1980. Between 1981 and 1984, I wrote several essays in which the term *postmodern* was central, including those published herein as chapters 3, 5, and 7, and founded the Center for a Postmodern World. In the meantime, Frederick Ferré had published *Shaping the Future: Resources for the Postmodern World* (San Francisco: Harper & Row, 1976), and "Religious World Modeling and Postmodern Science" (*Journal of Religion* 62/3 [July 1982], 261-70), although regretably I did not become aware of Ferré's use until, if I recall correctly, 1984. In any case, the use of the term *postmodern* grew naturally and independently within this tradition of philosophical theology, being traceable back to 1964.

6. See Donald W. Sherburne, "Whitehead Without God," *The Christian Scholar* 50 (1967), 251-72, reprinted in *Process Philosophy and Christian Thought*, Delwin Brown, Ralph E. James, Jr., and Gene Reeves, eds. (Indianapolis, Ind.: Bobbs-Merrill, 1971); also John B. Cobb, Jr., and Donald W. Sherburne, "The 'Whitehead Without God' Debate," *Process Studies* 1/2 (1971), 91-113.

7. See George Kline, "Form, Concrescence, and Concretum: A Neo-Whiteheadian Analysis," *Southern Journal of Philosophy* 7/4 (Winter 1969), 351-60. I should add that, as I learned in a recent conversation with Kline, his position is not based on a general rejection of influence at a distance. He, in fact, is open to the possibility of virtually instantaneous influence between spatially remote events, which would allow for parapsychological interactions and for the nonlocality proposed by physicists such as Henry Stapp and David Bohm. I have discussed this issue in the introduction to David Ray Griffin, ed., *The Reenchantment of Science: Postmodern Proposals* (Albany: State University of New York Press, 1988), 16-17.

8. I have discussed this issue in my essay review of Sheldrake's *A New Science of Life: The Hypothesis of Formative Causation* (London: Blond & Briggs, 1981) in *Process Studies* 12/1 (Spring 1982), 38-40.

CHAPTER 2
THE IMPORTANCE OF BEING HUMAN

1. This essay, which has been revised for inclusion in this volume, was originally prepared in 1984 for a lecture in a series on the theme "Preserving our Most Human Qualities," which was sponsored by the Santa Barbara City College Continuing Education Division.

2. Paul Tillich, *The Courage to Be* (New Haven, Conn.: Yale University Press), 143, 147, 175-76.

3. *The Basic Writings of Bertrand Russell 1903-1959*, Robert E. Enger and Lester E. Dennon, eds. (New York: Simon and Schuster, 1961), 67.

4. *Idem.*

5. *Ibid.*, 67, 70, 68.

6. *Ibid.*, 72.

7. Joseph Wood Krutch, *The Modern Temper: A Study and a Confession* (1929; New York: Harcourt, Brace & World, 1956).

8. *Ibid.*, xiii.

9. Robert Jay Lifton, *The Broken Connection: On Death and the Continuity of Life* (New York: Simon and Schuster, 1979).

10. This nihilistic postmodernism is treated at much greater length in a companion volume in this series, *Varieties of Postmodern Theology* (Albany: State University of New York Press, 1989), in essays by William Beardslee and me.

11. See, e.g., Huston Smith, *Forgotten Truth: The Primordial Tradition* (New York: Harper & Row, 1976), and *Beyond the Post-Modern Mind* (New York: Crossroad Publishing Co., 1982). A subsequent volume in this series will consist of a dialogue between Huston Smith and me.

12. See also my introduction to the first volume in this series, *The Reenchantment of Science: Postmodern Proposals* (Albany: State University of New York Press, 1988), section II.D.

13. I have described how revelation can be conceived without assuming supernaturalism in *A Process Christology* (Philadelphia: Westminster Press, 1973); "Is Revelation Coherent?" *Theology Today* 28 (October 1971), 278-94; and "Relativism, Divine Causation, and Biblical Theology," *Encounter* 36/4 (Autumn 1975), 342-60, reprinted in *God's Activity in the World: The Contemporary Problem*, Owen C. Thomas, ed. (Chico, Calif.: Scholars Press, 1983), 117-36.

14. Some thinkers, such as Albert Schweitzer and some "deep ecologists" (e.g., Bill Devall and George Sessions, *Deep Ecology: Living as if Nature Mattered* [New York: Peregrine Smith, 1985]), reject the idea of any theoretical "hierarchy of value" in which some creatures are said to have more intrinsic importance than others. This stance reflects an admirable rejection of anthropocentrism and an appreciation for the distinctive values of all species, which are to be respected. The affirmation of a "democracy of intrinsic value," however, provides no guidance for living, with its constant forced choices. In Schweitzer's case, the decision to save the lives of humans by taking the lives of microbes, mosquitoes, or lions was justified purely on the grounds that we naturally save our own kind. His ethical theory thereby left him bereft of any ethical principle in practice. Postmodern thought seeks to promote the same deep respect as do egalitarian ecologists for the ecological balance of nature in terms of the following three points: (1) Every individual creature has intrinsic value, meaning value for itself. Higher forms of individuals, having richer forms of experience, therefore by definition have greater intrinsic value. (2) Every individual also has ecological value, whether positive or negative, for the ecosystem. In general, the less an individual's intrinsic value, the greater the positive ecological value of its species for the ecosystem. For example, the ecosystem of the planet would get along very well without humans and dolphins (even *better* without humans), but not without plankton and earth-

worms. (3) In considering the overall value of each form of being, we should consider not only its value for itself and its value for other finite beings (finally the ecosystem) but also its value for the divine experience. This all-inclusive experience can be presumed to appreciate all the positive ecological values insofar as they enable the realization of intrinsic values, and to appreciate all intrinsic values for what they are. We can assume that the distinctively human qualities of experience contribute a special form of satisfaction to the divine experience (see note 15). In terms of this threefold point of view, we can completely reject anthropocentrism, which views the rest of nature in purely instrumental terms, without going to the other extreme of misanthropy or even ecological egalitarianism. For a more complete statement, see John B. Cobb, Jr., "Ecology, Science, and Religion: Toward a Postmodern Worldview," *The Reenchantment of Science*, David Ray Griffin, ed.

15. Alfred North Whitehead, *Adventures of Ideas* (1933; New York: Free Press, 1967), 11.

CHAPTER 3
CREATIVITY AND POSTMODERN RELIGION

1. Frances Yates, *Giordano Bruno and the Hermetic Tradition* (Chicago: University of Chicago Press, 1964), 155-56, 161. For further references on the Renaissance views and the early modern rejection of them summarized in the subsequent paragraphs, see notes 2-5 for chapter 4.

2. Newton's position on action at a distance is complex. There is no doubt that he believed in it. And his anti-Cartesian doctrine of multiple forces (both attractive and repulsive) that act at a distance probably, as Richard Westfall argues, "embodies the enduring influence of alchemy upon his scientific thought" ("Newton and Alchemy," *Occult and Scientific Mentalities in the Renaissance*, Brian Vickers, ed. [Cambridge: Cambridge University Press, 1984], 315-35, esp. 330). Newton in this sense reflected a Neoplatonic-Hermetic worldview. But Newton denied that these forces were inherent to matter. Fearing the charge of belief in "occult" powers, he sometimes took refuge in positivism, assigning a merely mathematical (rather than causal) meaning to the forces. At other times he described the forces as evidence of "active" and therefore "spiritual" agencies, which ultimately pointed to the agency of God. In any case, his particles of matter were no more capable of acting at a distance than was the matter of the Cartesians. Besides Westfall's article just cited, see also his monumental *Never at Rest: A Biography of Isaac Newton* (Cambridge and New York: Cambridge University Press, 1980), and Arnold Thakray, *Atoms and Powers: An Essay on Newtonian Matter-Theory and the Development of Chemistry* (Cambridge: Harvard University Press, 1970).

3. See Stephen Jay Gould, *The Panda's Thumb* (New York: W. W. Norton & Co., 1980), 71-78, and P. J. Bowler, "Darwinism and the Argument for Design: Suggestions for a Reevaluation," *Journal of History of Biology* 10/1 (Spring 1977), 29-43, esp. 31-32. For further references on Darwin's views, see the notes to chapter 5.

4. On Bergson's views, see Andrew G. Bjelland, "Evolutionary Epistemology, Durational Metaphysics, and Theoretical Physics: Čapek and the Bergsonian Tradition," *Physics and the Ultimate Significance of Time: Bohm, Prigogine, and Process Philosophy*, David Ray Griffin, ed. (Albany: State University of New York Press, 1986), 51-80; the "Introduction" in P. A. Y. Gunter, *Henri Bergson: A Bibliography* (Bowling Green, Ohio: Philosophy Documentation Center, 1974) or in Peter A. Y. Gunter, ed., *Bergson and the Evolution of Physics* (Knoxville: University of Tennessee Press, 1969); Milič Čapek, *Bergson and Modern Physics* (Vol. 7 of Boston Studies in the Philosophy of Science) (Dordrecht: D. Reidel; New York: Humanities Press, 1971).

5. Nicolas Berdyaev, *The Destiny of Man* (New York: Harper & Row, 1960), 22-35; *Truth and Revelation* (New York: Collier Books, 1962), 124.

6. *Truth and Revelation*, 59, 65.

7. *Ibid.*, 122, 114.

8. *Ibid.*, 15, 56.

9. *Ibid.*, 16, 17, 112, 120.

10. The difference occurs between Whitehead's Lowell Lectures in 1924 and their revision and expansion into *Science and the Modern World* (New York: Macmillan, 1925).

11. Perhaps in *Religion in the Making* (New York: Macmillan, 1926) and definitely in *Process and Reality*, which was first published in 1929.

12. Alfred North Whitehead, *Process and Reality*, corrected edition, David Ray Griffin and Donald W. Sherburne, eds. (New York: Free Press, 1978), 343.

13. John B. Cobb, Jr., "Buddhist Emptiness and the Christian God," *Journal of the American Academy of Religion* XLV/1 (March 1979), 11-26; *Beyond Dialogue: Toward a Mutual Transformation of Christianity and Buddhism* (Philadelphia: Fortress Press, 1982), esp. 42-43, 86-90, 110-14.

14. Whitehead, *Process and Reality*, 21.

15. Charles Hartshorne, *Creative Synthesis and Philosophic Method* (La Salle, Ill.: Open Court, 1970; Lanham, Md.: University Press of America, 1983), chap. VIII.

16. See John B. Cobb, Jr., "Beyond Anthropocentrism in Ethics and Religion," *On the Fifth Day: Animal Rights and Human Rights*, Richard Knowles Morris and Michael W. Fox, eds. (Washington, D. C.: Acropolis Books, 1978), 137-53.

CHAPTER 4
GOD IN THE POSTMODERN WORLD

1. Apologies to Woody Allen.

2. Boyle used matter's lack of the power of self-movement to prove God's existence: "[S]ince motion does not essentially belong to matter, . . . the motions of all bodies, at least at the beginnings of things, . . . were impressed upon them" (Boyle's *Works*, 1744, IV, 394). Newton says that, because matter must be moved from without, we are led to the belief in "a powerful ever-living Agent" who, "being in all Places, is . . . able by his Will to move the Bodies within his boundless uniform Sensorium" (Query 23 [31] to the Latin edition of *Opticks*). For a thorough discussion of Boyle and Newton on this topic, see Eugene Klaaren, *Religious Origins of Modern Science: Belief in Creation in Seventeenth-Century Thought* (Grand Rapids, Mich.: William B. Eerdmans, 1977; Lanham, Md.: University Press of America, 1985).

3. See *ibid.*; Frances Yates, *Giordano Bruno and the Hermetic Tradition* (Chicago: University of Chicago Press, 1964), and *The Rosicrucian Enlightenment* (1970; Boulder, Col.: Shambhala, 1978); Hugh Kearney, *Science and Change 1500-1700* (New York: McGraw-Hill, 1971); Carolyn Merchant, *The Death of Nature: Women, Ecology and the Scientific Revolution* (San Francisco: Harper & Row, 1980); J. R. Ravetz, "The Varieties of Scientific Experience," *The Sciences and Theology in the Twentieth Century*, Arthur Peacocke, ed. (Notre Dame, Ind.: University of Notre Dame, 1981); Margaret C. Jacob, *The Newtonians and the English Revolution 1689-1720* (Ithaca, N. Y.: Cornell University Press, 1976).

4. Robert Lenoble, *Mersenne ou la naissance du mécanisme* (Paris: Librairie Philosophique J. Vrin, 1943), 133, 157-58, 210, 375, 381; J. R. Jacob, *Robert Boyle and the English Revolution: A Study in Social and Intellectual Change* (New York: Franklin, Burt Publishers, 1978), 172.

5. On Newton, see Eugene Klaaren and Margaret Jacob (notes 2 and 3), and, on the tricky topic of action at a distance, note 2 of chap. 3, above.

6. See references in note 4.

7. Moody E. Prior, "Joseph Glanvill, Witchcraft and Seventeenth-Century Science," *Modern Philosophy* 30 (1932-33), 167-93; on Bacon, see Yates, *The Rosicrucian Enlightenment.*

8. John Locke, *An Essay Concerning Human Understanding*, Bk. II, Ch. I, 1-5; Bk. IV, Ch. X, 1-11.

9. Franklin L. Baumer, *Religion and the Rise of Scepticism* (New York: Harcourt, Brace & World, 1980), chap. 3; John Bowker, *The Sense of God: Sociological, Anthropological and Psychological Approaches to the Origin of the Sense of God* (Oxford: Clarendon, 1973).

10. Baumer, *Religion and the Rise of Scepticism*, chap. 5.

11. Martin Heidegger, "The Word of Nietzsche: 'God is Dead'," *The Question Concerning Technology: Heidegger's Critique of the Modern Age*, William Lovitt, trans. (New York: Harper & Row, 1977).

12. William James, *The Varieties of Religious Experience* (New York: Collier Books, 1961), 406.

13. Of course, there are non-Western frameworks of meaning, most notably various forms of Buddhism, that do not involve the generic idea of God. But typical Buddhist worldviews are far removed from modern Western atheism, and are not as devoid of theistic analogues as most textbook accounts suggest. It is even possible for a Western thinker to be atheistic without being nihilistic. For example, J. M. E. McTaggert denied God but affirmed reincarnation as the framework for the meaning of human life. But his Hegelianism was very different from the typical atheistic worldview of the modern age. Most post-theistic views *are* nihilistic.

14. Bertrand Russell, "A Free Man's Worship," *The Basic Writings of Bertrand Russell 1903-1959*, Robert E. Egner and Lester E. Dennon, eds. (New York: Simon and Schuster, 1961), 66-72. The passage is quoted above in section III of chapter 2.

15. Robert Jay Lifton and Richard Falk, *Indefensible Weapons: The Political and Psychological Case Against Nuclearism* (New York: Basic Books, 1982), 13-14, 88-89.

16. See the chapter "Spinoza: Everything is Simply Divine—Unorthodox Conclusion from Orthodox Premises" in David Ray Griffin, *God, Power, and Evil: A Process Theodicy* (Philadelphia: Westminster Press 1976); and James Gustafson, *Ethics from a Theocentric Perspective*, vol. I (Chicago: University of Chicago Press, 1981).

17. Paul Tillich, *Systematic Theology*, vol. I (Chicago: University of Chicago Press, 1951).

18. John Dewey, *A Common Faith* (New Haven, Conn.: Yale University Press, 1934); Donald Cupitt, *Taking Leave of God* (New York: Crossroad, 1981); Bertrand Russell, "A Free Man's Worship."

19. Russell, "A Free Man's Worship," 68: "Shall God exist and be evil, or shall he be recognized as the creation of our own conscience?"

20. For God as "linguisticality," see Gerhard Ebeling, *God and Word* (Philadelphia: Fortress Press, 1967); for God as our "co-humanity," see Herbert Braun, "The Problem of New Testament Theology," *The Bultmann School of Biblical Interpretation: New Directions?*, Robert Funk, ed. (New York: Harper & Row, 1965), 169-83; for God as "creative interchange," see Henry Nelson Wieman, *The Source of Human Good* (Chicago: University of Chicago Press, 1946).

21. "The operation of this God is as sovereign as Calvinist teaching describes it. In the strictest sense it is predestinating." Karl Barth, *Church Dogmatics*, vol. III/3, *The Doctrine of Creation*, G. W. Bromiley and R. J. Ehrlich, trans. (Edinburgh: T. & T. Clark, 1960), 131.

22. Rudolf Bultmann, *Jesus Christ and Mythology* (New York: Charles Scribner's Sons, 1958).

23. Patrick Sherry criticizes those, such as D. Z. Phillips, who employ Wittgenstein this way, in *Religion, Truth, and Language-Games* (New York: Barnes & Noble, 1977).

24. See Ian Barbour, *Issues in Science and Religion* (Englewood Cliffs, N. J.: Prentice-Hall, 1966), chap. 5; Frederick Ferré, *Language, Logic, and God* (New York: Harper, 1961).

25. For example, see Herbert Feigl, "Mind-Body, *Not* a Pseudoproblem," *Dimensions of Mind*, Sydney Hook, ed. (New York: New York University Press, 1969); J. C. C. Smart, "Sensations and Brain Processes," and "Materialism," *The Mind-Brain Identity Theory*, C. V. Borst, ed. (London: Macmillan, Ltd., 1979); R. C. Bennett, "Current Issues in the Philosophy of Mind," *American Philosophical Quarterly* 15/4 (October 1978), 249-59.

26. John Beloff, "The Identity Hypothesis: A Critique," *Brain and Mind*, J. R. Smythies, ed. (London: Routledge & Kegan Paul, 1965); Karl Popper and John C. Eccles, *The Self and Its Brain* (Heidelberg: Springer, 1977). This philosophical argument against materialism is developed more extensively in my introduction to *The Reenchantment of Science: Postmodern Proposals*, David Ray Griffin, ed. (Albany: State University of New York Press, 1988).

27. See notes 3-5. These studies are part of a larger effort to understand the extrascientific influences on scientific ideas. See, e.g., Paul Feyerabend, *Against Method: Outline of an Anarchistic Theory of Knowledge* (London: Verso, 1978), and Gary Gutting, ed., *Paradigms and Revolutions: Applications and Appraisals of Thomas Kuhn's Philosophy of Science* (Notre Dame, Ind.: University of Notre Dame Press, 1980). See also my extended discussion in the introduction to *The Reenchantment of Science*.

28. David Bohm, *Wholeness and the Implicate Order* (London: Routledge & Kegan Paul, 1980), 129, 186; Henry P. Stapp, "Einstein Time and Process Time," *Physics and the Ultimate Significance of Time: Bohm, Prigogine and Process Philosophy*, David Ray Griffin, ed. (Albany: State University of New York Press, 1986), 246-70, and "Bell's Theorem and the Foundations of Quantum Physics," *American Journal of Physics* 53 (1985), 306-17. For the historical background on this issue, see Mary Hesse, *Forces and Fields: The Concept of Action at a Distance in the History of Physics* (Totowa, N. J.: Littlefield, Adams, and Co., 1965). On Newtonian matter and action at a distance, see note 2 of chap. 3, above.

29. A. Goldbeter and D. E. Koshland, Jr., "Simple Molecular Model for Sensing and Adaptation Based on Receptor Modification with Application to Bacterial Chemotaxis," *Journal of Molecular Biology* 161/3 (1982), 395-416; Jeff Stock, Greg Kersulis, and Daniel E. Koshland, Jr., "Neither Methylating nor Demethylating Enzymes are Required for Bacterial Chemotaxis," *Cell* 42/2 (1985), 683-90.

30. Rupert Sheldrake, *A New Science of Life: The Hypothesis of Formative Causation* (London: Blond & Briggs, 1981).

31. J. E. Lovelock and Lynn Margulis, "Atmospheric Homeostasis by and for the Biosphere: the Gaia Hypothesis," *Tellus* 26/2 (1973); "Biological Modulation of the Earth's Atmosphere," *Icarus* 21/471 (1974); J. E. Lovelock, *Gaia: A New Look at Life on Earth* (Oxford: Oxford University Press, 1979). The scien-

tific developments pointing away from the modern worldview are discussed more extensively in my introduction to *The Reenchantment of Science*.

32. A. N. Whitehead spoke of our experience of ideals, "of ideals entertained, of ideals aimed at, of ideals achieved, of ideals defaced," as our "experience of the deity of the universe" (*Modes of Thought* [New York: Free Press, 1966], 103).

CHAPTER 5
EVOLUTION AND POSTMODERN THEISM

1. Peter J. Bowler, *The Eclipse of Darwinism: Anti-Darwinian Evolution Theories in the Decades Around 1900* (Baltimore, Md.: Johns Hopkins University Press, 1983), 27; Neal C. Gillespie, *Charles Darwin and the Problem of Creation* (Chicago: University of Chicago Press, 1979), 13, 16, 35, 40-41, 53-54, Epilogue.

2. Stephen Toulmin, *The Return to Cosmology: Postmodern Science and the Theology of Nature* (Berkeley: University of California Press), 8.

3. Gillespie, *Charles Darwin and the Problem of Creation*, 126-27; John C. Greene, *Science, Ideology, and World View: Essays in the History of Evolution Ideas* (Berkeley: University of California Press, 1981), 153.

4. Gillespie, *Charles Darwin and the Problem of Creation*, 127, 129-30.

5. *Ibid.*, 133.

6. *Ibid.*, 130.

7. Sandra Herbert, "The Place of Man in the Development of Darwin's Theory of Transmutation," *Journal of the History of Biology* 10/2 (Fall 1977), 155-227, esp. 207.

8. Gillespie, *Charles Darwin and the Problem of Creation*, 86, 123.

9. *Ibid.*, 86; for an example, see Stephen Jay Gould, *Ever Since Darwin* (New York: W. W. Norton & Co., 1977), 267.

10. Michael Ghiselin, *The Economy of Nature and the Evolution of Sex* (Berkeley: University of California Press, 1974), x.

11. Gillespie, *Charles Darwin and the Problem of Creation*, 55, 56, 120, 139-40.

12. *Ibid.*, 56; Theodosius Dobzhansky, "Chance and Creativity in Evolution," *Studies in the Philosophy of Biology*, Francisco J. Ayala and Theodosius Dobzhansky, eds. (Berkeley: University of California Press, 1974), 313-14, 316, 329. The word *chance* (or *random*) also has a more technical meaning, which is explained later in the text.

13. Gillespie, *Charles Darwin and the Problem of Creation*, 120.

14. *Ibid.*, 58.

15. *Ibid.*, 146-47.

16. Michael Ghiselin (*The Economy of Nature*, 13) says that the "total rejection of teleology" is the fundamental point of his book.

17. Stephen Jay Gould, *The Panda's Thumb* (New York: W. W. Norton & Co. 1980), 37-38.

18. Gould, *Ever Since Darwin*, 44.

19. Gould, *The Panda's Thumb*, 71-78; P. J. Bowler, "Darwinism and the Argument for Design: Suggestions for a Reevaluation," *Journal of the History of Biology* 10/1 (Spring 1977), 29-43, esp. 31-32; Sandra Herbert, "The Place of Man," 204.

20. Dobzhansky, "Chance and Creativity in Evolution," 313-14.

21. Stephen Jay Gould, *The Mismeasure of Man* (New York: W. W. Norton & Co., 1981), 325.

22. Stephen Jay Gould, *Hen's Teeth and Horse's Toes* (New York: W. W. Norton & Co., 1984), 138; *The Panda's Thumb*, 79; *Ever Since Darwin*, 12.

23. Gould, *Hen's Teeth and Horse's Toes*, 138.

24. Gillespie, *Charles Darwin and the Problem of Creation*, 107.

25. These features of what I call the "generic idea of God" are discussed more fully in chapter 4.

26. Toulmin, *The Return to Cosmology*, 13.

27. Gould, *The Panda's Thumb*, 50; *Ever Since Darwin*, 268-69; David J. Depew and Bruce H. Weber, eds., *Evolution at a Crossroads: The New Biology and the New Philosophy of Science* (Cambridge, Mass.: MIT Press, 1985), ix-xiii, 247-56; Mae-Wan Ho and Peter T. Saunders, eds., *Beyond Neo-Darwinism: An Introduction to the New Evolutionary Paradigm* (New York: Academic Press, 1984).

28. See Roger Sperry, *Science and Moral Priority: Merging Mind, Brain, and Human Values* (New York: Columbia University Press, 1983), 31-33, 66-67, 70, 79.

29. Although his evidence is controversial, E. J. Steele (*Somatic Selection and Adaptive Evolution: On the Inheritance of Acquired Characters*, second ed. [Chicago: University of Chicago Press, 1981], 95-96) suggests that the mind's ideas "can directly influence our genes" and thereby the inheritance of acquired characteristics. See also John H. Campbell, "An Organizational Interpretation of Evolution," *Evolution at the Crossroads*, Depew and Weber, eds., 133-67. Whitehead had long ago questioned the dogma of inviolable germ cells; see *Modes of Thought* (New York: Macmillan, 1938), 138.

30. Rupert Sheldrake, *A New Science of Life: The Hypothesis of Formative Causation* (London: Blond & Briggs, 1981).

31. Stephan Lackner, *Peaceable Nature: An Optimistic View of Life on Earth* (San Francisco: Harper & Row, 1984), 51.

CHAPTER 6
POSTMODERN ANIMISM AND
LIFE AFTER DEATH

1. On these Renaissance views, see Carolyn Merchant, *The Death of Nature: Women, Ecology and the Scientific Revolution* (San Francisco: Harper & Row, 1980); Hugh Kearney, *Science and Change 1500-1700* (New York: McGraw-Hill, 1971); Frances Yates, *The Rosicrucian Enlightenment* (Boulder, Col.: Shambhala, 1978); Morris Berman, *The Reenchantment of The World* (Ithaca, N. Y.: Cornell University Press, 1981); Brian Easlea, *Witch Hunting, Magic and the New Philosophy: An Introduction to Debates of the Scientific Revolution 1450-1750* (Atlantic Highlands, N. J.: Humanities Press, 1980); Margaret C. Jacob, *The Newtonians and the English Revolution 1689-1720* (Ithaca, N. Y.: Cornell University Press, 1976); James R. Jacob, *Robert Boyle and the English Revolution* (New York: Franklin, Burt Publishers, 1978).

2. I have summarized the general motives for the adoption of the mechanistic view in the second section of the introduction to *The Reenchantment of Science: Postmodern Proposals*, David Ray Griffin, ed. (Albany: State University of New York Press, 1988). With regard to dualism and mortalism in particular, see James R. Jacob, *Robert Boyle and the English Revolution*, 172, and Brian Easlea, *Witch Hunting, Magic and the New Philosophy*, 113, 234-35.

3. Eugene Klaaren, *Religious Origins of Modern Science: Belief in Creation in Seventeenth-Century Thought* (Grand Rapids, Mich.: William B. Eerdmans, 1977; Lanham, Md.: University Press of America, 1985), 98-99, 149; Brian Easlea, *Witch Hunting, Magic and the New Philosophy*, 112, 138.

4. Easlea, *op. cit.*, 94-95, 108-15, 132, 135, 138, 158, 210; James R. Jacob, *Robert Boyle and the English Revolution*, 161-76; Robert Lenoble, *Mersenne ou la naissance du mécanisme* (Paris: Librairie Philosophique J. Vrin, 1943), 133, 157-58, 210, 375, 381.

5. A. Goldbeter and D. E. Koshland, Jr., "Simple Molecular Model for Sensing and Adaptation Based on Receptor Modification with Application to Bacterial Chemotaxis," *Journal of Molecular Biology* 161/3 (1982), 395-416; Jess Stock, Greg Kersulis and Daniel E. Koshland, Jr., "Neither Methylating nor Demethylating Enzymes are Required for Bacterial Chemotaxis," *Cell* 42/2 (1985), 683-90.

6. See Bernard Rensch, "Arguments for Panpsychistic Identism," *Mind in Nature: Essays on the Interface of Science and Philosophy*, John B. Cobb, Jr.,

and David Ray Griffin, eds. (Washington, D. C.: University Press of America, 1977), 70-78.

7. See Raymond A. Moody, Jr., *Life After Life* (Covington, Ga.: Mockingbird Books, 1975), and *Reflections on Life After Life* (Covington, Ga.: Mockingbird Books, 1977); Kenneth Ring, *Life at Death* (New York: Coward, McCann & Geoghegan, 1980), and *Heading Toward Omega* (New York: William Morrow & Co., 1984); and M. B. Sabom, *Recollections of Death* (New York: Harper & Row, 1982).

8. For the best surveys of studies in a wide range of areas of parapsychological research, see Benjamin Wolman, ed., *Handbook of Parapsychology* (New York: Van Nostrand Reinhold, 1977); Hoyt L. Edge, Robert L. Morris, John Palmer, and Joseph H. Rush, *Foundations of Parapsychology* (Boston and London: Routledge & Kegan Paul, 1986); and the series, *Advances in Parapsychological Research*, Stanley Krippner, ed. (New York: Plenum Press), esp. vol. I, *Psychokinesis* (1977) and vol. II, *Extrasensory Perception* (1978). For evaluations by capable philosophers, see *William James on Psychical Research*, Gardner Murphy and Robert Ballou, eds. (New York: Viking Press, 1960; Clifton, N. J.: Augustus M. Kelley, 1973); C. D. Broad, *Religion, Philosophy and Psychical Research* (London: Routledge & Kegan Paul, 1953; New York: Humanities Press, 1969); and Stephen Braude, *ESP and Psychokinesis: A Philosophical Examination* (Philadelphia: Temple University Press, 1979) and *The Limits of Influence: Psychokinesis and the Philosophy of Science* (New York and London: Routledge & Kegan Paul, 1986).

9. Experiments in which a subject's involuntary physiological responses are monitored suggest that people have an unconscious awareness of things of which they have no conscious knowledge. See Charles T. Tart, "Physiological Correlates of Psi Cognition," *International Journal of Parapsychology* 5 (1963), 375-86, and E. D. Dean and C. B. Nash, "Coincident Plethysmograph Results under Controlled Conditions," *Journal of the Society of Psychical Research* 44 (1967), 1-14. For a philosophical psychiatrist's conviction that paranormal relations occur continually at the unconscious level, see Jule Eisenbud, *Parapsychology and the Unconscious* (Berkeley, Calif.: North Atlantic Books, 1983), 21, 22, 36, 40, 125, 157-58, 162, 167, 183. See also the supporting opinion of Stephen Braude in *ESP and Psychokinesis* and *The Limits of Influence*.

10. See Kenneth R. Pelletier, *Mind as Healer, Mind as Slayer: A Holistic Approach to Preventing Stress Disorders* (New York: Dell Publishing Co., 1977) and Norman Cousins, *The Healing Heart: Antidotes to Panic and Helplessness* (New York: W. W. Norton & Co., 1983). I have discussed psychosomatic relations in "Of Minds and Molecules: Postmodern Medicine in a Psychosomatic Universe" in *The Reenchantment of Science*; this essay was published earlier in slightly different form in Marcus P. Ford, ed., *A Process Theory of Medicine: Interdisciplinary Essays* (Lewiston, N. Y.: Edwin Mellen Press, 1987).

11. See Joseph H. Rush, "Findings from Experimental PK Research," in Hoyt L. Edge, Robert L. Morris, John Palmer, and Joseph H. Rush, *Foundations of Parapsychology*, 237-75; Stanley Krippner, ed., *Psychokinesis*; and, for

a particularly dramatic account of "psychic photography," Jule Eisenbud, *The World of Ted Serios: "Thoughtographic" Studies of an Extraordinary Mind* (1967; New York: Pocket Books, 1968).

12. Charles T. Tart, "Out-of-the-Body Experiences," in *Psychic Explorations*, Edgar Mitchell and John White, eds. (New York: Putnam's 1974); D. Scott Rogo, ed., *Mind Beyond the Body: The Mystery of ESP Projection* (New York: Penguin Books, 1978).

13. Rogo, *op. cit.*

14. For surveys and evaluations of the various types of evidence, see F. W. H. Myers, *Human Personality and Its Survival of Bodily Death* (London: Longmans, Green, 1903); Hornell Hart, *The Enigma of Survival: The Case for and against Life after Death* (Springfield, Ill.: Charles Thomas, 1959); C. D. Broad, *Human Personality and the Possibility of its Survival* (Berkeley: University of California Press, 1955); C. J. Ducasse, *A Critical Examination of the Belief in Life after Death* (Springfield, Ill.: Charles Thomas, 1961). See also Hoyt L. Edge's circumspect conclusion, after a survey of evidence: "There is no doubt that survival has not been *proved*, as alternative explanations exist. That does not, however, negate the fact that there is interesting empirical evidence that can be interpreted as supporting the hypothesis," "Survival and Other Philosophical Questions," Hoyt L. Edge, *et al.*, *Foundations of Parapsychology*, 325-60, esp. 347.

15. See note 7.

16. See Karlis Osis and Erlandur Haraldsson, *At the Hour of Death* (New York: Avon Books, 1977).

17. *Ibid.*, 197-91; Kenneth Ring, *Life at Death*, 210-17.

18. See Eleanor M. Sidgwick, *Phantasms of the Living* (1918; New York: Arno Press, 1975); G. N. M. Tyrrell, *Apparitions* (1942; New York: Macmillan, 1962); Celia Green and Charles McCreery, *Apparitions* (London: Hamish Hamilton, 1975); Hornell Hart, *et al.*, "Six Theories about Apparitions," *Proceedings of the Society for Psychical Research* 50 (1956), 153-239; and Ian Stevenson, "The Contribution of Apparitions to the Evidence for Survival," *Journal of the American Society for Psychical Research* 76 (1982), 341-58.

19. See G. N. M. Tyrrell's complex explanation for collective veridical apparitions in *Apparitions*, chap. III.

20. On the "super-ESP hypothesis" see Hoyt Edge, *et al.*, *Foundations of Parapsychology*, 338-47.

21. See H. F. Saltmarsh, *Evidence of Personal Survival from Cross-Correspondences* (London: G. Bell, 1939).

22. See Ian Stevenson, *Twenty Cases Suggestive of Reincarnation* (Charlottesville: University Press of Virginia, 1974), and his several volumes entitled *Cases of the Reincarnation Type*, beginning with Volume I, *Ten Cases in India* (Charlottesville: University Press of Virginia, 1975).

23. See Jonathan Schell, *The Fate of the Earth* (New York: Avon Books, 1982), 155, 164-71.

24. Schell recognizes that his humanistic, nontheistic view, which makes all meaning dependent upon human beings, creates a problem. Having asked who will miss human life when it is extinguished, he replies: "The only honest answer is: Nobody. . . . [W]e have to admit that extinction is no loss, since there cannot be a loss when there is no loser" (*ibid.*, 171).

25. Charles Hartshorne, *The Logic of Perfection and Other Essays in Neoclassical Metaphysics* (Lasalle, Ill.: Open Court, 1962), 146.

26. See, e.g., Hartshorne, *Omnipotence and Other Theological Mistakes* (Albany: State University of New York Press, 1984), 4.

27. Hartshorne, *The Logic of Perfection*, 253; *Reality as Social Process* (Glencoe, Ill.: Free Press, 1953), 143; also personal correspondence.

Chapter 7
Spiritual Discipline in the Medieval, Modern, and Postmodern Worlds

1. Peter Brown, *Augustine of Hippo* (Berkeley: University of California Press, 1969), 51-53. My discussion of Augustine throughout the first section of this chapter is heavily indebted to Brown's book.

2. For an extended discussion of Augustine's doctrine of divine omnipotence, see the chapter on Augustine in my *God, Power, and Evil: A Process Theodicy* (Philadelphia: Westminster Press, 1976).

3. St. Augustine, *On Baptism: Against the Donatists*, bk. 3, chap. 19.

4. St. Augustine, *Answer to Petilian*, bk. 3, chap. 50.

5. I have argued this in the chapter, "Thomas Aquinas: Divine Simplicity and Theological Complexity," in *God, Power, and Evil: A Process Theodicy.*

6. See *ibid.*, the chapters on Luther and Calvin.

7. See *ibid.*, the chapter on Karl Barth.

8. Here I refer only to divine grace in the sense of liberating, transforming, sanctifying grace, which Reinhold Niebuhr called "grace in us." The effectiveness of grace in this sense depends upon our response. The situation is quite otherwise with forgiving grace, or "grace over us," meaning God's unconditional forgiveness, compassion, and everlasting cherishing of us. In this sense our relation to God is determined by God alone. Many of the problems in Christian theology have resulted from speaking about grace in us in terms that are appropriate only to grace over us.

CHAPTER 8
IMPERIALISM, NUCLEARISM,
AND POSTMODERN THEISM

1. See Delwin Brown, *To Set at Liberty: Christian Faith and Human Freedom* (Maryknoll, N.Y.: Orbis Books, 1981).

2. When the first version of this essay was written, Gordon Kaufman's *Theology for a Nuclear Age* (Philadelphia: Westminster Press, 1985) had just been published. Since that time, two more important theological books have appeared: G. Clarke Chapman's *Facing the Nuclear Heresy: A Call to Reformation* (Elgin, Ill.: Brethren Press, 1986), and Sallie McFague's *Models of God: Theology for an Ecological, Nuclear Age* (Philadelphia: Fortress Press, 1987). Some of the most important earlier books are Dale Aukerman, *Darkening Valley: A Biblical Perspective on Nuclear War* (New York: Seabury, 1981); Duane Beachey, *Faith in a Nuclear Age: A Christian Response to War* (Scottdale, Penn.: Herald Press, 1978); Robert F. Drinan, S. J., *Vietnam and Armageddon: Peace, War and the Christian Conscience* (New York: Sheed & Ward, 1970); Jim Garrison, *The Darkness of God: Theology after Hiroshima* (Grand Rapids, Mich.: William B. Eerdmans, 1982); Alan Geyer, *The Idea of Disarmament! Rethinking the Unthinkable* (Elgin, Ill.: Brethren Press, 1982); Donald Kraybill, *Facing Nuclear War: A Plea for Christian Witness* (Scottdale, Penn.: Herald Press, 1982); Jean Lasserre, *War and the Gospel* (Scottdale, Penn.: Herald Press, 1962); Thomas Merton, *Original Child Bomb: Points of Meditation to be Scratched on the Walls of a Cave* (Greenboro, N. C.: Unicorn Press, 1962); *Thomas Merton on Peace*, Introduction by Gordon C. Zahn (New York: McCall Publ. Co., 1971); and Ronald J. Sider and Richard K. Taylor, *Nuclear Holocaust & Christian Hope: A Book for Christian Peacemakers* (Downsgrove, Ill.: InterVarsity Press, 1982). Two important books written from a religious studies viewpoint are James A. Aho, *Religious Mythology and the Art of War: Comparative Religious Symbolisms of Military Violence* (Westport, Conn.: Greenwood Press, 1981) and Ira Chernus, *Dr. Strangegod: On the Symbolic Meaning of Nuclear Weapons* (Columbia: University of South Carolina Press, 1986).

3. Whereas some naturalistic views of deity have denied divine freedom altogether, the naturalistic theism of postmodern theology involves a moderate voluntarism. God, being essentially the soul of the universe, decides neither whether there will be a realm of finite beings nor the fundamental way of interacting with these beings, just as God (as even the most extreme voluntarists agree) does not freely decide whether to exist. But within this given structure, much room for free choice can be assumed.

4. For an excellent examination of the development of voluntarism from the nominalists through the Protestant reformers to the legal-mechanical worldview of Boyle and Newton, see Eugene M. Klaaren, *Religious Origins of Modern Science: Belief in Creation in Seventeenth-Century Thought* (Grand Rapids, Mich.: William B. Eerdmans, 1977; Lanham, Md.: University Press of America, 1985).

5. See the chapter "Thomas Aquinas: Divine Simplicity and Theological Complexity" in my *God, Power, and Evil: A Process Theodicy* (Philadelphia: Westminster Press, 1976).

6. See the chapter "Luther: The Explicit Denial of Creaturely Freedom" in *ibid.*

7. The term *bipolar* (or *dipolar*) is used by Whiteheadian philosophers in a positive sense to refer to dualities that are not dualisms. The dualism of physical and mental substances is replaced by dipolar actual occasions, each of which has a physical and a mental pole. Whitehead and Hartshorne both speak of God as dipolar, having a primordial nature (or, for Hartshorne, an abstract essence) and a consequent nature (or, for Hartshorne, consequent states). In this essay, however, I use the term *bipolar* in a different, negative sense. My usage here is rooted in discussions of a bipolar political worldview, in which virtually everything of importance that happens on the world scene involves the competition between two superpowers. My point is that this bipolar view (in distinction from a more realistic multipolar or multilateral view) is rooted in part in a particular version of the dualistic theological view of the world as (provisionally) the battleground between cosmic forces of good and evil.

8. Hal Lindsey, *The Late Great Planet Earth* (Grand Rapids, Mich.: Zondervan, 1970), 168.

9. *Idem.* The complacency of this theological position was illustrated humorously by a billboard in front of a church in Joplin, Missouri, which I saw while proof-reading this manuscript. It read: "The Rapture—Fly the Friendly Skies!"

10. My view of the American attitude and behavior has been influenced by Robert Jewett's discussion of the Puritan tradition in shaping a "Captain America complex" (*The Captain America Complex: The Dilemma of Zealous Nationalism*, second edition [Santa Fe: Bear & Company, 1984]). He argues for the need to replace zealotry with realism. Jewett, however, does not seem to appreciate the degree to which this zealous complex is a result of the supernaturalistic idea of God itself, so that it cannot be overcome by an act of will apart from a fundamental change in our idea of God.

11. Richard J. Barnet, *The Roots of War: The Men and Institutions Behind U. S. Foreign Policy* (New York: Penguin Books, 1973) and *The Alliance: America-Europe-Japan: Makers of the Postwar World* (New York: Simon and Schuster, 1983); Alan Wolfe, *The Rise and Fall of the Soviet Threat: Domestic Sources of the Cold War Consensus* (Boston: South End Press, 1984); and Jerry W. Sanders, *Peddlers of Crisis: The Committee on the Present Danger and the Politics of Containment* (Boston: South End Press, 1983).

12. See Daniel Ellsberg, "Introduction: Call to Mutiny," *Protest and Survive*, E. P. Thompson and Ian Smith, eds. (New York: Monthly Review Press, 1981); Noam Chomsky, "Interventionism and Nuclear War," *Beyond Survival: New Directions for the Disarmament Movement*, Michael Albert and David Dellinger, eds. (Boston: South End Press, 1983); Richard Barnet, "Ultimate Terrorism:

The Real Meaning of Nuclear Strategies," *Waging Peace: A Handbook for the Struggle to Abolish Nuclear Weapons*, Jim Wallis, ed. (San Francisco: Harper & Row, 1982); and Richard Falk's portion of *Indefensible Weapons: The Political and Psychological Case Against Nuclearism* (New York: Basic Books, 1982), coauthored with Robert Jay Lifton. For an account of U. S. plans to attack the Soviet Union, based on recently declassified documents, see Michio Kaku and Daniel Axelrod, *To Win a Nuclear War: The Pentagon's Secret War Plans* (Boston: South End Press, 1987).

13. See the sources cited in note 12, plus Robert Aldridge, "The Deadly Race: A Look at U.S.-U.S.S.R. Nuclear Capabilities and Intentions," *Waging Peace*, Jim Wallis, ed.

14. See Kaku and Axelrod, *To Win a Nuclear War*, chap. 12, "Star Wars: Missing Link to a First Strike."

15. Louis Agassiz, who believed that the world in essentially its present form was the product of a supernatural creation, characterized the Darwinian alternative as the view that it arose through "the omnipotence of matter" (*American Journal of Science*, July 1860, 147-49; cited by Asa Gray in Philip Appleman, ed., *Darwin: A Norton Critical Edition* [New York: W. W. Norton & Co., 1970], 431). The term *omnipotent matter* was also used by Bertrand Russell in a passage cited above in chapter 2 (text to note 6).

16. See Richard Hofstadter, *Social Darwinism in American Thought*, revised edition (Boston: Beacon Press, 1955); on Darwin's own views, see John C. Greene, *Science, Ideology, and World View: Essays in the History of Evolutionary Ideas* (Berkeley: University of California Press, 1981), chap. 5.

17. Alfred North Whitehead, *Adventures of Ideas* (1933; New York: Free Press, 1967), 168.

18. *Idem.*

19. Whitehead, *Process and Reality*, corrected edition, David Ray Griffin and Donald W. Sherburne, eds. (New York: Free Press, 1978), 95, 96.

20. *Ibid.*, 21.

21. *Ibid.*, 225.

22. *Adventures of Ideas*, 166.

23. When Whitehead is not contrasting two views of divine power, but is instead contrasting the power of material forces as "senseless agencies" with the power of ideals as "persuasive agencies," he refers to the former type of power as "compulsion" even though it includes forms of causal influence that do not totally determine the outcomes and hence would not constitute finite examples of the "coercive power" ascribed to God by traditional theologians; see *ibid.*, chap. I.

24. *Ibid.*, 169.

25. *Process and Reality*, 343.

26. Whitehead, *Religion in the Making* (1926; Cleveland, Ohio: World Publishing Co., 1960), 56.

27. *Process and Reality*, 342.

28. *Ibid.*, 346.

29. P. H. Nowell-Smith, "Morality: Religious and Secular," *Christian Ethics and Contemporary Philosophy*, Ian T. Ramsey, ed. (London: SCM Press, 1966), 95-112, esp. 97. Henry David Aiken, "God and Evil: A Study of Some Relations Between Faith and Morals," *Ethics* 68/2 (January 1958), 77-97, esp. 82.

30. *Process and Reality*, 162.

31. Charles Hartshorne, *Reality as Social Process: Studies in Metaphysics and Religion* (New York: Free Press, 1968), 205.

32. Hartshorne, *Man's Vision of God and the Logic of Theism* (1941; Hamden, Conn.: Archon Books, 1964), 169.

33. Hartshorne, *Beyond Humanism: Essays in the New Philosophy of Nature* (1937; Lincoln: University of Nebraska Press, 1968), 148.

34. *Idem.*

35. *Man's Vision of God*, 162-63.

NOTE ON CENTERS

This series is published under the auspices of the Center for a Postmodern World and the Center for Process Studies.

The Center for a Postmodern World is an independent nonprofit organization in Santa Barbara, California, founded by David Ray Griffin. It promotes the awareness and exploration of the postmodern worldview and encourages reflection about a postmodern world, from postmodern art, spirituality, and education to a postmodern world order, with all this implies for economics, ecology, and security. One of its major projects is to produce a collaborative study that marshals the numerous facts supportive of a postmodern worldview and provides a portrayal of a postmodern world order toward which we can realistically move. It is located at 2060 Alameda Padre Serra, Suite 101, Santa Barbara, California 93103.

The Center for Process Studies is a research organization affiliated with the School of Theology at Claremont and Claremont University Center and Graduate School. It was founded by John B. Cobb, Jr., Director, and David Ray Griffin, Executive Director. It encourages research and reflection upon the process philosophy of Alfred North Whitehead, Charles Hartshorne, and related thinkers, and upon the application and testing of this viewpoint in all areas of thought and practice. This center sponsors conferences, welcomes visiting scholars to use its library, and publishes a scholarly journal, *Process Studies,* and a quarterly *Newsletter.* It is located at 1325 North College, Claremont, California 91711.

Both centers gratefully accept (tax-deductible) contributions to support their work.

INDEX